THE EMERGENCE OF PROSE

THE EMERGENCE OF PROSE
an essay in prosaics

Wlad Godzich and Jeffrey Kittay

University of Minnesota Press, Minneapolis

The University of Minnesota Press gratefully acknowledges
assistance provided by the Andrew W. Mellon Foundation for
publication of this book.

Quotations from Ernst Robert Curtius *European Literature and the Latin Middle
Ages* translated by Willard R. Trask, Bollingen Series XXXVI (c) 1953, (c) 1981
renewed by Princeton University Press, excerpted from pp. 147-49, reprinted
by permission of Princeton University Press.

Quotations from the introduction to Malory, *Works,* edited by Eugène Vinaver,
2nd edition, Oxford University Press, 1971, (c) Eugène Vinaver 1971, pp. vii-
ix, reprinted by permission of Oxford University Press.

Quotations from Louis Aragon's *Je n'ai jamais appris à écrire, ou les iincipits,*
pp. 10-13, (c) Editions d'Art Albert Skira S.A., Geneva.

Published by the University of Minnesota Press
2037 University Avenue Southeast, Minneapolis, MN 55414.
Published simultaneously in Canada
by Fitzhenry & Whiteside Limited, Markham.
Printed in the United States of America.

Library of Congress Cataloging-in-Publication Data

Godzich, Wlad.
    The emergence of prose.
    Includes index.
    1. French prose literature—To 1500—History and
criticism. 2. French language—Style. I. Kittay,
Jeffrey. II. Title.
PQ607.G6 1987   848'.108'09   87-5079
ISBN 0-8166-1572-1
ISBN 0-8166-1574-8 (pbk.)

Contents

Preface

Our inquiry into the beginnings of prose started with fairly traditional questions. As we proceeded, however, the object of our focus seemed continually to pull the rug out from under our feet. We were led, along the way, to reexamine the grounds of the questions with which we started. What we have finally produced is a distillate of the several paths taken. In spite of the many confident assertions our reader will encounter, we offer here no final answers, just viable modes of approach.

Most studies in our field either are focused on a set of texts, which engage an individual scholar's analytic ability, or are theoretical, asserting an individual argument. Looking at prose, however, raised questions about the appropriate tools to understand an object not yet clearly constituted. The result was the opening up of a dialogic space between the theoretical and the analytic. Such a space is more easily investigated by more than one individual. The book is the product of a collaboration. Chapters were written together. Nothing should be taken as singly authored. It is often claimed that collaboration is difficult in the humanities. We can attest to the fact that it is not easy, but its personal rewards are great indeed.

Note to the Reader: The superscripts in this text refer to notes at the back of the volume. Although the notes contain scholarly apparatus, they are for the most part discursive and are integral to the book as a whole. We urge you to follow along with them.

Introduction

Any inquiry into prose inevitably meets the perplexing example of an illustrious predecessor, M. Jourdain, the famous bourgeois *gentilhomme* from Molière's play of the same name. Moved to write an amorous epistle to an unattainable lady, the bourgeois hires a master of philosophy to instruct him in this arcane skill. The master first asks him whether the letter is to be written in verse. Bourgeois that he is, Jourdain rejects that out of hand. "You want only prose?" asks the master. "No, I want neither prose nor verse," answers the bourgeois, who merely wants a seductive note to be casually dropped at the feet of the lady. But the master is less concerned with the pragmatics or effects of the note than with taxonomic distinctions. "It must be one or the other," he insists. Expression admits of no other possible forms. Asked why, the master provides the following rule: "Tout ce qui n'est point prose est vers; et tout ce qui n'est point vers est prose" (Everything that is not prose is verse, and everything that is not verse is prose).[1] M. Jourdain then wonders what it is that he is speaking. "Prose" is the reply. "And when I say: 'Nicole, bring me my slippers, and give me my nightcap', is that prose?" At the master's affirmative answer, Jourdain marvels at a competence he did not know he had: "For over forty years I have been speaking prose without suspecting it in the least." He returns, however, to his primary concern, the composition of the note. He suggests its content, a simple cliché, and asks the master to change it around, to couch it in a more gallant manner. The master essays various permutations on the original suggestion but winds up admitting that

Jourdain's initial version was the best, which leads Jourdain to say: "And yet I did not study, and I've done this on the first try" (Act 2, scene 4).

Even by the master's lights (dim as they are), M. Jourdain intuitively arrives at correct expression for his purposes. So what has he learned by learning that he was speaking in prose? No insight was gained here, only a label to be applied to an activity that had not called attention to itself and showed no need of doing so. Yet once the label is available, it becomes a weapon in the arsenal of knowledge that M. Jourdain can now wield to affirm his superiority over those from whom he seeks to differentiate himself. Thus, when his wife reprimands him for his foolishness, he retorts by beginning to quiz her (Act 3, scene3): "Do you know what you are talking at this moment?" Madame Jourdain clearly has no idea what her husband is talking about. To his now more refined linguistic sensibility, she appears to be obtusely concerned with matters of content, of evaluation, of pragmatics. "What is that called?" M. Jourdain insists. "That is called whatever one wants to call it," she replies. Clearly, she fails to understand the value of a label, subscribing to a theory that sees naming as arbitrary. She knows there is no knowledge to be gained here, just some verbal posturing. "C'est de la prose, ignorante" (It is prose, stupid), says the gentleman in triumph, who then goes on to restate for her the opposition proffered by the master that divides the expression of the world into two universes. But whereas the master had offered two mutually exclusive possibilities, M. Jourdain, whose intuitive powers have been ratified by the correctness of his own version of the love letters, now unwittingly deconstructs this opposition by showing that verse and prose are not in a relationship of opposition and territorial dominion. He delivers the rule to his wife as follows: "Tout ce qui est prose n'est point vers; et tout ce qui n'est point vers n'est point prose" (Everything that is prose is not verse; and everything that is not verse is not prose). We may laugh at the bourgeois's inability to parrot his master's lesson, but we may well wonder whether, just as he has been speaking prose unwittingly, he may unwittingly state a truth about it (a truth to which there is a great resistance: as simple as this statement is, translators have occasionally mistranslated it into its opposite).[2] We may also wonder whether the ridicule, rather than accruing to Jourdain, should be heaped upon the master, who believes that prose and verse represent territorial dominions. Of course the statement may very well mean that what Jourdain has been speaking is not prose either.

The discussion of prose in the *Bourgeois Gentilhomme* thus leaves us with a short lesson. The word prose carries little meaning, and taxonomic approaches to it will bring only ridicule. This may be why there has been so little study of prose as such, in a world dominated by the taxonomic approaches of poetics.

From the very beginning, we have to admit that literary scholarship has not known what prose is. Some thirty years ago, when Northrop Frye set out, in his *Anatomy of Criticism*, to address the fundamental problems of critical thought, he had to straightaway concede that he could not write the first two pages of the book, for the notions they were meant to deal with defied treatment. The first page was supposed to define literature. The second was to address the verse and prose distinction.[3] For a critic of Frye's interests, the inability of critical discourse to come to grips with these two notions, although embarrassing, is not fatal. For the most part, he can proceed as if he knew what both literature and prose were, and not suffer in the process. For a student of the Middle Ages—and more broadly for anyone who is concerned with the historical sweep of literature—these questions must loom large indeed.

In all the theories of literature at our disposal, from Aristotle's *Poetics* onward, we have been taught that verse is a form of discourse more elaborate than prose, which suggests two things: first, that verse is the result of work on a discourse that is taken to be prose and, second, that prose is anterior to verse. The various poetics, including medieval ones, take prose for granted, treating it as if it were natural, artless, just a given, and turn their attention to verse, which is seen as an artifice, and whose degree of "artfulness" has to be analyzed and described. Frye provides confirmation by stating: "Any attempt to give literary dignity to prose is likely to give it some of the characteristics of verse" (p. 263). Unwittingly, Frye justifies the blindness of the poetics to prose by claiming that prose is interesting only to the extent that it ceases to be "just prose." There is to be no interest *inherent* in prose. It is for this reason that we have so many studies of versification and none of prosification. Prose is everything else. It is what there is. We have all, along with M. Jourdain, been speaking it since birth. There is no such term as prosification because prose is understood to be a natural output of our language activity. We know, however, that anything communally considered to have the status of natural is most likely the locus of powerful semiotic mechanisms.

The view of prose as natural, which has commanded assent, is at odds with a set of facts that are undisputable. Literary scholarship is well aware that prose is not omnipresent. It has not always been present in all cultures, even in all literate ones. Historical evidence shows that it is verse that precedes prose. In the linguistic traditions of Hebrew, Greek, Latin, Arabic, Old Icelandic, English, Spanish, German, Wolof, and Pulaar, and on and on and on, prose comes after verse. There is an epoch in each of these traditions in which there is no prose, and apparently never had been. There is then, subsequently, a time in which prose appears. And the appearance of prose does not at all coincide with the appearance of writing. It is subsequent to the appearance of writing. There are many cultures that have verse and have writing but that have no prose.[4]

To the extent that a general description can be said to exist concerning these matters, it runs as follows: first there is oral verse, and then there is a writing down of oral verse (and other oral discourses). And then, somehow, there are works written in prose, which tend to proliferate until they seem to become the dominant mode of written communication. This description scarcely constitutes a satisfactory understanding of the phenomenon, and it is incumbent on literary theory to provide one. To do so, literary theory cannot afford to continue to ignore the weight of the historical evidence and its implications.

Ideally, such a study should approach the phenomenon comparatively, taking into account all instances, and especially ancient ones. Such an approach, however, presupposes an ability to identify the constant amid the variations, and we are very far from being in that position. Our inquiry will take as its point of departure the emergence of prose in France in the Middle Ages. The French tradition, which has left to us an exceptionally large number of manuscripts, is the one we are best equipped to inquire into. It is also a fact that such limited scholarship as exists on the subject agrees in seeing the modern emergence of prose in the West as occurring in the linguistic tradition of French. Furthermore, it is significant that through the years, while researching this subject, we have come across no suggestion, from either primary or secondary sources, that the emergence of prose in France was influenced by prose in any neighboring vernacular. On the contrary:

> C'est dire assez qu'au XIIe siècle, la prose romane en France est une singularité. Elle n'était pas née encore en Italie où elle ne verra le jour que vers 1300, lorsque Bartolomeo da San Concordio, un moine de Pise, traduira deux livres historiques de Salluste. Elle n'était pas née en Espagne où elle n'apparaît que dans la seconde moitié du XIIIe siècle.[5]

> It can be said that in the twelfth century, vernacular prose in France is a unique event. It had not yet been born in Italy, where it will see the light of day only around 1300, when Bartolomeo da San Corcordio, a monk from Pisa, will translate two historical works of Sallustus. It had not been born in Spain where it will appear only in the second half of the thirteenth century.

To consider prose at one historical moment requires certain adjustments in the handling of terms and conceptions that were developed in the absence of such considerations. First and foremost, this affects the term verse and our conceptions of it, which must be equally historicized. We are very much affected by the predominance of prose today—prose considered as a given or natural state of written language. Our world is a literally prosaic one, full of prose. We do not realize that we live in a world transformed by the historical event of prose's emergence and subsequent spread. We are already, fully, *après prose.* To adopt a historical perspective, we must ask our readers to consider our remarks in the context of early thirteenth-century France, in which there is French verse but not as yet French prose. Bear in mind that when we use the term verse, then, we are not referring to modern verse, which has already adjusted to the presence of prose, but to verse in the High Middle Ages, which did not know of its existence. Modern verse is very much conditioned by prose. Once prose emerges, prose and verse become interdependent through time. We even have texts that the nineteenth century calls prose poems. This is why we have chosen to examine prose at a particular historical moment, *in situ,* rather than in the abstract. Our use of the term verse throughout most of this book should be interpreted as *pre-prose* verse, not *post-prose* verse, which entertains a very complex and contaminated relationship to modern prose.

Poetics has not provided us with adequate terminology for the designation of verse and prose because these terms exceed the scope of the broadest category of poetics: genre. In fact, we commonly recognize the existence of genres *within* prose and verse. We have found it useful to speak of both prose and verse as *signifying practices,* a category that will have additional members. Its nature will become more evident as our study of prose progresses.

In 1202, an obscure court writer, Nicolas de Senlis, found himself the recipient of a strange request, which led him to translate into French a Latin text then known as the *Chronicle of Turpin* and falsely attributed to the famous archbishop, the killer of Saracens in the *Chanson de Roland.* The request for the translation itself was unremarkable at the time: the end of the twelfth and the beginning of the thirteenth century was a period characterized by the feudal lords' attempts to consolidate the political and ideological foundations of their power, so translations of texts that justified the power of individuals or their families were in growing demand.[6] This was what the lord of Senlis, Baudouin V, Count of Flanders, had in mind. What was unusual is the request by his sister Yolande, Countess of Saint Pol, that the translation be in prose, or, in the very words of the translator, *en romans sans rime:* "in the vernacular, unrhymed." Here is the prologue of what is now known as the *Pseudo-Turpin* by Senlis:

> En l'enor nostre Segnior qui est Peres e Fils e Saint Esperis et qui est un Dex en trois personnes, e au nom de la gloriose mere madame saincte Marie, voil commencier l'estoire si cum li bons empereires Kar-

lemaines en ala en Espagnie por la terre conquerre sour les Sarasins. Maintes gens si en ont oï conter et chanter, mes n'est si mençonge non ço qu'il en dient e en chantent, cil chanteor ni cil jogleor. Nus contes rimés n'est verais; tot est mençongie ço qu'il en dient; car il n'en sievent riens for quant pour oïr dire. Li bons Baudouins, li cuens de Chainau, si ama most Karlemaines. Ni ne vout onque croire chose que l'on en chantast; ainz fist cercher totes les bones abeïes de France e garder par totes les aumaires por saver si l'om i troveroit la veraie ystoire; ne onques trover ne li porent li cler. Tant avint que uns sis clers si ala en Borgognie por l'estoire querre eissi cum à Deu plot: si la trova à Sans en Borgognie, icele istoire meismement que Turpins li bons arcevesques de Reins escrit en Espagnie, qui avec le bon empereur Karlemaines fu e tot les miracles, e tot le conquest qu'il fit, por so qu'il sot que vers fu, si les escrivit par nuit et par jor quant il en vait lisir, si cum il li avenoient le jor. Dont on feist mieux cil à croire qui i fu, qui le vit, que ne font cil qui riens n'en sevent fors quant par oïr dire. Li clers au bon comte Baudouin contrescrit l'estoire et à son segnor l'aporta, qui most la tint en grant cherté tant que il vesqui. E quant il sot qu'il dut mourir, si envoia son livre à son seror, la bonne Yolande la comtesse de Saint-Pou, e si li manda que par amor de lui gardast le livre cum ele vivroit. La bone comtesse ha gardé le livre jusqu'à ore. Or si me proie que je le mete de latin en romans sans rime; por ço que teus set de letre qui de latin ne le seust eslire, e por ce que par romans sera il mieus gardés. Or se orés qui li bons arcevesques en raconte.[7]

In honor of our Lord who is Father and Son and Holy Spirit and is one God in three persons, and in the name of the glorious mother, our lady holy Mary, I want to begin the story of how the good emperor Charlemagne went to Spain to conquer the land over the Saracens. Many people have heard it told and sung, but it is nothing but lies that they tell and sing, these singers and jongleurs. No rhymed tale is true; everything they say is a lie for they know nothing of it except through hearsay. The good Baudouin, Count of Chainau, loved Charlemagne very much. He did not want to ever believe anything that would be sung about him, and so he had all the good abbeys of France searched and all the cabinets looked into in order to find the true story, but the clerks could not find it. And so it happened that one of his clerks went to Burgundy to look for the story, and it pleased God and he found in Sens in Burgundy the very story that Turpin, the good archbishop of Rheims wrote in Spain, the very Turpin who accompanied the good emperor Charlemagne and who wrote down day or night, as he had time and as they happened, all the miracles and all the conquests of Charles that he knew to be true. And it is therefore better to believe the one who was there, and who saw it all, than those who know nothing beyond hear-say. Good count Baudouin's clerk recopied the story and brought it to his lord, who held it most dear as long as he lived.

And when he knew he had to die, he sent the book to his sister, the good Yolande, Countess of Saint-Pol, and asked that for the love of him she keep the book as long as she lived. The good countess has kept the book until now. And now she is asking me to put it from Latin into rhymeless *roman* because there are those who know letters but cannot read Latin and because in *roman* it will be better kept. And now listen to what the good archbishop tells.

Up to that time, all translations into the vernacular were done into verses of eight, ten, or 12 syllables, and that was regardless of the form of the original Latin. Even Latin prose, when translated into French, was translated into verse.[8] This request is the oldest instance that we have in the French language of a stated preference, a motivated choice, of nonverse over verse, and it thus marks a milestone in what we have come to see as the emergence of prose.

Baudouin's request was but the first of many. There were five versions of the translated *Pseudo-Turpin*. Other translations into prose were commissioned, and little by little the vogue of prose became so great that one began to transpose into prose not only Latin texts but also texts that were already in French, such as the old *chansons de geste,* which in their written form had been in verse. These are the famous *dérimages,* or derhymed texts (not unrhymed but de-rhymed), of the Middle Ages. And it is possible to study this phenomenon today because both the original verse version and the subsequent *remaniement en prose* (reworking in prose) have come down to us in a number of instances.

The deliberate choice of prose over verse represents a critique, if not an outright refusal, of verse. What motivates this critique? Let us examine the words of Nicolas de Senlis. "Many people have heard it told and sung, but it is nothing but lies that they tell and sing, these singers and jongleurs. No rhymed tale is true; everything they say is a lie for they know nothing of it except through hearsay." The conclusion is an important epistemological one: the whole system of transmission of the oral tradition is under attack. The weak link in that system is seen to be the jongleur, and therefore it behooves us to look at what motivated the disqualification of this individual and of the signifying practice that is centered around him.

This is not the first appearance of an attack on jongleurs: the church, after all, had begun to denounce them a century earlier, but from a different set of concerns. For the church, the jongleur, whose itinerant lifestyle already did not set a very edifying example for the congregation, represented a competitor. The jongleur not only trafficked in news from one city to the next, thus playing a certain political role that competed with the church's monopoly on the flow and distribution of news through its own network of abbeys and parishes, but also stimulated the imagination of the audience with his stories, songs, dances, and accompaniments, thereby distracting their attention from the Faith and its works. His ecclesiastical critics were threatened by his way of life and his ability to distract: the argument to discredit the jongleur was a moral one. Until the appearance of an alternative signifying practice such as prose, however, the jongleur was able to withstand this line of attack and preserve his credit.

What was the credit the jongleur enjoyed? In the High Middle Ages, in a mostly illiterate society, the jongleur, by means of his trained memory and what it stored, represented an important cultural institution. The texts, epic and otherwise, that were his stock-in-trade constituted the cultural patrimony of the collectivity: its originating myths and legends, the treasure trove of precedents, and other explanatory regresses. His function, particularly at the beginning, was not to innovate or add to his patrimony but to preserve it. We know that the audience of a performed *chanson de geste* was looking not for novelty but for something it already knew, presented in an effective and entertaining manner. The jongleur was judged not on the content of his recitations and songs, which in any case the audience was familiar with, but on the style of his presentations. He was believable because his performance evidenced that he had served his apprenticeship, that he had been trained by others who "knew," that he was "in the know." He had to be a master at the complex task of performing a narrative, as well as of reciting other forms of discourse. And it was the way in which he fulfilled these expectations that showed him to be a keeper of tradition, a transmitter of law, a person worthy of credit and, therefore, one whose authority is not put into question.

And as we have just seen, he manages to hold on to this authority during the early feudal period, in spite of the church's hostility. But as soon as the earlier collectivities become stratified in a new order of estates and even emergent classes, there is no longer a locus that is universally agreed upon for the jongleur to occupy. In this new social order, the jongleur is increasingly dependent on members of the seigneurial class, and he soon finds himself sought after by embryonic bourgeois communities as well. No longer able to function as the depository of the entire collectivity, he will be called upon by powerful private or municipal patrons whose ambitions he is to justify—for compensation of course. In other words, he sells his authority, his credit, and lets himself be taken over by individuals who use for their own ends the fact that the jongleur's discourse had not up to that time been subject to question on the grounds of truth. His credit does not prove to be unlimited, though: the more he sells it, the less he has. All his *collective* authority is gone: he can affirm only a personal authority, which makes him vulnerable to all attackers, and finally even to the moral attacks of the church. Baudouin's search for written authority and Yolande's interdiction of rhyme mark the jongleur's bankruptcy.[9]

The development of the feudal system, and the founding of the estate system which it marks, precipitates the commodification of the jongleur, which will stigmatize his services, his performance. We might ask, however, why Yolande would not have been content with a translation into written verse, free of the vagaries of the individual jongleur and his performance? Why is it that it is *verse* that lies? We know that verse does not die out; in fact, some of the early attacks on verse were themselves in verse. Here is the versified prologue of a prose chronicle dated 1226:

> Issi vos an fere le conte
> Non pas rime, qui an droit conte
> Si con li livres Lancelot
> Ou il na de rime un seul mot,
> Por mielz dire la verite
> Et por tretier sans fausete;
> Quar anviz puet estre rimee
> Estoire ou n'ait ajostee
> Manconge por fere la rime.[10]

> Here I will tell you the tale
> But not rhymed, but in straight telling
> Just like the book of Lancelot
> Where of rhyme there is not a one,
> In order to better tell the truth
> And speak without falsehood;
> For there never can be rhymed
> A story where there has not been added
> A lie to get a rhyme.

Verse still has a future (what we know as the lyric, for example), but the particular needs it satisfies are not those of Baudouin and Yolande. Verse is not removed from the configuration of signifying practices that make up communication. It is just that its extension is restricted. The domain of signifying practices is remapped. Prose appears and claims a territory of its own.

Written verse bears witness to the performance of the jongleur, and that performance is the communicative framework in which written verse is understood. Readers at the time understood written verse because of what they understood of performance (see chap. 2). When we watch performance and the writing to which it was reduced be removed by prose from a position of dominance, it becomes clear that they had been Truth but are Truth no longer or, more precisely, that there are certain kinds of truth to which the signifying practice of performance no longer had the power to lend authority. In an oral culture, performances of the same story by different jongleurs vary greatly, but that variability of the text (in the large sense of this term) was accepted, as long as there was a bona fide jongleur who put it into action, who guaranteed it. (In fact, in a totally oral culture there is no system of verification, as it is not really possible to compare systematically two different performances.) But when jongleurs are seen as newly unreliable, they alone cannot guarantee the veracity of their message. Here, the variability of their performances becomes particularly disturbing. To be authoritative, a text must be verifiable, exclusive of its jongleur. The issue becomes verifiability, which is connected in a new modern sense to stability. Truth (again, the truth to which Baudouin and Yolande are looking) resides no longer in a movable tradition but (and this is just part of it, as we shall see) in a self-sameness, an unalterability, a document.

The jongleur, in *his* self-sameness, contained changing time and, thus, withdrew from view its destabilizing impact on what was to be transmitted. But when the status of the jongleur changes, that is, when the jongleur himself reacts with and within time, a different source of stability must be found. (Yet, as will be clear as this book unfolds, the jongleur is always at our back and we will return to him again and again in our effort to understand what succeeds him.) The move to documentary truth acknowledges the impossibility of containing time and its changes but manages to locate a form of preserving identity within it, namely an unchanging piece of paper.

This development is no doubt related to the contemporaneous shift in the concept of jurisprudence to Latin models, that is, to written texts, to documents. Quite possibly, the move to a documentary truth may have been part of the desire to transcribe performances in the first place. But the total jongleur performance, implicit and necessary to the understanding and credibility of verse transcription, turns out to be superfluous as the origin of documents because the kind of document we are speaking about is that form of writing that is precisely not to be understood as a supplement to and parasitic on an originating act of performance. The jongleur as originator is no longer a communally authorized guarantor, he is just a drag on the authority of the document. There needs to be a truth that is not vulnerable to the now questionable authority of the jongleur, who discredits rather than accredits.

As the signifying practice of performance falls (and that of written verse encounters problems of legitimacy), another signifying practice, prose, is taking its place. Again we stress that this is not a wholesale replacement—performance and verse are still around—but a new mapping of the domains in which certain signifying practices hold sway over others.

Thus far, we have yet to see prose emerge. What we have seen is a discrediting of verse and the shift to an apparent literal opposite: nonverse. What is clear so far is that there is a loss. The first, most easily constatable loss is that of verse. (This is the formal difference, and it conforms to Jeremy Bentham's succinct and minimal definition of prose: prose is that writing which runs on to the edge of the page.) But we know that nonverse marks the loss of performance, the loss of the jongleur, his training and his tradition, the loss of the institution that guaranteed which utterances among all utterances command assent.

Take away verse and what is left? Without a jongleur, what mechanism ensures the responsibility of the text? What is the mechanism by which the text has the ability to actualize itself? Derhyming seems to us moderns, *après prose*, to be an easy process, but the first *dérimeurs* would occasionally abandon the attempt to paraphrase the original, and they would fall back on the verse. For them, difficult questions must have arisen: it no longer sounds like a jongleur. How is it supposed to *sound*, or is that no longer important? Who literally *stands* behind this text, or is that also now unimportant? In the signifying practice of performance, the text by itself is outside the realm of authority because it is the accredited jongleur who brings authority to the performance, and this authority then devolves upon the text that is part of the performance. Prose as a signifying practice has no corresponding accrediting agency. It has no fount of authority outside itself on which to draw and thus authorize the text that constitutes all its practice. If unrhymed vernacular, *romans sans rime*, is not to be understood within a framework of performance, because the authority ensured by that framework is put into question, how is it to be understood? What is its guarantee? How is this new kind of text going to command assent? Or, to put it another way, why would anyone think that a rhymeless, jongleurless text would ever command assent?

Writers of prose had to examine its considerable limitations and see what could be drawn from them in terms of new narrative and cognitive possibilities, see what prose could utter that a jongleur would never sing. All this to make prose more believable, more real, in a world in which notions of truth and reality were rapidly changing.[11]

The eight chapters of this book are divided into three parts. In the first part, we lay down certain historical and theoretical lines, while we examine signifying practices, some of the consequences as they change in a culture, and the place of written verse. In the second part, we look at three kinds of texts in which prose emerges, to develop some tools through close textual analysis and to extend our understanding. With the conceptual and textual work behind us, we indicate in the third part how one might think about prose.

Prorsa is the name of the Roman goddess who presides over births in which the head of the infant is presented first. Her name comes from the Latin adjective *prorsus* meaning "straightforward." It would be nice to think that prose, like a perfect homunculus, itself undergoes such an unproblematic and natural birth. But, as the chapter titles in part 2 suggest, prose's emergence is through a series of mutations: slightly freakish, somewhat unnatural. Prose does not emerge ready-made.

Part I

Chapter 1
Signifying Practice

Communication is very simple to understand, if we take it to be only some kind of physical channel that links two or more sentient beings. But when we look closely at any one signifying practice—speech, for example, which is most immediate and familiar to us—its structure and components are revealed as unendingly complex.

> Speech, as a means of communication, cannot strictly be divorced from the rest of Man's communicative activity. The operations of the speech organs and of the ear form an integral part of the functioning of the whole body and brain. When we hear a man speak, we usually see him too, his facial expressions and gestures; we communicate in a complex physical environment, against a particular social and cultural background. But the study and understanding of the whole communication process is, as yet, an unattainable ideal.[1]

One kind of communication entails other kinds of communication. A signifying act is a mixture of types of communication. To understand the communication process is to understand what kind of mixture each act is and what fundamental differences exist between different kinds of acts, different *signifying practices*. Insofar as it is the cultural sphere that governs the behavior of individuals who belong within it, it is the cultural sphere that puts into operation certain rules with respect to communication and signification. The signifying act is a shared, social act, an act of social signification.

If we begin with a synchronic view of a culture, or if we look at what could be considered an unchanging culture, questions can already be posed.

Which kinds of messages are transmitted through which kinds of signifying practices? What are the differences among signifying practices, and why is one kind of message rather than another relegated to one signifying practice rather than another? Is the message meant to be permanent or evanescent, verbatim or approximate? Is the skill of encoding to be domestically assimilated or formally learned? Is this message appropriate for use at any time or only on certain occasions? Is it usually exchanged among males or females? Is it to be used between single individuals, between an individual and a collectivity, or only among a collectivity? Is it appropriate only to certain groups or classes in a culture, or available to all? Is it to be communicated between physical, bodily presences or via inert signs? Is it meant to be esoteric or easily retrieved, and must one travel through some predetermined sequence to get to it or can one retrieve it selectively (e.g., look it up)? Is it meant for proximate or long-distance communication? Is it to be understood as personally guaranteed (e.g., signed, sealed, sworn) or as essentially anonymous (e.g., applause, riot, graffitti)? Is it meant to be questioned or believed?

There is no limit to how finely drawn these distinctions can get. For certain cultures, many of them would be meaningless: information is simply not needed, or carried, for the same purposes. These distinctions do not constitute a universal grid of communicative criteria; rather, if they say anything about a specific culture, they bespeak the configuration of our own signifying practices, the one in which this book is written and of which it is a part. As Edmund Leach has said so simply: "Culture communicates." Much of what distinguishes one culture from another is the inner distinctions that the culture has established among its kinds of messages. And (here we adopt a diachronic perspective) new distinctions emerge, become meaningful; certain kinds of messages merge with others; other kinds disappear. In each culture, there is an explicit and implicit configuration, explicit and implicit rules of distribution of the signifying practices: what needs to be communicated and how that can or should be accomplished. One kind of message is in the domain of one signifying practice, another kind is in the domain of another. To understand the emergence of prose is to understand the way in which the configuration of signifying practices changes.

There are needs to be communicated and materials and their accompanying technologies to satisfy those needs. But the means of communication are not purely instrumental, responding only to previously attested need. Different signifying practices evolve and come to the attention of a culture in a variety of ways; they find themselves at the disposal of a culture and invite that culture to make use of them, allowing it the opportunity for new kinds of distinctions in its messages, inviting it to modify and nuance the kinds of meaningful behavior that can be communicated and to create kinds of messages that would be previously unimaginable. An African tribe may communicate with a neighboring village only by messenger. It may then discover that its drums (a technological invention) are audible at great distance and enable it to communicate with that village without the use of a messenger. While providing a new channel, the drum will also demand a different kind of code, "drum language."[2] Although this can be seen in one sense only as a simple recoding of what a messenger would otherwise "say," the new code, as such, represents a new possibility to that culture, offered up to the culture by technology alone (rather than responding to a preexisting need for a new code). The culture could impart to "drum language" a meaning and a social significance different from that of "messenger language." Drum language becomes available, to be exploited or not by the culture. Of course, questions may arise about authority: is a drum to be believed the way a messenger is to be believed? Is a drum more or less authoritative? What would it mean if a certain message were *still* sent by messenger? How does drum language "fit in"? How does it change things? How has the configuration of signifying practices been modified?[3]

It is difficult to have a total awareness of the implications of different modes of message conveyance in one's own culture. It is virtually impossible to classify exhaustively the types of messages utilized in one culture at one time. They are seen as natural—natural responses to natural needs. The shifts that allow new signifying practices to emerge are gradual shifts of configuration, which then make it difficult to picture the situation before the shift. Messages are often taken to be at one with the medium in which they are delivered ("I know so because I read it in the paper"), therefore, the truth, the very meaning and importance, of a message tends to become associated with, and even dependent on, the signifying practice used to convey it. This puts a very large investment in the present configuration of signifying practices, makes that configuration appear natural and unquestionable, and renders problematic the effort to penetrate the way in which dominating contemporary signifying practices work.

By looking back through history, or at other cultures, we get a keener sense of what actually happens when communication changes, when a signifying practice emerges or disappears. We are at all times in and among a play of forces, manifest or incipient, some in current use, some not fully exploited, and some on their way to abandonment, forces that distinguish and define kinds of messages and kinds of meanings. In a diachronic dimension, in the *change* of communication such as that of the emergence of prose, there is the opportunity to overcome the resistance to taking these phenomena as other than natural; there is the opportunity to unmask precise communicative practices.

The change that we seek to analyze is not single, it is complex. And our goal is not necessarily a clear linear development of events, for this may well be inappropriate in a situation in which the very ground of signification shifts. In and among a play of forces, we are to see how one component of existing signifying practices (specifically, the verbal) takes advantage of certain of its material properties (as writing it can be transmitted *hors situation* and yet as language it can *construct situation* among its discourses, deictically and otherwise) to emerge as a new signifying practice and thereby to redraw the configuration of signifying practices in its culture.

To talk of emergence raises problems by its very terms: in such change, on such shifting ground, it is difficult to know what to hold on to, for as the signifying practice that carries authority changes, the kind of authority, the kind of truth it represents changes. What will remain steadily knowable in what we sense to be the beginning of an epistemological shift? We can identify a moment of change, but we have, strictly speaking, no language of change, there is no *truth*. Things become less able to be judged by criteria of truth, more amorphous, less formulatable. When considerations of truth change, from, say, something having to do with stability over time to something having to do with the adequation of language to a notion of "fact" or reality that does not have a language of its own, how do we describe what accounts for the passage from one to the other? Can such a description be as faithful as possible to both kinds of truth and still be *in truth*?

At any moment in a culture, various kinds of signifying practice are in use. Many are relegated to specific levels in a social hierarchy. One way to make a division among signifying practices is to suggest that there are two camps, one containing those practices that treat everyday or contingent occurrences (such as what is often called "common speech") and are judged primarily on their immediate pragmatic usefulness, and one containing those that are understood to be an imparting of the culture's *ethos* and *nomos*, its "ascendant truths," those messages that are held to be preeminent in influence and power and which a culture has a crucial stake in transmitting from generation to generation. This is the distinction usually understood as that between the profane and the sacred. Although the distinction seems universal, it is no more simple than others to delineate finely in any given culture. There is fertilization across the boundary separating communication that is ephemeral and that is retained, communication that is spontaneous and that is contrived, and such a boundary changes through time. The distinction is operative, however (even if any given message is not necessarily and unequivocally classifiable thereby), for it is in the retained and repeated messages, in these "truths," that the culture locates, preserves, and protects its own identity, founds *its* distinction from others, as well as its own notion of truth.[4] Retained messages are often assigned to a special kind of signifying practice, which operates at a higher level in the social hierarchy. Social hierarchies change through history, and there is an opportunity to observe the birth, life and death of signifying practices when the signifying practice of the retained or "sacred" falls from authority and another signifying practice rises to replace it. (That is, to retain the still sacred, the same content, presumably. But that, of course, is one of the interesting questions.)

An instance of change in the configuration of signifying practices is the subject of this study. When such a shift occurs, either because of a redistribution among existing signifying practices or because of the emergence of a "new" one, or some combination of these two factors, certain functions of signifying practice, which were understood or taken as "natural" in the earlier signifying practice, come to light, surface, become distinct. For example, in speech the use of the demonstrative, of certain tenses, or of first- and second-person pronouns may not be seen as different from other expressions, but when that speech is transcribed (or even merely repeated in different situations), demonstratives and pronouns become problematic: who is "I"? Where is "here"? When is "now"? What do we do with such deixis, which was not, previously, a problem? So that the shift from the event of a speech to the transcription of that speech, or even to oral repetition in a situation seen as different, brings to light certain discursive functions "buried" in speech, and then the question becomes: what happens to them? They must (1) be understood differently or used in a new way, (2) become archaic or mysterious, (3) be transposed or translated in some manner, or (4) be sacrificed or rejected. The study of a shift of signifying practice makes distinct certain functions of the earlier signifying practice. (Again, the study is not exhaustive; certain functions are successfully retained or replicated through the shift, and so can remain masked.)

When a new signifying practice replaces an old one, the replacement is rarely wholesale. Rather, there is a gradual shift of emphasis. What results in a new signifying practice often begins as a supplement to the old, so that the final new signifying practice builds off the former one, possesses many characteristics of the former, and may even retain the earlier practice (as a formal whole) within it. A new signifying practice may—perhaps must — initially pretend to "hold" the old, to contain it.[5] This often makes it difficult to define exactly when a signifying practice changes, when, for example, the written dialogue of a play ceases to be the notation of an actual or virtual performance (understood as such) and begins to be a signifying practice all its own (e.g., closet dramas, written to be read). On such shifting sands, periodization becomes a risky business.

Prose was endowed relatively quickly with great authoritative power. But scrutiny of early prose shows that it was full of uncertainties. Nothing demonstrates this more than the presence of a great number of versiprosa texts (in which verse and prose alternate), one of which we will examine later. Suffice it to say for the moment that the versiprosa texts show that prose was not unequivocally and immediately adopted as a *full-blown* way of communicating. Verse was disqualified, but it was a partial disqualification; the advent of prose marked the recognition of verse as insufficient, but verse continued to be seen as frequently necessary. The question poses itself: necessary for what? What can prose not do? or not yet do? Clearly it is not just that "verse lies," for verse is retained. What kind of lies, what kind of truth is denied of verse, and what kind of truth remains within its exclusive domain? We shall see that, rather than a rejection, there has been a reassignment of responsibility. The world of signifying practice has increased in complexity, and the monopoly of verse over a large part of the spectrum of cultural communication has been breached. Verse must share.

We have previously said that a culture has a great stake in preserving certain messages it considers crucial to its own identity and continuity. Needless to say, the signifying practice used for these kinds of messages occupies a privileged position in the configuration of signifying practices, one to be defended at great cost. As the "truth" of these vital messages becomes a product both of some "content" and of their signifying practice, and as that "truth" and that practice can, and almost always do, become the property of one caste or class versus another in a society, we see how signifying practices make possible internal distinctions and establish or help perpetuate social hierarchies. A change of signifying practice is an attack on authenticity and authority.[6] As a consequence, the arrival of another kind of signifying practice that proves to be more fitting for those kinds of messages, the redrawing of the configuration of signifying practices to limit the area in which the previously privileged practice held sway, is an event with enormous consequences. Let us review some signifying practices that have held the place of that highest authority.

In early cases, one would go to the place of access to divine message, an oracle, and there one could get the information sought. At the oldest oracle of Zeus, at Dodona, divination comes in the form of the whispering leaves of a sacred oak. Most frequently, the seat of prophecy is an inspired person, through whose voice the gods speak. For instance, the ancient vates and his female counterpart, the sibyl, were individuals who did not possess any particular knowledge in and of themselves (and are indeed often depicted as generally silent or at least suffering from some form of speech impediment when speaking ordinarily: e.g., Moses). And when the vates speaks in his capacity as vates, he is universally described as being "visited by language." The oracle, the vates, the sibyl, were understood as the place where language of divine message *takes place*. The sibyl does not really speak "in the first person": she is a container for the divine personage. Language happens to her; it takes place by means of her, there, then.[7] Hers is a human voice. It comes through her speech. She is a concrete individual in a here and now; she is the nonverbal factor that sets the place for the verbal to come through. And the verbal is believed by virtue of the fact that it takes place that way.

The sibyl will have many successors: the rhapsode, the prophet, the aede, the bard, and eventually the jongleur. There are differences between them, to be sure, because the societies and cultures in which they occur think differently of the origin of the language that issues from them. Thus the gods speak through the vates, God through the prophets, a mythical past through the rhapsode, the collective memory through the jongleur. And there are formal differences: the sibyl can be obscure, the jongleur cannot; the bard talks of the past, the prophet of the future. In each of these instances, the speaker, as the vehicle of the language, is the means whereby that language *instantiates itself* in the concreteness of the here and now of a certain audience. It is for them that language takes place there and then.

The sibyl is but an instance in which we see language take place, where its taking place is thematized as a visitation upon an individual. Another instance is provided by ritual, wherein a protocol of actions induces the divine action. This is a collective making of a here and now, which, if successful, will validate that here and now. What is sought by a highly choreographed set of gestures, settings, et cetera, is an effect of divine presence. To the extent that the ritual is successful, the divine will make itself present. It will thus verify, legitimate the actions that were effected to bring it about.

Ritual thought distinguishes between two sets of actions: ordinary actions undertaken by individuals in the course of everyday affairs, and actions that constitute sacred events inasmuch as they modify an existing state of being in a desired way. The latter type is seen as in need of careful preparation. Such preparation includes but is not limited to the selection of participants, a site, a setting, a propitious time period, and the conduct and observance of a behavior both verbal and nonverbal. All these preparatory acts will be perceived as successful if they result in the desired state coming into being. If a ritual is seen not to work, the defectiveness tends to fall upon the circumstances or the participants of the ritual on that particular occasion (e.g., a woman who is menstruating and thus may be judged unclean) and not upon the ritual itself. The relationship between what will be deemed to be the event and its preparation is conceived of along lines of temporality and causality. Cause will produce effect, and in return effect will validate cause. The desired state of affairs comes into being, that is, takes place, and thus affirms the validity of all the preparatory actions. They have been adequate to its occurrence, they have set the stage for its happening: in fact, in the mind of the performers and cocelebrants of the ritual, the carrying-out of the constitutive part of the ritual is seen as triggering the occurrence of the desired event, and thus as holding power over it. Ritual is a means of constraining the gods inasmuch as it sets the stage upon which they must produce themselves. The constitutive elements of the ritual are thus *indexes* delimiting a space and time for this divine production. They are not, in the minds of the practitioners, the production itself; they are the *hic et nunc* within which the production must take place.

It is our understanding that what was at an earlier time communicated and affirmed by means of ritual was gradually taken over by performance. Considerable anthropological evidence could be adduced on this point,[8] but it would be inappropriate here. We can take as an instance a story told by S. J. Agnon to Gershom Scholem.[9]

When the Baal Shem had a difficult task before him, he would go to a certain place in the woods, light a fire and meditate in prayer—and what he had set out to perform was done. When a generation later the "Maggid" of Meseritz was faced with the same task, he would go to the same place in the woods and say: We can no longer light the fire, but we can still speak the prayers—and what he wanted done became reality. Again a generation later Rabbi Moshe Lieb of Sassov had to perform this task. And he too went to the woods and said: We can no longer light a fire, nor do we know the secret meditations belonging to the prayer, but we do know the place in the woods to which it all belongs—and that must be sufficient; and sufficient it was. But when another generation had passed and Rabbi Israel of Rishin was called upon to perform the task, he sat down on his golden chair in his castle and said: We cannot light the fire, we cannot speak the prayers, we do not know the place, but we can tell the story of how it was done. And, the story-teller adds, the story which he [Rabbi Israel] told had the same effect as the actions of the other three.

If we look at the shift from the ritual—the trip to the woods, the lighting of the fire, and the prayer—to the storytelling as paradigmatic of a change in signifying practice, we can begin to examine what kind of issues are involved in such a shift. The ritual is reduced to fewer and fewer elements whose significance is lost as well, so that the effectiveness of the ritual comes to depend entirely upon its formal elements. There was a place, an action, and words (although uttered silently); then a place and words, then just a place, and then only the story of it all. The ritual is lost, but its efficacy can be recouped by the ability to spin a story from the loss. We cannot light the fire, but we can sit in a golden chair and tell of the fire. The need is the same, and can be satisfied, but through a different set of techniques, a different kind of understanding. This is the story not of a loss but of the replacement of the celebrant's skill by the storyteller's skill. It is a change in signifying practice.

We can talk at great length about what is lost in ritual, and how its goals are to some extent lost but also to a great extent recouped, even surpassed, in performance, and about all that has changed to bring this to pass, including the fashioning of the new skills that any performer had to have. We will make only a few remarks here.

One function of ritual is *telos*. Ritual has an objective efficacy: it draws the divine communication, or brings rain, appeases the gods, initiates a man or a woman. If it is done correctly, the ritual never fails. One who is accurately dubbed a knight is a knight. Herein lies its tie with magic (as well as with performatives). Ritual is a productive event: one reaps from it something other than itself.

A second function of ritual is its *protocol*. It prescribes certain actions (*ritus*), it lays down rules which must be followed. Although a ritual may allow varying degrees of freedom, its success comes from a set of actions that is determined and imposed. Furthermore, its protocol is a group protocol. Participants are not merely spectators (although the ritual may have spectators as well); all have a necessary place and role. Ritual engages all who choose to participate in it; it is inclusive. It may be hierarchized, there may be someone, or some group, who leads, initiates, sets the protocol in motion, et cetera (for simplicity, we will call the leader of a ritual the priest), but the protocol stipulates necessary sets of acts, necessary roles, for all those for whom the ritual is meant.

If ritual is displaced by the performance of a singer of tales, we notice first of all that the criterion of success of the performance is not some objective efficacy, some production other than represented action. This is not to say that the performer is ineffective. He may have powerful mimetic gifts or impart a good deal of historical, biographical, or technical information. He may even succeed in eliciting certain sought-after emotional reactions. It is just that he has not produced results that are tangible in the minds of his audience. That is not his *telos*.

And what of the performer? Does he replace the priest of ritual? Actually, he replaces the priest and much of what the participants of ritual were doing, insofar as they were cocelebrants. The great part of the collective signifying functions, shared by the group, are now bestowed upon an individual. It is the performer who initiates, recounts, moves, recites, brings relevant information to bear. The other participants are, in a more modern sense, the audience. They do have a necessary role: they react, signal their willing participation, comprehension, and appreciation, and thus determine a good deal of the performer's behavior. But their reactions, although perhaps formalized, are not determined by a protocol (although elements of protocol persist: one can see it in modern theater with the bow, the applause, in opera with the flowers, the rotten fruit). Their role is to be a pragmatic indicator of successful communication. Their reactions may vary.[10] Likewise, the performer, unlike the priest, varies his act, tailors his communication to the time, place, and audience, which, although still within a situation of telling that retains certain formalized characteristics and even protocol, are variable.

The retention of certain characteristics is central to the shift in the first place. But those characteristics can become formalized, known only as form, and so fall into discredit or disuse, unless a new role is found for them, for example, as a marker of a valued past. Given the gradual shift of emphasis and the retention of formal characteristics, certain signifying activity might be difficult to classify as "either" ritual or performance. This is not a problem if one willingly espouses a diachronic view that sees signifying practices in gradual shifts.

Some messages might never be cleansed of parts of their earlier signifying practice. Dennis Tedlock is an anthropologist particularly sensitive to the distortions performance undergoes in a written medium. His translation "A Zuñi Story: The Girl and the Protector" ends with the following remarks:

> A number of people have told me of their difficulty in deciding just what these stories should finally sound like, a problem which the further elaboration of specific instructions seems unlikely to remedy. [In other words, for this he cannot find more discourse.] Let me put it this way: the reader should not sound like someone making a speech (unless a character in the story is making a speech), but like someone telling a story at the hearthside.
>
> And now a word of warning. The written meaning gives us unlimited access to words that are really appropriate or effective only for certain times of the day or year. A Zuñi story like this one should be told late at night; if you tell it during the day you will hasten the coming of darkness. If you tell it after the snakes have come out in the spring and before they go underground in the fall, take care to omit the first and last lines and to hold a flower in one hand while you speak. Otherwise the story may attract the attention of the snakes.[11]

Sometimes, aspects of earlier practices do not remain just "residue". They can come back to haunt us. Even a reader can get a chill here. Tellers are lucky: they know the rules. What are the rules about writing the story down, publishing it, reading it? Did Tedlock take any precautions? How did he get away with it? Can just writing or reading the story escape these sanctions, or might they have their own kinds of danger? Does not reading have protocols as well, or, since the double act of writing and reading shares no unique moment or space, is reading's lack of eventfulness simply presumed to have some special talismanic value that disarms such protocols?

Communication in performance centers upon a representation, with basically a single agent responsible for constructing and maintaining a represented world. Protocols of concerted action by a community have given way to the repertoire of an individual who becomes, in performance, the *locus* of different representative functions, and whose skill (for this is the new *tekhne*) allows him to shift from one to the other and still hold together the representation, still constitute a continuity in his own body and presence. He learns to do that difficult task of *performing a narrative*. It all happens in the place he creates and engages around him. The distribution of communicative functions among individuals has become interiorized in a single individual. As a corollary, the "sacred" ritual space has become more abstract, less a templum and more a stage, held together by the singer's skill in shifts of function. Whereas in ritual he as a participant would be *assigned* a position, in performance he *negotiates* one.

The shift of signifying practice has imposed a different cleavage among the participants. To one participant (newly skilled) has fallen the function of presentation and representation as a whole. Other participants have been sheared off: no longer cocelebrants, they are retained only for specific cuing functions. The cleavage has brought with it a measure of new autonomy to both sides.[12]

It is important to understand what a jongleur does, so that when his performance is, in its turn, replaced by, or "contained within," another signifying practice, we can get a sense of the burdens placed on the successor signifying practice. The jongleur's performance will be transcribed and it will be read. (At least, this is how we understand early written verse.) With the disappearance of the substance and presence of the jongleur, with the disappearance of that which located, contained, and continuously sustained the performance in its shifts among all the different types of discourse that any sustained fabula will require, what will the burdens be on that piece of writing when it evolves into a new signifying practice all its own?

Writing is a *tekhne*, like the drum: it is used for varying purposes, endowed with different kinds of power according to the signifying practice in which it takes part. As performance becomes written, verbal behavior will become potentially more powerful than nonverbal behavior. It is up to the culture to allow that to happen. The question is: to the extent that the voice, body, and presence of the jongleur is the *nonverbal* anchor, the taking-place of the truth, the seat of the utterance (as in the seat of prophesy), how can the written embrace it? How can discourse embrace its own uttering subject and circumstances?

Chapter 2
Written Verse

The linguistic history of the peoples inhabiting the territory that came to be known as France is a particularly murky one. The original inhabitants of the land, the Gauls, had adopted Latin as their vehicle of communication. This Latin, however, was of the soldier, the trader, and not of the learned classes, and thus it differed considerably from that found in the texts of Latin culture. From the fifth to the eighth century, this territory was invaded primarily by people of Germanic origins who spoke a variety of Germanic dialects. In contact with Gallo-Roman culture, they preserved some of their own institutions, notably their conceptions of law, but they adopted the vulgar Latin then spoken in the territory as their main vehicle. We do not know and are never likely to be able to establish how long the cultural artifacts, such as epic songs, of these Germanic tribes were preserved in the Germanic dialects. These dialects were not written and have therefore left no textual evidence. All writing was done in Latin, usually under the auspices of the church, which saw itself as the rightful heir to the cultural heritage of the Roman Empire.

The church itself was forced to acknowledge that its dedication to the preservation of Latin could form an obstacle to its evangelical mission, for it became quite apparent that the vulgar language was evolving further and further away from the canons of Latin, which were becoming incomprehensible to the population. At the Council of Tours, in 813, the church thus authorized the preaching of sermons in the vulgar language, yet in accordance with its conception of itself as a universal church, it preserved Latin as the vehicle of all written and learned communication. Therefore, two cultures were established, one learned, relying on the written word and for which Latin was the language of choice, and the other oral, speaking a bewildering diversity of languages without formalized grammars or, indeed, codes for their orthographic transcription. We may never understand what led to the decision to begin writing down some of the cultural artifacts of this oral culture, for example, what we call epics. Nor are we likely to be able to reconstruct the process by which the codes for recording these artifacts were elaborated. We simply have to acknowledge their existence as something that materialized with growing intensity from the tenth century onward.

All these early artifacts are written in verse, and there has been a strong tendency on the part of medievalists and philologists to take them as mere transcriptions of the verbal component of prior oral performances. Such a view can proceed only from an ignorance of the nature of writing. Writing is never merely transcription: it is a system that involves codes, rules of inclusion and exclusion, as well as all sorts of markers.[1] The very decision to write in a vernacular tongue grants that tongue a status that bears at least some analogy to that of Latin. It begins to change that tongue and to explicitly formalize its grammar. It reflects a perception of the social and communicative importance of the tongue and inevitably raises issues of hegemony of one tongue over others, which will then be considered only as dialects or variants of this *koine*, undeserving of such permanence. There is thus constituted an emergent written culture in the vernacular, with still very close ties to the oral culture inasmuch as most members of this culture are preliterate. With that as the case, the vast majority of the population still relies on performance, or on performed reading. A purely oral culture is now becoming more of an aural culture, and reading will be useful only if understood as within the communicative framework of performance, as a script, deriving its ethos from the here and now of performance and not from the written. That is, the text to be read is a virtuality to be actualized in the performance. The very fact that most of this verse was read out loud in a transitional form of performance further obfuscated the issue.

In this type of culture, let us recognize two different levels of literacy, one that applies to those who have the skill and are empowered to actualize a text into a performance, namely, the jongleur, and one that applies to others who cannot actualize the text as performance but are able to read the text as virtual performance. Literacy for the jongleur is the ability both to decode the script and to enact it according to the conventions of the tradition into which it fits. For a nonjongleur to be literate with respect to these texts, he or she would presumably have to have been a spectator of a number of performances, with a cultural competence based on the knowledge of and ethos of performances. He or she could then provide, by an act of imagination fed by memory, the unwritten components of performance, including specifically the assignment of the jongleur as that which occupies the position of enunciating subject. Such an assignment of the appropriate position is a condition of any utterance's proper comprehension and meaning.[2] We present-day readers also can assign "jongleur" to that position, but we cannot really read him in, as can a reader contemporary to performance, because we are ignorant of all that he stands for, all that he is a part of. Our lack of cultural competence stands in the way of our understanding of early medieval texts.

In the movement from performance to text, there is both a sense of loss and a sense of excess, and the reader will perceive an incommensurateness between the text and the performance and will apply all his or her cultural competence to mitigate its effects. The abundance of written verse, and the recycling of some of it through derhyming, testifies to the fact that it must have enjoyed a certain measure of success as communication despite such difficulties. There is much we do not understand when we read medieval epics because all we have is the text (and what we know of modern performance practice). Contemporary readers possessed the necessary competence, which we do not have. Our task is to reconstruct that competence, but we can get an idea of the magnitude of that task by taking stock of our own difficulties in specifying with precision the performance aspects of texts derived from modern performance. We are not even in a position to know totally how much we are missing.

We do feel certain lacks, such as the absence of transitional material in the epics (this is the famous problem of the *raccords* in scholarly discussion). For example, the texts did not have quotation marks, and they did not always clearly distinguish between when the jongleur is reciting the dialogue of one speaker as opposed to another. Such a shift is easy enough for a jongleur to signal nonverbally. The diverse functions that the jongleur assumes are not limited to his change in role, from the "voice" of one character to that of another. Dialogue, repeating the "speech" of a character, is just one of many distinctive discourses, distinctive enunciative modalities signaled by a variety of semiotic means (such as mimicry, dance, stance, voice levels, gaze) that the jongleur routinely manipulates. He has to have the ability to go from the narrative of a battle to the *planctus* on the death of the hero and, thereafter, to another mode. Music, rhythm, and even the pause of silence were mobilized to achieve these distinct modalities without sacrificing the coherence of the whole. We readers attempt to gain what coherence we can, deprived as we are of these nonverbal behaviors.

As written texts of performance overtake and surpass performance itself as a conveyance for certain kinds of messages between generations, such problems as those we have just outlined must have begun to affect the contemporary reader as well. Any reader for whom performance weakens in the memory begins to feel the physical absence of the utterer and the lack of continuity in space and time between utterer and addressee, which is characteristic of performance and which the sole written verse of that performance does not enjoy. The reader must rely on the verbal alone and thus is faced with what must have then appeared brutally paratactic, lacking in all the means that ensure the cohesion and smooth flow of a performance, in which the embedding of one discourse into another is frequently handled by nondiscursive means. As is the case with all forms of writing, verse does not control the conditions of its reception. Yet the verse, written and recopied over the next few centuries, does not address this issue at all.[3] The explanation lies in the fact that verse remains beholden to performance. It is only in a truly jongleurless text, in which the assigned position is not that of the jongleur and the understood situation is not that of the performance, that the issue will be raised. And it is prose that will face it squarely.

If we, and gradually the medieval readership as well, face written texts at a distance from performance, how are they to be read? What new kind of literacy is necessary? Perhaps its fundamental principle is the ability to distinguish between the jongleur as a flesh-and-blood practitioner of performance and the jongleur as the locus and articulator of an aggregate of verbal and nonverbal semiotic codes. What is required is the ability to abstract the *function* from the *agent* of communication, a process of abstraction and analysis which we link to prose literacy. To use a technology (which writing and reading is) to undermine a signifying practice (e.g., performance) in terms of the centerpiece of that signifying practice (e.g., the jongleur) is very cumbersome and requires constant adjustments. The development of prose, we claim, represents the attempt to provide a signifying practice commensurate with the available technology.

A simple solution for the "jongleurless" verse script would be to somehow "add" the jongleur, to add the deictic expression "he said: ' . . . '." But just the understanding, which was implicit anyway, that this is jongleurian language is clearly not sufficient in the absence of his other behavior, his extralinguistic situation, and so on. A transcriber could then, in the next logical step, proceed to record aspects of the jongleur's accompanying nonverbal activity, for example, "and then the jongleur turned toward the mountains, shaded his eyes, and shouted". But who can do this? The jongleur describes his characters' actions all the time, he supplements their dialogue, he is authorized to do that, and he knows what we are looking for. But there is no *rapporteur,* no agent trained to do this with respect to the jongleur. In a culture still primarily oral, why would one have to be trained to jot down the jongleur's behavior when, if you were there, you could simply imitate him? In other words, there were no means at the time for delivering a performance as such *in absentia.*

And if one attempted to recount the behavior of the jongleur and add it to a script, how much would be sufficient? Would only one code, his gross body movement, or his tone of voice, do? Or would one have to use several? What would hold them together? Inscribing the jongleur poses formidable problems of semiotic transcription. Even today, we lack the vocabulary and, indeed, the codes for "writing down a performance," and that very phrase is more the expression of a wish than a possibility. The question is then: how is *he* to be written so as to be understood? In performance, he is the final agent, there is no other who contains and embraces him. *He* is the deixis, the underlying deictic condition, both the utterer and that which draws in anything else when necessary. All that can be described of the jongleur is, through some kind of analytics, a limited account of some of the ways he functions. The jongleur, as a flesh-and-blood professional practitioner with a broad repertoire of skills, falls victim to the new technology of reading.

If a *rapporteur* records the jongleur's activity as well as his words, there could be confusion: when is it the jongleur and when is it the *rapporteur* talking? Quotation marks were introduced by sixteenth-century scholars and were named *guillemets* after the French printer Guillaume in 1677. (Any provenance they may have would be from *Latin* manuscripts of *commentary,* not vernacular texts of performance.)[4] Even if there were quotation marks, what sort of "voice" could there be? Is there at that time a sort of "neutral" voice? The jongleur can move nimbly "in" and "out" of the characters he presents, but that is a particular skill of his, which completely depends on his physical presence and has nothing to do with writing. Voice was allowed to fluctuate within boundaries known to him. This is built into the signifying practice of performance: it is how it works.

The encoding of the jongleur's nonverbal behavior and other reportorial problems could have been solved had there been an established status of *rapporteur,* that is, had there evolved a new signifying practice concerning reports of performance (including words, performer, setting, etc.). That written verse did not so evolve shows prose to have emerged not just from some technical difficulty or entanglement in verse itself but from a slow, irreversible movement away from (even encapsulated or narrated) performance as the signifying practice of record for these kinds of messages.

The inability to *write* the jongleur shows that one cannot establish a signifying practice, or recoup a waning one, by means of deictic expressions alone. A deictic expression is that portion of a verbal string that refers to its outside, its own ground, but mere reference to the ground by such an expression, or by what we will call the larger category of deictic (any communicative means, verbal or otherwise, whereby the space, time, origin, and circumstance of that communication is referred to), will not suffice.[5]

From the Greek definition "pointing" or "indicating," deixis usually means the function of certain grammatical and lexical features that relate utterances to the spatiotemporal coordinates of the act of utterance. For example, "I," "here," "now," and "you," "there," "then," as well as verb tenses, mean only the "who" and "where" and "when" of the utterance, which is often given nonverbally. As Agamben points out, Thomas of Erfurt (1340), in his *grammatica speculativa,* distinguishes between two types of *demonstratio* or deixis: the first type makes reference to the senses *(demonstratio ad sensum),* in which case it signifies what it indicates, it is ostensive, and thus accomplishes a coincidence of showing and telling; the second type makes reference to the intellect *(demonstratio ad intellectum),* in which case it does not signify what it shows but something else. According to Thomas of Erfurt, this is the *modus significandi* of proper names as well: "Ut si dicam, demonstrato Joanne, iste fuit Joannes, hic unum demonstratur et aliud in numeros significatur" (So that if I am to say, showing John, this here was John, one is being shown here, and another is being signified in signs [numbers]). Where does this *aliud* come from, this otherness that is in play in the second form of deixis?

Benveniste has pointed out that there is more complexity in deixis than one might think because each act of utterance is unique, and so these words have no stable referent; their meaning is determinable only by means of the instance of discourse in which they occur.[6] In so doing, however, they refer not to that which the utterance contains but to that which it does not contain (otherwise the utterance would not have to use a deictic expression): deixis indicates, in a fashion that is in some sense wordless (that is, it assigns no labels), that which surrounds it and contains it. Deixis refers to that for which the discourse has no name but on which it depends; deictic expressions indicate only what is outside the discourse, but their reference draws one right back to the discourse. Benveniste activates the Saussurian distinction to conclude that deictics are the verbal mechanism that permits language to become discourse, that they effect the passage from the virtuality of *langue* to the actuality of *parole.* Roman Jakobson's analysis of deictics, which he calls "shifters," is quite similar, although it originates in, and indeed closely espouses, Piercian categories of symbol and index.[7] What is interesting about this theory of deixis is that it appears to run counter to what seemed to be the very core of the problem. On the one hand, the indicational capability of deixis, its ability to indicate a here and now, had been taken as the very bedrock of referentiality. This is where language encountered the *resistance* of what it talked about, and thus it has cognitive value; it apprehended the world. On the other hand, once the mechanism at work in deixis is investigated and described, it turns out that deictics do not refer to anything tangible, to anything that has any resistance, as is clear from the very instability of the terms themselves: "I" becomes "you" when you address me, and "here" turns into "there," et cetera. That deictics refer to the instance of discourse is a dismal finding for those who placed their hopes in the referential capacity of language, for it is clear that deictics were the great hope of referentiality. But it is too soon to conclude that, as a result, deictics lock us into language.

Deixis can be a condition of truth. "The cat is on the mat" problem is a problem of deixis: the sentence is true only insofar as the utterer refers to a given cat, that is, the cat is a cat that has been referred to or otherwise brought to the attention of the addressee. For all practical purposes, the sentence must be taken to mean something like: "This cat that you and I are aware of is now on this mat that you and I are aware of." Of course no one talks this way, but the proper functioning of the discourse that we wield *presupposes that sort of structural capacity to specify deixis*. The history of languages is instructive in this regard: it is well known that the present-day articles of Romance languages are descendants of Latin demonstratives (e.g., *le* from *ille*), and the medieval forms of these articles still have the strong demonstrative capabilities and have to be translated as such. Many utterances can be evaluated in terms of their claims to truthfulness only when this deictic dimension is brought into consideration. Neither the logical nor the grammatical structure of a sentence suffices for these purposes; they may provide assurances of well-formedness, but they are helpless to determine whether the sentence is true with respect to a certain state of affairs. So deictics do refer; they refer to the fact that language has taken place and that it is something that takes place, that it is even something that offers resistance. Benveniste's reliance upon the Saussurian terminology and its Aristotelian overtones ought not to blind us to the fact that *deictics are the means by which language makes itself into something that can be referred to,* and it is from this inaugural act of reference that all other forms of discourse reference will flow.[8]

Deixis shows the very instance of discourse; it shows that discourse is *taking place.* It is a way that discourse can make reference to its own eventfulness, something that can be referred to, something that has taken place. Insofar as the place that discourse takes is a condition of its meaning, deixis is a condition of meaning. To understand discourse is to understand its situation, its taking-place, its set of pragmatic indexes, its *deixis,* which we will take to be that which situates and holds the utterance, that to which its deictic expressions refer.[9]

Anything in communication that connects a piece of signifying behavior to its situation, like the gesture of pointing, we will call a deictic. Any grammatical or lexical feature that acts in such a way is a subclass of deictic, which we will call a *deictic expression.* And deixis, as we use it, has this double character: it shows a dependence, one to which we will repeatedly return, of discourse upon its outside, what contains it; and also the ability of an instrument (discourse) to gesture to and in its particular way embrace (although in varying degrees of completeness, and never completely) precisely that which is excluded from it.

A deictic expression is an index out of word and into situation. It is a place in the lexicon and grammar for recognizing that which is excluded by *verba* (the extralinguistic) but necessary to it (because, in enunciation, *verba* must be engaged in situation). Whether there is a deictic (an operator) at the surface of the communication or not, every utterance must have a deixis: it is where the utterance is understood to take place, it surrounds the utterance and so is necessary to its meaning. When referring to this condition, we will occasionally substitute for it another term more appropriate to the discussion: the assigned subject, the enunciative instance, the discourse, the situation or circumstances, the perspective, the context. These terms are not interchangeable—they each approach the condition of deixis from their *own* contexts and sets of mechanisms—but they all participate in the establishment of necessary deixis.

Deixis for us, then, will not be just a deictic expression linking an instance of *langue* with its instantiation as utterance, as, say, attributable voice. It will more broadly be the grounding of utterance or other particular signifying behavior in whatever coexisting and coextensive circumstances are necessary to empower it and give it meaning (and, of course, if those vary, its meaning varies). Now, when an utterer stands in a given place at a given time, with us, when we the receivers of the verbal message also receive everything necessary to know about the empowerment of the situation, there is no deictic expression or particular deictic behavior necessary to mark that deixis. The deixis is *implicit.* As a structural part of successful communication, we depend on it without necessarily being able to point to the ways in which we have been made aware of it. In fact, deixis is difficult to limit in scope: for most complex communications, it may extend beyond our range and our ability to be analytically exhaustive with respect to it. Therefore there may very well be deictics that we have not yet recognized as such, that is, referring to as yet unrecognized aspects of deixis. How far we go in identifying deictics is really a measure of our total analytic scope. Another measure of our analytic success is the ability to cut off the deictic search, concluding with confidence that the deictics (and deixis, since deictics would be a way of plotting deixis) need go no further. How can we go about drawing such kinds of conclusions? The best way to analyze deictics is to take something out of its place—displace it—make it take place but not let it take *its* place, keep certain things in the message constant but uproot the message from other surrounding circumstances, and see what happens. When writing transcribed speech, the functioning of certain deictics became clear: who is "I"? Where is "here"? Yet, if the writing is just to be recited by the original or equivalent speaker, under functionally equivalent circumstances (i.e., the same deixis), such questions would not have been asked, there having occurred a change by means of a new *tekhne* but as yet no change of signifying practice. In the emergence of a new signifying practice, questions of deixis become central.

Utterances are multisemiotic. One either experiences them in all their heterogeneous components or takes them through a smaller number of semiotic systems in which, as previously said, some components are set aside, assumed, referred to, or called on from time to time, and links are established when necessary. A signifying practice manages manifold semiotic systems to its particular end. It establishes some implicit whole, which it involves, and has to have some principle of exclusion that separates the relevant from the irrelevant in the ambient cacaphony. So one thing a signifying practice is concerned with is minimalities. The verbal component of a signifying practice is relatively easy to isolate (although problems are inherent in that, too); nonverbal components are more difficult. How are they codified? How do they intertwine? What is important and what is not? And of the important, what needs to operate on the surface, be recognized as important, as opposed to that which can remain assumed and implicit?

We asked how the medieval reader could continue to read verse texts, finding himself or herself at an increasing distance from performance. The question can be restated as follows: as an utterance is distanced from its empowering ground and situation, and as it is reduced from the multisemioticity of its former setting to a limited number of codes that cannot include everything that was part of its former setting, what happens? If this kind of utterance is to retain its importance, if the culture considers the utterance to hold that which is meant to be preserved, then a new signifying practice will emerge around the utterance. That new signifying practice will, *grosso modo* (1) be able to compensate for the loss of certain original and empowering aspects, (2) willingly leave other aspects for lost, and (3) realize new gains from what is newly available to it.

The most striking result is that some nonverbal factors in the previous signifying practice are replaced by new discourses or discourses newly employed.[10] This usually takes the general form of description, or of the recounting of action, *diegesis*. In the words of the Baal Shem story, "We cannot light the fire, we cannot speak the prayers, we do not know the place, but we can tell the story of how it was done." Although the Baal Shem himself had no need of a *discourse about* lighting fires or a *discourse about* finding a certain place in the woods—he just knew how to do it, had a method that was lost to succeeding generations—for the storyteller, these aspects must be given in voice.[11] The emerging signifying practice will establish a new ground on which the different arrangement of verbal and nonverbal behavior can "take place." Performance is such a new ground, on which the jongleur can *represent* the multisemiotic of the handed-down act or ritual (those aspects that remained meaningful) by all the means materially and technically available to him, not only through his language but through *all that is multisemiotic in his situation and at his disposal:* his body as signifying in various ways and his engagement with time and surroundings. Much of this is unavoidable: he is already there; these things stand around him. He need not constantly and consciously use deictics or deictic expressions: he is an operator of deixis merely by doing what he is doing. He is always implicitly pointing to some of these things. At one time the ground on which he is standing is understood to be the stony floor of a castle, at another time, the bloody field of battle. It is by virtue of his presence that the ground can be different and yet the same. He can draw the ground in, and change its identity, without ever isolating it as such. He need not enact an explicit decoupage, stating or encapsulating the necessary factors of his surroundings: he simply engages them for the purposes of meaning-making.

There is a strong strategy of implicities and minimalities in signifying practices: just enough to keep portrayals locally consistent.[12] Performance is a new ground on which different sets of discourses and different sets of nonverbal signifying behavior and settings can meet because the jongleur is heir to a tradition that has found a way to reestablish necessary deixis. Of course we are in historical change, so what *is* necessary deixis changes.[13] The new discourses, the different and differing perspectives that tend to compensate for a distancing from a waning signifying practice, can cohere only on the new ground of a new signifying practice. Just as this happens in the movement toward performance, it happens again in the movement away from it.

The success of performance depends on the actions and soma of the subject, the jongleur, as the operator of its deixis. When he seems to fail to readers of today or of the fourteenth and fifteenth centuries, we who encounter seeming incoherencies, it is most likely because we do not share that situation, we have only the writing of his words, in which there are not enough deictic expressions (nor could deictics alone be the answer) to draw us back into the deixis of performance. We are at too great a distance from his circumstances. As mentioned earlier, the jongleur *could* still survive, as character, say, in a possible emerging signifying practice that successfully conveys performance, but he does not because the way performance sees things, and the way it knows them, whether the performance is enacted *or* written, can no longer hold sway. This will become clear as our study progresses.

Part II

Chapter 3
Dérimage

To walk well it is not enough that a man abstain from dancing.

Thomas de Quincy

Prose:—Plus facile à faire que les vers.

Gustave Flaubert, *Dictionnaire des idées reçues*

A certain neglected class of texts from the thirteenth century onward provides a privileged domain of inquiry. After the impetus of the Dukes of Flanders, the demand for prose was so strong and so immediate that it could not be satisfied by the original prose that appeared. Written culture was now reaching for a new stage and conducting a purge of written artifacts still beholden to the culture of performance, assigning a new place to those that would become full-fledged members of written culture as it was being defined. Writers were asked to produce prose works by derhyming already existing rhymed works. There arose the profession of the *dérimeur*, one who could "transpose" rhymed *chansons de geste* and *romans d'avanture* into nonverse. The *dérimeur* would be, then, at the center of the motivated choice of nonverse over verse, a choice essential to the evolution of prose.

The few scholars who have compared rhymed and derhymed versions[1] have remarked on the frequency with which the *dérimeur* left intact whole verses and even couplets in his "prosification." Occasionally a *dérimeur* would fall back into verse proper. Perhaps derhyming was not as simple a task for them as it would be for us today. Perhaps we see here a hesitancy to derhyme, a difficulty these writers had in detaching themselves from the versified form, and a trepidation about plunging into the less articulated, more amorphous material that is prose, Cicero's term for which is *oratio soluta*: "loosened," "unfettered," "free". The *dérimeurs* might not have considered prose to be natural, neutral, or perhaps even formless. They might have seen it as exacting its own demands. They can problematize for us what "prose-work" is and, thus, what prose may be.

The task that imposes itself is to compare original verse and subsequent unrhymed material. Even though many such derhymings were conducted, very few instances of both the rhymed and derhymed text have been handed down to us, and in even fewer cases do we have the corresponding passages of the derhymed to the rhymed to permit analysis. One of the better known ones is *Bérinus*, an anonymous *roman d'avanture* of which we have two fragments of a verse manuscript from the thirteenth century and an anonymous, complete derhymed version dating between 1350 and 1380.[2] We will be looking at five pairs of passages that give us the central narrative core of the more extensive verse fragment.

Our first passage recounts the end of a combat between the hero, Aigres, and a count. They have both been thrown off their horses.

> *Verse*
>
> N'avoit pas chascon la moitie
> De tote s'armeure [e]ntere,
> Mes, a la fin, par de derrere,
> Li gette Ai[gres] un entredous
> Ki de costes le trencha dous.
> Le brant d'acier el cors li baigne:
> Cil n'a poeir qu[e] il se plaigne,
> Ki a la mort estoit feruz;
> A la terre est tantost chauz.
>
> *Aigres le veit, si li disoit:*
> "Sire vassals, si ore endroit
> La duchoyse ne clamez quite,
> Vostre vie ert mult petite."
> Mes a co qu Ai[gres] l'aresone,

Cil qui mort fut [nul] mot ne sone.
Ai[gres] quide qu'il [ne] se feigne;
Tote s'espee el cors li baigne,
A son bliaut l'a essuie.

Verse

Each did not have half
Of his suit of armor unscathed;
Finally Aigres strikes
A blow from behind
That cut through two of his ribs.
He plunges the steel blade in the body.
The count, who was struck to death,
Does not have the strength to utter a complaint;
He falls to the ground.
Aigres saw this and told him:
"Lord vassal, if right here
You do not pledge the duchess free of your claims,
Your life will be very short."
But in reply to Aigres's speech
He who was dead made no sound.
Aigres thinks that he is pretending;
He plunges all of his sword into his body,
He wiped it on his tunic.

Prose

Ne nul d'eulx deux n'avoit pas la moitie de ses armeures, tant que,
en la fin, Aigres jetta un coup en travers au conte, si lui coupa deux
de ses costes. Et quant il senti que le coup ala au roit, si bouta avant
et lui baigna l'espee dedens le corps, dont fut si attaint que de lui plain-
dre n'ot pouoir, ains cheÿ a terre comme cellui qui estoit ferus a mort.
*Et Aigres, qui ne se donnoit garde que le comte feust si durement navrez,
si lui dist:* "Ha! vassal, maintenant vous convient il la duchesse quitte
clamer de son heritage, ou vous avrez courte duree." Mais pour chose
que Aigres deïst, le conte ne lui sonna mot, car l'ame en estoit ja partie.
Et Aigres, qui cuidoit qu'il ne feust pas mort, lui bouta son espee parmi
le corps, puis l'essuya et la mist dedens le fourrel. (2.207-8.144-45)[3]

Prose

Neither of them had half of his suit of armor unscathed, and finally
Aigres dealt the count a cross blow, and he cut two of his ribs. And
when he felt that the blow was going sideways, he pushed forward and
plunged the sword into the body, which blow so affected the count
that he did not have the strength to complain, and he fell to the ground
like one who is struck to death. *And Aigres, who did not notice that*

the count was so severely wounded, told him: "Ah! vassal, now you must proclaim the duchess free of your claims to her inheritance or you will last but a short time." But whatever Aigres may have told him, the count did not utter a word, for his soul had already departed. And Aigres, who thought he was not dead, thrust his sword into his body, and then wiped it and put it into his scabbard.

The two passages markedly differ in two respects: their characterization of what Aigres saw and of the manner of his apprehension. In the verse, the count is described as "a la mort feruz" (struck [or wounded] to death) and as subsequently falling to the ground. Aigres, we are told, sees "him," "it," or "this"—the Old French "Aigres le veit" does not permit us to specify. The prose, by contrast, describes the count as falling "like one who is struck to death" and Aigres as unaware of the severity of the count's wound. This difference is substantial: the prose motivates Aigres's second blow inflicted to a man already dead by indicating the limits of Aigres's knowledge of the count's true condition. In the verse, Aigres's predicament—what is the count's exact condition?—is shared by the reader as well.

The phrase "a la mort feruz" is supremely ambiguous. It states that death is caused by a wound, but it says nothing about the length of time between the inflicting of the wound and the cessation of life. There is thus established, through the aforesaid phase, a temporal indeterminacy. It is language that opens this temporal gap between the cause of death and its effect.

In both texts, this temporal gap is exploited for reasons having to do with the movement of the plot: Aigres seeks from his defeated enemy a pledge of renunciation with respect to his claims over the lady, a pledge that would effectively bring all hostilities to an end and ensure that no revenge would be sought, either by the count, should he recover from his wound, or by his followers in the event of his death. In other words, Aigres seeks a final disposition of the conflict. Such a disposition is of course not available to him because there is no time for such an act of renunciation.[4] The count is dead, the text belatedly lets us know unequivocally.

The reader of the verse is in a bind: he or she reads that the count is fatally wounded but does not know whether that means that the count is dead. He or she reads that Aigres issues an ultimatum to the count and that he strikes him again as the latter lies dead. The count's death is confirmed now, but too late, as it were. The uncertainty about the count's actual condition while he is addressed by Aigres is shared equally by the reader and Aigres. Neither knows how to read "mortally wounded." Either the count is already dead at the moment when Aigres is talking to him (and then Aigres should know this) or else the count dies during Aigres's speech, and Aigres should notice this. The problem lies in the verbal expression "a la mort feruz," which occults the moment of the death.

Prose dispels this confusion yet leaves all Aigres's uncertainty intact. And it does so by means that are purely verbal. The written verse (and this is what we mean by "written verse" in this context), we see by contrast to the subsequent prose, cannot dispel the confusion because it is doubly lacking: first, in the nonverbal resources of performance and, second, in the deeper language analytics (to which we will return) of prose. This is why written verse is precarious.

Prose can unpack the distinction between the punctual and the resultant qualities of a mortal wound. First, prose modulates the expression "a la mort feruz" with a "like," which places the entire phenomenon into the realm of perception: that is, first of all, out of assertion (where verse had it) and into something that calls for a reading and an interpretation. In fact, the fall, which in the verse follows as a consequence of the mortal wound, in the prose is itself subject to interpretation and classed as only resembling the class of falls caused by mortal wounds. Second, prose tells us what the limitations upon Aigres's perception are. He is careless in establishing the severity of the count's wound. Aigres's subsequent comportment is comprehensible and behaviorally coherent. And, more importantly, the entire scene makes sense to the reader, who understands the whole sequence once he or she understands Aigres as laboring under a misapprehension, whereas in the verse, it appears that Aigres's misapprehension can be maintained only at the cost of a corresponding confusion in the reader. This brings us to the striking difference: in verse Aigres sees; in prose he does not notice. Prose can function with blindness.

In the passage that follows the inflicting of the fatal wound, Aigres heads back to the castle, but he is without his horse, Morel. Orchas, his companion, comes to his aid.

Verse

Mes il n'a mie de Morel,
Si fust venuz tart al chastel,
S[e] il n'eüst socors mult tost,
Kar [c]ulvert pres furent repost,
Li home al conte en un boschet.
Quand il voient que Ai[gres] se vait
E que lor sires est occis,
Apres lui vont tuit ademis,
Si le suient plus que le pas.
Quant sis conpainz le veit, Orchas,

Avint tost [monté] sor Morel,
Ke a la porte del chastel
Trova, quant il se [en]fuï
E Aigres de sor lui chaï.
Quand il voit cels venir le cors,
Lors point pur faire Ai[gre] socors,
Ki de curre failloit l'aleine.
Mes Orchas le destrier le meine;
Quand il l'encontre, si descent,
Le destrier par le freint le rent,
E Ai[gres] sor le destrier monte;
Einz que venist la gent al conte,
Sailli Orchas derere lui.
E quant il sun monté amdui,
Plus tost que ne destent quarrels
Les [en] enporteroit Morels,
Tant qu[e] il vindrent el chastel,
[Ou sa]chez que mult en fu bel
A la duchoise e a ses genz.

Verse

But he did not have Morel,
And he would have reached the castle late
If he did not receive assistance very soon;
The count's men were resting
In some woods nearby.
When they saw that Aigres was leaving
And that their lord was killed,
They set out after him
And they followed him more than apace.
When his companion Orchas saw this,
He came immediately riding Morel
Whom he had found by the castle's gate
Where the latter had fled
When Aigres had fallen off him.
When he [Orchas] saw them coming,
He spurred the horse to bring help to Aigres who
Was getting out of breath from running.
Orchas brings the mount forward;
When he meets him he dismounts
And hands the horse over by the bridle
And Aigres mounts the horse;
Just as the count's men came
Orchas jumped behind him.
And when they both had been mounted

Morel carried them away
Faster than a fight breaks out,
So much so that they arrived at the castle,
Which, you should know, pleased
The duchess and her followers.

Prose

Et atant il s'en cuida retourner a pié, quand les hommes du conte qui estoient dedens le bois embuschiez, coururent aprés lui, car moult avoint grant duel de leur seigner qu'il avoit occiz, et croy qu'ilz *l'eüssent* rataint et retenu, quant Orchas son compaignon, qui bien avoit veü que on le chassoit, lui amena Moreau son cheval. Si monta sus moult viguereusement et puis brocherent tant que ilz vindrent ou chastel ou Aigres fut receü a moult grant joie de la duchesse et de ses gens. (2.208-9.145)

Prose

And so he thought of making his way back on foot when the count's men, who were laying in ambush in the woods, ran after him for they were very aggrieved with the loss of their lord whom he had killed, and he thought they *would* catch up to him and hold him when his companion Orchas, who saw indeed that he was being chased, brought him his horse Morel. He mounted it speedily and they spurred it on until they arrived at the castle where Aigres was received with great joy by the duchess and her followers.

In the verse we are given Aigres's moves, the soldiers' perceptions, and their moves. We then get Orchas's perceptions when he sees his companion. A recalling of the fact that Aigres was thrown off his horse is involved. Orchas sees the pursuers, bent on revenge, sees Aigres tiring, and brings him the horse. Then the handing-over of the horse is recounted, at the moment when the men are approaching.

In the prose, Orchas is not introduced until Aigres is in imminent danger. Orchas is then brought in, as one who sees "qu'on le chassait." "On le chassait" is a distillation of the preceding information. Orchas is presented as understanding the situation, but the situation is not constructed along the discrete units of this character's apprehension.

A present-day reader experiences a certain amount of difficulty in following the details of the action in the verse version. This type of difficulty is a standard occurrence in narrative medieval texts and is recognized by the learned editors of these texts, who frequently offer synopses of the action. The difficulty is attributed to a certain lack of precision in the reference of pronouns. It would be absurd to suppose that medieval readers were as confused, and we ought not to assume, as some have suggested, that they simply

accommodated themselves to this imprecision. Thus the only reasonable conclusion is that they read differently from the way we do. We have already
suggested that readers of written verse had a literacy anchored around the
practice of performance. If we recall that the forms of the pronouns as well
as those of the articles in Old French derived from Latin demonstratives (e.g.,
le from *ille*), we will see in the texts that they have a reference that is strongly
ostensive and suggest a gestural articulation of the space of representation.
Thus, where you have in two consecutive lines one "il" referring to the horse
Morel and another referring to Orchas, the difference in their antecedents
and referents does not lend itself to confusion as long as one "sees" them
as occupying different loci in a space of representation where the finger of
the performer affixes them.[5]

When the culture moves further away from performance-based communication, this mode of reading will begin to vanish, and such texts will in fact
become confusing for lack of competent readers. Once again, the prose text
will relieve their confusion. As far as the pronouns themselves are concerned,
prose will reverse the weight between reference and antecedence in favor of
the latter, which is much more easily ascertainable in a dimension that is now
purely textual, and deprive the pronouns of their demonstrative value in favor
of their endophoric potentialities as text binders.[6] Prose operates in a space
of its own making, a purely textual space, rather than one of performance.

The other major difference is the number of main clauses. The growing
complexity of the sentence as it develops in Old French has long been noted.
Yet the reasons for such a development have remained uncertain and are
best explained as a natural process of maturation. The verse and prose passages juxtaposed here may help us understand what determines such an evolution.

Each of the verbs of the written verse stands for a discrete action: it gives
each event its own space and its own time. And these elements of space fit
into the real space of the performance, that is, here is Aigres, here are the
men, here is Orchas, here is the horse. The "here is" is not necessary in the
speech of the jongleur: the space of which it is a question is a natural space
that is merely acknowledged by the language taking place there. Similarly,
time here is also natural time and, whereas the duration of each event may
admit of some shortening or lengthening, the consecution continues to obey
the irreversibility of natural time. Once again, language merely takes note
of this natural time. In other words, we are in a monoplanar space and in a
unilinear time, which are the distinctive features of the world of performance.
Here action and cognition of that action are treated equally.

In the prose, the verbs of action are subordinated to main clause verbs
of cognition and perception ("cuida," "croy," "voir"). Thus the representation of the action is articulated not by the natural unfolding of the events

but by acts of cognition that give each event a place and a time determined by the cognition thereof. Space and time are no longer universal and natural but rather a functor of the cognition and therefore variable according to the latter's needs. In other words, prose constructs its own space and time according to local needs.

In the verse, the rescue is possible because of a necessary preparation that gives each element its equal due, endowing cognition with the same space and time as action. (This is one cause of the monoplanar quality, the "flatness," of written epic.) Prose by contrast has neither the resources of the representation of natural space and time by natural space and time nor the constraints thereby imposed. In fact, the temporality and spatiality of prose have nothing natural about them, their being not that of a natural consciousness but of Aigres, who is nothing but a character in the text. Prose constructs its own space and time, a textual space and time, according to the needs of the immediate textual environment. Cognition enjoys no special privilege in this respect: it is but a means to that construction. Put differently, the rescue in prose is constructed around the cognition of Aigres. Because cognition (or anything else for that matter) in prose is not wedded to a discrete naturalistic place and time, it can be used here as the organizer of a textual spatiality and temporality, where syntagms admit of consecution based on dependencies and inequalities. Elements are introduced—and can, at that *textual* time and place, be explained or motivated—only as they impinge on a focus—Aigres the potential victim—which is untenable in the written verse alone, based as it is on performance.

Syntactic subordination in prose effects an articulation and a hierarchization that is of a logical nature (not according to some sort of universal logic but according to the logic of a given text); it constructs space and time according to its needs. Events as well as acts of cognition have spatial and temporal extension and localization in a space and time *in the making* rather than given, a space and time constructed by the reader in the course of the reading. Space is no longer real and monoplanar but textual and tabular. Time is no longer unilinear and irreversible but a complex of diverse temporalities capable of countless articulations. At the climactic moment in the action, note the shift from the verse "einz" ("just as . . . right at the moment when [the men found Aigres, he was rescued]") to the prose "eussent" ("[they] would have [caught him, when he was rescued]"). "Einz" designates the space and time in which the hero is on the verge of being captured. It is indicative: they and Aigres are to be understood as having been seen there then, the latter just beyond the grasp of the former. The imperfect subjunctive "eussent" provides the probable consequence of not being rescued. No less frightening, perhaps, but not pinning down space and time. Who saw this? Was this *ever* seen?

The dependence of written verse on the real time and space of performance leads it to grant a textual weight to elements that from the point of view
of the plot or meaning seem quite secondary. A good example is provided
in our text by the description of the handing-over of the horse from Orchas
to Aigres. We are told how Orchas, having ridden the horse up to his lord,
dismounts and hands the reins to Aigres, who then mounts the horse, after
which Orchas finally remounts behind him. Such attention to consecutive
details is easily understandable in real space and time but may strike the
reader as excessive and distracting under the circumstances. Prose ignores
these discrete elements of the rescue. It finds them entangling.

Further on in the fragment, Aigres and his friend Orchas are out riding
when a messenger comes up. The messenger does not know Aigres's name.
He confides to him that he bears a message from the daughter of the emperor
but cannot find the man to whom the message is addressed. Aigres, who
loves the daughter, named Nulie, but has been separated from her for a long
time, anxiously asks the messenger for the name of the person sought. The
message is, as luck would have it, for Aigres. Our passage begins in the middle
of the messenger's speech and then shifts to Aigres's speech.

Verse

Mes el refuse toz a orne,
Kar sis pensers alliors li torne
En autre ou ele a son corage,
Pur qui jo ai fet cest grant vaage,
Mes ne trois pas ço que jo quier.
"Messager, frere, or te requier
En servise e en geredon
Ke de celui me dites le non
Ki tu si longement as quis."

Verse

But she refuses one after the other,
For her thoughts turn elsewhere
To another on whom she has her heart set
And for whom I have made this great journey.
But I do not find what I am looking for.
"Brother messenger, I ask
As a service and as a boon
That you tell me the name of the one
That you have sought for so long."

Prose

"Elle n'en veult riens faire, car elle a donné son courage et son amour

a un chevalier qui n'est mis ou païs, pour lequel j'ay ceste voie em-
prinse, mais je ne le puis trouver, dont il me poise durement pour vray."

Quand Aigres oÿ nommer le nom de s'amie, *si luy fremy toute la
char*, et dist lors au messagier: "Frere, je te prie et requir en guerredon
et en service que tu me dïes le nom de cellui que tu as si longuement
quis." (2.214-15.150)

Prose

She does not want to do it for she has given her heart and her love to
a knight who is no longer in the country and for whom I have undertaken this trip, but I cannot find him, which truly chagrins me."

When Aigres heard the name of his beloved mentioned, *all of his
flesh trembled*, and he then said to the messenger: "Brother, I pray and
ask that as a boon and as a service you tell me the name of the one
you sought for so long."

We first note that the derhymer shifts to diegesis for the shift of locutor:
it adds the deictic expression, the *inquit*[7], "Aigres said to the messenger."
For the jongleur, the shift of locutor is clear in the vocative: "Messager."[8]
The relationship between cited speech and other discourses in prose is a
particularly intriguing one. (Keep in mind that most punctuation marks, including quotation marks, have been added by the modern editor.)

In the prose, Aigres's response to the messenger's statement includes a
nonverbal reaction that is not present in the verse. We know that because
it is given verbally. This sort of observation in the prose is, of course, not
limited to nonrhyme, but it is interesting that it is exploited in the process
of unrhyming, in the process of moving away from a communicative framework where voice and body are so central. It recalls Aigres's reaction upon
hearing the messenger say the name of his lady (but one for which the messenger's speech was not interrupted at the time). It is, among other things,
a supplement to the moment of the speech, for we have both the action of
the addresser and the (meant to be simultaneous) action of the addressee.
It is also conjunctive, linking and motivating Aigres's request, and coloring
it with emotion (again, in what is now a silent communicative framework).
In the verse version, by the way, there is no mention of Nulie's *name* in the
earlier part of the messenger's speech, it just says: emperor's daughter. In
the derhymed version, the name is put in earlier, and that fact, plus the added
reaction of Aigres as the (textualized) hearer, constructs an emotional dimension that is not in the directly cited speech. It is silent, and so calls for a
writing that is silent. Again, an emotional dimension *can be* included in directly cited speech, but maybe it was there already, in the way the jongleur
delivered it.

The reaction is given in terms of a gesture: the hero's flesh trembled. The rhymed version has no gesture. What sort of gesture is this? Who could testify, as jongleur, to this? Who saw this, who *could* see this, or is it only Aigres who felt it? The visible, the manifest is not an absolute criterion for existence in this represented universe. The perception is of a private and internalized movement. Furthermore, in terms of the framework of communication of prose—writing and reading, in which bodily imitation is excluded—"frémir la char" does not invite, rather it discourages, its own imitation.

Contrast this with the moment when the count's men discover their slain leader:

Verse

Mais cil defors n'[en o]nt talent,
Ki por le conte sunt dolent.
Quant lor seignor trove[re]nt mort,
Chascon ses poinz tire e atort,
assez l'unt plaint e regreté;
En son escu l'[en] unt porté,
Si l'enfoierent en sa terre.

Verse

But those outside have no desire for it,
Who grieve for the count.
When they found their lord dead,
Each one wrung his hands.
And they mourned and regretted his loss at length.
They carried him away on his shield
And they buried him on his land.

Prose

Et ceulx de dehors estoient dolens et courrouciez pour leur seigneur que ilz trouverent mort; adonc prindrent le corps de leur seigneur et l'emporterent en sa terre, ou il fut moult plaint et regreté. (2.209.146)

Prose

And those outside were grieving and angry for their lord whom they had found dead; and so they took their lord's body and carried it to his land where he was mourned and regretted.

The gesture inscribed in the verse—the wringing of hands—is suppressed in the prose. What kind of gesture is it? It is a gesture of such explicit visibility that it has become iconic for "grief," and this visibility makes it useful to the jongleur, who is functioning as a witness to the action he is recounting: "You could *see* the grief," the jongleur seems to say, "they wrung their hands." Can "grief" be seen? Yes, when people wring their hands. A witness is more viable as a recounter of action the more the action is perceivable and ostensive, *gestae*, the more it is "einz" rather than "eussent." But involved in the "wringing of hands" is not just a certain mode of perception, on the part of the narrator, of the represented universe. The jongleur vis-à-vis his audience, in the frame of communication that is his performance, has his body, his hands at this command, and also acts as a mime of the actions he recounts. The words "wringing of hands" provide him with visible action that his spectators can witness: action as imitable gesture.

We are not making exclusive, essentialist claims that prose has *inquits* but verse does not, that "wringing of hands" cannot occur in prose, that "trembling of flesh" cannot occur in verse. Language is fungible: any words that are said can be written; anything that is written can be said. We are suggesting that the observed difference in the inscription of locutor and the inscription of gesture as exemplified in these brief passages has to do with differences in communicative function (e.g., mime vs. not mime) and in signifying practice. In the case of gesture, these passages illustrate the way in which verse tends to treat action as nonproblematic from the point of view of perception: what is seen is there; what is there is seen. (For that reason, verse does have a problem with a character who cannot see what is there: Aigres facing the fatal wound.) As a corollary, the jongleur not only bears witness to events (i.e., states what he has seen or what he has "heard tell" as having been seen) but also, within his communicational framework, is furnished with easily mimable, easily voiceable acts, vis-à-vis his audience. He can, he must (to a certain extent), identify with his characters, mime or "mark" their voice,[9] and orient the action he is recounting around himself in space, as either witness or actor. But prose does not exist under the same conditions. It cannot orient a represented action around itself. It has no voice and cannot mime. Its stake in the visible and the audible is smaller, for it can neither portray the visible, give voice to the audible as the jongleur does, nor get from them what the jongleur gets, a reinforcement of his own visibility and presence, and the pervasion of the jongleur's own voice by the voices of his characters.

Verse, in nostalgia of the presence of performance, re-presents the representable. The representable is not a limit for prose. We can understand now why "frémir la char" might be added by prose.

Our final example from *Bérinus* shows prose more appropriate to certain tasks than verse. In this passage, the messenger gives Aigres the letter from Lady Nulie.

Verse

E li vallez, qui fu senez,
Si li baillie un seel de cire

Ke la pucele ont fait escrire.
Il en a la cire brisee,
Si a la chartre desploie[e],
E le parchemin desploia;
Mult sout bien tost quanqu'il i a.
Al commencement le salue
La gentle Nulie sa drue,
Come a celui qui a son quer,
E si li mande que, a nul fuer,
Nel tienge plus, einz le report
A s'amie, qui nul confort
Ne poet avoir si de lui non.
D'empereor avra le non,
Si tost come il vendra a Rome;
Ele ne lerroit, pur nul home
Ne por chose que seit el mond,
Puis que fin Amor l'en somont.
E s[e] il velt le bref mescroire
E que la chartre ne soit voire,
Les paroles i sunt escrites,
Les deraines que furent dites
Le jor que Ai[gres] parti de lui;
Mult ourent coroz e ennui,
Quant a desevrir le covint.
Einsint Ai[gres], qui le bref tint,
Si l'a l[e]ü de chef en chief;
Mult trove bien escrit le bref.

Verse

And the attendant, who was a man of experience,
Handed over to him a message sealed with wax
That the young lady had ordered written.
He broke the wax seal
And unfolded the letter
And unfolded the parchment
And soon knew well what was in it.
At the beginning the noble Nulie,
His beloved, greets him
Like someone whom she holds in her heart,
And then she tells him that she cares for nothing
So much as for his reporting
To her who can have
No comfort but from him.
He will have the title of emperor
As soon as he will come to Rome.

She would not leave him for any man
Or anything in the world
Since courtly Love enjoins her.
And if he wants to disbelieve the message
And [think] that the letter is not true,
There are written in it the words
That were spoken last on the day
that Aigres left her;
They had much unhappiness and distress
When they had to separate.
And so Aigres who was holding the message
Read it from beginning to end,
And he found the message well written.

Prose

Quand le messagier qui estoit sages et avisez, ot certainement enquiz et entendu qu'il avoit trouvé ce que il queroit, si ot grant joie et puis bailla a Aigres unes lettres seellees de par la fille de l'empereur. Et tantost que Aigres les tint, il les ouvry et leut ce qu'il y avoit dedens escript, si trouva en escript que s'amie lui mandoit salut comme celle qui avoit eü moult a souffrir pour lui. Aprés il vist que elle lui prioit par fines amours que, celle lettre veüe, il ne laissast en nulle maniere qu'il ne venist a Romme, et lui affermoit en la lettre que, si tost comme il seroit venu a Romme, elle le feroit empereur, car l'empire lui estoit escheü; et pour la chose fere plus creable, elle lui mandoit enseignes telles qu'il recongnut bien. Et avecques tout ce, la damoiselle lui fist mencion en la lettre de tout son estat, et comment les barons la voulloient marïer a force.

Aprés ce que Aigres ot la lettre leüe tout a loisir, il fut tout esbahis. (2.215-16.150-51)

Prose

When the messenger, who was wise and circumspect, had inquired and heard that he had found the one whom he was looking for, he was most happy and he gave Aigres a sealed letter from the emperor's daughter. And as soon as Aigres held it, he opened it and read what was written in it and he found written that his beloved sent him greetings in the manner of someone who had much to suffer on his account. And then he saw that she begged him, in the name of courtly love, to do nothing as soon as he read the letter but come to Rome, and she asserted in the letter that as soon as he would arrive in Rome, she would have him made emperor for the empire had fallen to her, and to make the whole thing more credible she sent him such signs that he easily recognized. And with all this the damsel made mention of her own situation in the letter and of how the barons wanted to force her into marriage.

After Aigres had read the letter at leisure, he was stunned.

Aigres receives a letter. What does it "say," how do we get its message? Although the letter is communication itself, it is also silent. (It is *inscription*, which is intended only to be read. Reading can use presence and representation but on its own terms.) The verse chooses not to quote the letter, which within the conventions of oral performance would be to give it voice and to introduce Nulie into a scene that is clearly marked by her absence. Furthermore, no one else on the scene reads it out loud, *viva voce*, or comments on it, including Aigres (more on this later), and it is not offered to view, so in a performance a jongleur-witness would have no means of perceiving it. We have the paradoxical situation in which one wants to represent a character decoding a message, and it is via that decoding that one would normally get to the message, but the action of decoding itself cannot be witnessed and subsequently represented, for in performance such a decoding would be taken as recitation. Because reading is not representable, the jongleur must give up the representation of its verbal message to provide a diegetized version of it. He recounts it not as Nulie writing or uttering but as Nulie *acting*: "The noble Nulie greets him."

Let us compare this to the modern problem of the reading of a letter in film. Were the jongleur to turn into a modern writer of screenplays, say, he would still have to "break" his scene, but he could establish another perspective, "unreal" but nonetheless necessary, because the audience of a film *has* to have one. The screenwriter, to reveal to the audience the contents of a letter that one character is reading silently, would resort to either audio or visual displacement, either by adding a voice-over providing us with the imaginary "speaking" of the sender or what is "heard" by the receiver, which is a concrete instance of "giving of voice," or by indirect camera action, such that the camera coincides with the view of the represented reader, allowing us to read the letter as if we were Aigres (or, say looking over his shoulder). In both instances, film can do what the jongleur cannot do: simultaneously represent Aigres reading and what he is reading. Performance-bound reading of the passage must ask itself: who reads? Is it the jongleur or Aigres, and how will the content be known? There are subtle limits on a jongleur's powers: he can imitate, but it is difficult for him to mediate by proxy. He can represent, but, standing as he does and where he does, he runs into problems if he *delegates* representation.

Let us suppose that Aigres read the letter out loud. The problem would be one of confusion, for we would have the jongleur playing Aigres playing Nulie, a layering of three voices in one, where the structural uniqueness entailed by presence would deprive us of knowing who exactly was being represented. (A problem with dialogue: it has difficulty preserving the layering of speech upon speech.) The credibility of an out-loud reading would be enhanced if Aigres interrupted it to comment on it, but this would weaken representation at least as much as it would enhance it because it would add a considerable amount of syntagmatic heterogeneity (the shifting of a single voice) to the paradigmatic heterogeneity (the layering of voices), making it difficult to know *who* was making the metalinguistic comment: Aigres? the jongleur? or perhaps even Nulie? The verse of oral performance is clearly reaching a limit here. If you have *parole*, it must be attributed (to a speaker? to a witness?). This is a problem for written verse.

Another possibility is for Aigres to summarize, diegetize the letter. This might not fully prevent the problem of the interference of the comment with the content of the letter. But we do see how such a device can get a narrator out of certain difficulties and how "confidants" are very useful in such a case. (Orchas could so serve.) Neither version opts for that solution, which is flawed on other grounds: because Nulie wants to prove to Aigres that her letters is authentic, she quotes in it words they exchanged at their last parting (lines 285-88), presumably known to no one else (nor need the words themselves be of any specific interest to anyone else—they are merely a signature, not representation, and call only for a re-cognition). Can Aigres quote himself talking *to* Nulie when he receives a message *from* her?[10] Clearly, the voice of Aigres gets in the way, it is entangling, whether from without the message itself, or from within it.

We should not fail to notice that the decisive blow to the representation comes from its very strength: it cannot have Aigres (represented by the jongleur) give his voice to himself on stage, the Aigres quoted in Nulie's letter, for the single reason that representation's commitment to, and reliance on, a unique present (rendering the absent present) prevents it from representing its own past at the same time as, or as a function of, its present. It cannot *stage* the Aigres of then with the Aigres of now. Such a presentation of the past in another space would deconstruct the presence of Aigres in the here and now of the performance.[11]

So verse must diegetize the action represented in the letter; consequently, it is forced to skip the reading and the reader, as well as the utterer *as writer*. Strange as it may seem, the verse must eliminate the actual words exchanged to avert the temporal and spatial assault we have just described on the "presence" of representation. (This is strange because if one considers verse as written, it obviously can represent other written words. But this verse, although it comes down to us in writing, is not understood as written and, in fact, has difficulties coping with the representation of writing.) It would have been preferable for Nulie to have bid that the message be delivered orally, although even then the citation of Aigres's earlier words would still be a prob-lem.[12] By eliminating the words exchanged, the verse avoids Aigres's obliga-tion to comment on his own words. Aigres is not represented as perceiving the letter. The jongleur has Nulie acting, not writing, and so avoids both her (present/absent) voice and the silent mediation of the receiver of what it says. For the jongleur realizes that with regard to this written communication, the presence of his characters is only an obstacle to representation. They are an entanglement.

A reading bound to rules of performance discovers that the only way of representing silent reading is not to represent it but to diegetize it, for to give voice to the words of the letter, whether at the moment of the writing or at the moment of the reading, is to violate the essence of a letter, which is. as inscription, to be silent. The letter cannot be spoken, it can only be spoken of. A performance-bound reading cannot read the letter: it can read only around it. The letter as a piece of writing sticks in the throat of any perform-ance-oriented reading.

The entire setup of representation, based as it is on a presence—whether that of a jongleur qua jongleur or as a persona—escapes from total dissolu-tion, in this *emblematic encounter with the written,* only because it renounces it own specificity. The verse text can function here because Nulie has been rendered absent as text originator (as a consequence, she has been rendered present), and Aigres has been rendered absent as mediator of the text. Al-though the strength of performance is in its ability to represent conditions of utterance, here its representation succeeds only to the extent that it elimi-nates (from the communicational framework) every reference to the condi-tions of utterance (in this case, writing). (In other words, as we shall see, oral representation here succeeds only insofar as it takes on the characteris-tics of prose.)

The prose version does have the capacity to transmit the letter through Aigres. Aigres is both a patient of the action of the letter (it speaks to him) and an agent in the reading (it is he who decodes it). Prose can conflate these dual roles of the hero—it has no stake in a unique perspective or in keeping them separate—such that Aigres can mediate for us the content of the letter. We have it neither as Nulie "said" it nor as Nulie "did" it but as Aigres understood it: Aigres "trouva en escript que". There is a possible representa-tion of Aigres that need not be mediated by a performance model of represen-tation: Aigres is not enacted. He can read what the text says but still partici-pate in, be a function of the reading. And the reading can be a function of him. In prose, his perceptions, as well as his actions, can be inscribed: "Et pour la chose fere plus creable, elle lui mandoit enseignes telles qu'il re-congnut bien." Credibility depends on the recognition of signs, on the decod-ing. But such signs and such recognition need not be played out (meaningless to us anyway): they can simply be asserted. In the verse, we are told that Aigres is given the last words said. We are tempted to ask irreverently, "Who says they are the last words?" But the prose (not referring to particular parting words, just "signs") tells us that there were signs in the letter and that *Aigres* recognized them. It does not commit itself to knowing them to be the last words; it did not have to hear them; it did not have to be there.

Clearly, there is nothing about the language in verse or prose that would expressly preclude it from representing the reading of a letter. The question for us here is not one of *diction*. One could find, in either verse or prose, (1) the "text" of the letter, (2) the diegetized acts of the originator, or (3) the reactions of its receiver. Language can handle it, there are discourses for it, but how is the task handled by one signifying practice as opposed to another? How much must a signifying practice modify its own presuppositions? A performance-bound reading is not friendly to the silent reading of a letter; it can do it only by abandoning the protocol of performance, thereby opening the way to a textual reading, which will be that of prose.

Chapter 4
Versiprosa

The technique of versiprosa texts (also called *prosametrum*), which alternate passages of prose and verse, had been known in medieval Latin since at least the time of Boethius, and it would be improper to speak of them as an invention of fifteenth-century France; they are more of a discovery. Their inherent interest for us lies in the fact that they represent a stage of development that is superior to derhyming because the prose passages they contain are not of verse origin but are meant to stand side by side with verse and thus must self-consciously differ from them.

Our text will be taken from the works of the Grands Rhétoriqueurs, the school of writers that flourished at the Burgundian court in the fifteenth century. The works of this school have been much maligned and little studied;[1] their prose, moreover, has attracted even less attention than their verse. The Grands Rhétoriqueurs found themselves at an important juncture in the history of discursive forms: the large edifice of medieval genres and styles was either exhibiting formal sclerosis[2] or beginning to dissolve both at the formal level and at the level of content.[3] As a result, theirs was a period of intense experimentation that can be best described as a systematic inquiry into the combinatorial possibilities of the language. Exhibiting a rare thoroughness and an admirable willingness to take risks, the Rhétoriqueurs frequently produced works that have struck critics as artificial and uninteresting,[4] but these works must be seen as rigorous explorations of uncharted territory or systematic exploitation of until then only partially understood devices. That such a strategy would produce frequent failures is not unexpected but is in fact a reason for adopting it: the sifting-out and stabilization of forms that occur in the sixteenth century would scarcely have been possible had the Rhétoriqueurs not indicated which lines of inquiry were promising and which were likely to prove unproductive. For our purposes, the works of the Grands Rhétoriqueurs provide the additional attraction of not stifling a given development simply because it contravenes handed-down tradition. Thus, when their texts encounter difficulties, *these difficulties may be presumed to be specific to the form at that stage of development* and all the more valuable for our present inquiry.

Our text is *La Ressource du Petit Peuple* by Jean Molinet (1435?-1507),[5] one to which Paul Zumthor has recently devoted some attention, although from concerns quite different from ours. *La Ressource du Petit Peuple*, dated by its editor, Noël Dupire, 1 May 1481, is a political allegory in the form of a pageant, which deplores the condition of Common Folk, the Petit Peuple of the title, in this, the 95th year of the Hundred Years War.

The text begins with an utterer, transparently identified by a conceit based on "molinet," or work-mill, who witnesses the eruption from the bowels of the earth, of a scourge, later identified as Tyranny, and its subsequent work of terrible devastation. The point of view shifts to a lady of "grant auctorite," who comes upon the heartrending scene of a trampled and beleaguered mother holding a starving infant. The lady recognizes the characters of the Pietà-like scene: they are her cousin Justice and the latter's child, Petit Peuple (Common Folk). The lady, it turns out, is none other than Truth. All this is told in a 92-line introductory passage of prose, which is followed by a 144-line speech in verse by Truth, a speech in which she denounces the princes responsible for the current condition of Justice and her child. There then occurs a 15-line prose section attributed to *Acteur*, whom we will discuss later.

An audience is said to have formed around Truth, and from it she selects her old friend Conseil (Counsel) and addresses him in 69 prose lines, in the traditional rhetoric of encomium, urging him to take Justice and Common Folk under his care. *Acteur* returns to give us a 12-line prose description of the ministrations of Counsel to Justice, after which the latter is asked to tell her tale, which she proceeds to do over 144 lines of verse. Counsel then dispenses his advice in 95 lines of prose, urging prayer and reliance upon the two "Margarets" of York and of Burgundy. Justice briefly inquires, in 6 prose lines, where Might can be found, in order to effect the changes that are deemed necessary, and Counsel replies in 80 prose lines with a description of Burgundian power, ending once again with an exhortation to prayer.

Acteur then gives a 30-line prose account of the departure of Counsel and the subsequent departure and travels of Truth, Justice, and Common Folk, on their way to Might, with a stopover at Good Hope, where Justice prays in 51 lines of verse. *Acteur* brings the text to a close, with 15 lines of verse, finally urging the audience to add their prayers to those of Justice.

The alternation of prose and verse does not suggest any immediate conclusions: all the "characters," except Counsel, "speak" in both. Nor do considerations of length or subject matter provide sufficient basis for the elaboration of hypotheses.

This is where an approach that would be more characteristic of what we have taken to call prosaics may be called for. Trained as we are to perceive texts as totalities, we seek to apprehend their structure and, in the description of that structure, to assert our mastery over the text. Prosaics seeks instead to espouse the movement of the text as it manages the economy of its discourses, to establish where thresholds of decision arise, what the decisions are, and what their motivations and determinations as well as their consequences have been. In other words, we must learn to follow the processive threading of the text. To do so, we will divide the text into extended passages, *lexies*, and comment on each, allowing us to look at the work as it unfolds as a whole. In this kind of development, we are dependent on our *lexie* for what we say. This chapter is a series of statements provoked by a linear textual reading. Thus, what unfolds here is in the form neither of a hypothetical or deductive argument nor of a historical reconstruction.

We will be citing the prose passages. The whole work, including the verse passages, is provided in the appendix to this book.

> Pour ce que naguaires vent failli aux volans de mon molinet, qui multitude de nouvelles histoires debvoit tourner entre ses meules, pour en tirer fleur et farine, pensant oublier merancolie, je me tiray aux champs.

> Where once there was no wind for the sails of my little mill, which was supposed to grind out plenty of new stories in its stones to extract their germ and flower, in order to forget melancholy, I set out in the country.

The text begins with what critical convention dictates we call first-person narrative: the subject of the "je" of the main verb refers to the subject of the utterance, and the transparent conceit of "mon molinet," combining the anaphoric "mon" with the homonymic "molinet" establishes the identity of the subject with the author of the text. This is an example of a presentatory discourse, anchoring the text in an extratextual subject, that of the writer Jean Molinet, who appears to be the presenter of the story.

> Et, ainsi que, par admiration, je reguardoye les plaisanz flouritures dont les preaulx herbus estoient ricement parez, soubdainement s'ouvri la terre, se vis ung tres parfond abisme.

And while I was thus looking with admiration at the pleasant flowerings that ornamented the green meadows, suddenly the earth opened up and there could be seen a very deep abyss.

The presentatory discourse here gives way to a witness discourse. The "je" is now the witness of an event, a function commonly assumed by jongleurs. Both of these are discourses that jongleurs exploited: as presenters, they appear to be protagonists, but they rapidly shift to the recounting of something that they have seen or heard (always on good authority, of course): they are content to play the role of a witness: we get *res gestae*, observed happenstance. Such a shift from one discourse to another is relatively unproblematic in the case of the jongleur, who relies on his physical presence, and the *jeu de scène* that it makes possible, to provide a bridge between the two.

Most texts, whether of jongleur or prose origin, provide evidence of a third discourse, namely an interpretive one, which stands in a relation of characterization to other parts of the text, such as a comment or a reaction.

. . . duquel, aveuc feu, flame et fumee qui premiere en sailli, sourdi sur piez une tres laide, espoentable satrape, fille de perdicion, fiere de regard, horrible de face, difforme de corpz, perverse de coeur, robuste de bras et ravissant des mains: elle avoit le chief cornu, les oreilles pendans, les yeux ardans, la bouche moult tortue, les dens agus, la langue serpentine, les poings de fer, la pance boursouflee, le dos velu, la queue venimeuse et estoit puissamment montee sur ung estrange monstre a maniere de leuserve fort et corageux a merveilles, jettant feu par la geule, chaulx et soufre par les narines, chargie a tous letz d'espees, couteaulx, dolequins, rasoirs, soyes, faulx, dagues, planchons, paffus, picques, pinces, pouchons, forches, fourches, ars, dars, hars, licolz, chaines, cordes et cagnons, ensemble pluseurs instrumens convenables a son office et portoit sus la crupe ung bariseau plain d'escorpions, riagal, arsenic, uuille, plong boulant, harpois, azil et morteles poisons.

Quand ceste plutonique matrosne se trouva sur les rendz, accompagnie de Crudelité, Famine, Fraude, Rapine, Sacriliege, Conspiration, Mutre, et Felonnie, elle appella par propres noms pour conduire son oost Cacus, Nemproth, Denys, Dyoscorus, Datien, Marchien, Simphronien, Rictiovaire, Olibrius, Agricolan, Matrocolus, Elmoradach, avec Neron qui portoit l'estandart, lesquelz impetueusement yssus de ce tres puissant gouffre, hydeux, crueux, et fantasticques, crochus, bochus et noirs que Moriens, montez touttevoyes sus elephans, giraffes, tigres, griffons, serpens, dragons et cocodrilles, se rengerent en grosse bataille, esleverent ung terrible tonnoire, criminel fourdre et dure pestilence et en courant le plat pays commencherent a sanc espandre, bruler eglises, mutiler innocens, deflorer vierges, rostir petis enfans, fourdroier villes et patibuler gens.

. . . from which, in a burst of fire, flame and smoke, there rose a very ugly and frightful despot, the daughter of damnation, with savage look, horrible face, deformed body, perverted heart, powerful arms and clutching hands: she had a horned head, folded-back ears, burning eyes, a most distorted mouth, sharpened teeth, a snakelike tongue, iron fists, a bloated belly, a hairy back and a poisonous tail. She was masterfully riding on a strange monster not unlike a powerful and incredibly daring lynx, breathing fire through its mouth, lime and sulphur through its nostrils, and loaded all over with swords, knives, dirks, razors, saws, scythes, daggers, spears, broadswords, pikes, pincers, stakes, forks, bows, arrows, ropes, knots, chains, stringed knives [?] with other instruments of similar nature, and on its back it carried a handful of scorpions, sulfur, arsenic, oil, molten lead, flammable pitch, vinegar, and deadly poisons.
When this Plutonic crone lined up along with her companions Cruelty, Famine, Fraud, Plunder, Sacrilege, Conspiracy, Murder, and Felony to lead out her army, she called out their names: Cacus, Nemrod, Denys, Dioscorus, Dacius, Marchius, Symphronian, Rictovarius, Olibrius, Agricola, Matroclus, Elmoradachus, and Nero who was the standard bearer, all of whom suddenly emerged from this mighty abyss, hideous, cruel, fantastic, hooked, hump-backed, blacker than Moors, mounted on elephants, giraffes, tigers, gryphons, serpents, dragons, and crocodiles; they lined up in battle, raised horrific thunder, criminal lightning, and harsh pestilence, and, running over the flat lands, began to spill blood, burn churches, mutilate the innocent, deflower virgins, roast little children, blast cities, and gibbet people.

The most striking feature of these passages for us is the seemingly endless listing. List-making is frequently seen as peculiar to the medieval mind: lists also occur in verse texts meant for performance, such as the *Dit de l'Herberie* of Rutebeuf. All modern readers seem to agree, though, that the Grands Rhétoriqueurs, Molinet foremost among them, push lists to their limit. Critical discourse, without exception, has seen this as one of the most reprehensible aspects of their writing: an unnecessarily ostentatious display of verbal extravagance, a lack of the famed Gallic sense of measure and restraint (no doubt accounted for by the Burgundian loyalties of the Rhétoriqueurs), a luxuriant overgrowth in need of severe pruning. From the perspective of classical French writers, it is these very long enumerative lists that made the Rhétoriqueurs unreadable; even Rabelais did not escape censure for relying on them excessively, although in his case allowance is made for the fact that they produce a comic effect. The propensity for list-making, if it is that, requires some attention.

It has been noted that Old French style favors a sort of synonymic overcoding: a warrior will be called "fier et superbe" (proud and haughty), a horse "isnel et rapide" (quick and swift). To speak tagmemically, it is as if, in each instance, it was not enough, in the construction of the syntagmatic chain, to draw one member from the paradigmatic set most appropriate to that slot; one must *cite* the entire set. Although this is not the place to argue it, one may well consider this compositional device as part of a larger strategy in which the progression of the syntagma is the result of a generalized *citing* of paradigms, motifs, themes, et cetera, in an effort to make the text, or its performance, a repository of the culture.[6]

The functioning of enumeration is not tied to either verse or prose.[7] Oral societies are known for storing, in the memory of their storytellers, long lists of nominalized data. But oral lists differ from written ones in their principle of organization, as Jack Goody points out.[8] Lists transmitted orally present serious problems of memory, and so they had mnemonic devices built into them. But the moment they are written and thus preserved verbatim, other modes of articulation and organization, around taxonomies or categories of thought, can be explored.

Goody distinguishes only between written and oral, but we must go on to distinguish within the written between lists in verse and lists in prose. An oral list, based on either alliterative or rhyming composition, partakes of composition by citation: it operates exclusively with material already organized in paradigms. It will soon exhaust its paradigm (although that paradigm maye be quite large). A written list meant for performance (in verse) also exhibits paradigmatic characteristics. Prose lists need not do so. Although undeniably still part of the cultural memory, they can be explorative devices through which new paradigms, new alignments can be created, alignments and paradigms that were not inscribed in the culture until then.[9] Thus decontextualized, arbitrariness seems to preside over their constitution. For example, in our passage it is impossible to decide whether the order of the companions of the "plutonicque matrosne" is significant or not. Prose is not exclusive, like verse (which excludes the foreign, the unassimilated), rather, it is inclusive, being able to frame paradigms and go beyond them, taking an exhausted paradigm and creating a new one along the syntagmatic mechanism. Prose can create new paradigms altogether, whereas the only level of creativity that oral or written verse have in this respect is that one can add an item to a paradigm.

These two types of text construction are parallel to two different kinds of social practices: the first, list-making by paradigmatic exhaustion, belongs to an economy of display, of conspicuous consumption, manifested in such other medieval cultural practices and values as pageants, largess, almsgiving, and feast-making. The second is in an economy that we would like to call conspicuous production. That it should occur in texts dating from the famine- and plague-infested years of the Hundred Years War is a clear indication of its compensatory character. But we should not stay there, limiting our- selves to a traditional view of literature as escape from the scarcities and difficulties in everyday life. Rather, we ought to recognize in it a practice of the emerging state, which begins to be less concerned with the distribution of available goods than with the verbal record-keeping of them, drawing from its lists claims of riches that, true as GNP, do little for those who experience scarcity. We will have further occasion to reflect on this mechanism, which is conceivable only if there exists a bureaucratic state apparatus for its con- duct. Whereas the first is more interested in the display of control over known wealth, the second holds the promise of the production of more wealth, pre- sumably to satisfy the needs and desires of those who experience its absence, thus, neatly avoiding the disquieting issue of what is happening to known and recorded wealth. The first partakes of an ideology of community, the second locates itself in the aftermath of the dissolution of the community and the institution of competing estates and classes, as we shall see in *Aucas- sin et Nicolette.*

This passage gives us the sight of a witness, but it is clearly an object that exceeds the bounds of such a sight, for the creature described here is fabu- lous. The description combines physical details ("yeux ardans") that a wit- ness can reasonably observe, with moral ones ("perverse de coeur") that can result only from interpretation. The mode of representation that we have here is allegorese, which permits the admixture of witnessing and interpretive discourses.

> Et tant exploiterent de detestables et execrables faix que l'hystoire au loing recitee donroit piteuses lermes aux yeulx des escoutans.

> And they committed so many hateful and dastardly deeds that the story told at length would cause tears of pity in the eyes of listeners.

The witness discourse has come to an end, and we are given an interpretation instead: "hateful," " dastardly," "pitiful," and a reference to addressees, "lis- teners."

With this shift to a discourse describing reaction of addressees, a *first bid* toward authority is made. The bid is one toward the authority of the earlier signifying practice. In the absence of a characterization of its own communi- cational situation, the text posits a fictitious one modeled on that of perform- ance: *if* this story were told to listeners, they *would* visibly react in such and such a way. But this story is not being told; there are no "escoutans" here. This is the first of many instances in which the prose writer has struck upon the device of figuring hearers, readers, and other reactors in the text and,

thus, creating interpretation, horizons of success, and a space for reader identification. Were we in performance, says this text, "you" as audience would
be reacting with tears.[10]

But let us examine the structure of this bid. In a contrary-to-fact conditional
mood ("donroit"), an effect is described (tears in the eyes of listeners), and
the mode of delivery of performance (story told at length) is adduced as the
enabling condition of that effect. The important thing is that while using the
topos of brevity, the text is drawing the reader toward a reaction by associating the reader with the audience of a performance, or offering for the reader's
observation the audience of performance. There is no audience of performance, there are no listeners; they have been put there for the benefit of the
reader. Although this can be called a nostalgia for performance (and we have
seen how written verse inherently depends on the cultural competence that
the audience of a performance had), what is happening here is also a turning-
of-one's-back on performance, a progressive detachment of the prose text
from the conditions of utterance of performance, whose extratextual presences, which seemed necessary to it at its beginning, can be done without,
done without because they can be brought within: prose will find a discourse
for them. By moving from presentational and witness discourses to interpretive discourses and discourses describing reactors, in the absence of the jongleur's soma, which enabled him to make such shifts, and also of an audience, the text makes a first bid at having authority stand independently of
presence. I can bring you, through my grammar (i.e., my shifts of discourse,
including discourses of audience, of reaction), to reactions modeled on those
of the pragmatics of performance. This bid suggests that the grammatical apparatus of the signifying practice of prose is a match for the particular pragmatic underpinnings of the signifying practice of performance. If that is true,
the absence of the jongleur is not fatal to prose's effectiveness.

Now, extratextual entities (addressers, addressees, authorities), rather than
being that which introduces the text and from which the authority of the
text is derived, can be introduced by the text, in the text. They will thereby
be intratextual, authorized by the text and at the text's disposal. In the next
passage, one such authority is introduced.

> Sy tost que la lice rabice eut perpetré ce dolent vasselage par ses mi-
> gnons qui le nommoient Tirannie, avec sieute de boutefeus, gibelins,
> pirates, satellites, fueillars, bringars, nacquez, laronceaulx, cavestreaux,
> quoquineaulx, paillardeaux et ribaudeaux qui se fourerent en la queue
> de son armee, au tres grant prejudice et desercion desdis pays, et que
> ycelle se fut ung petit eslongee de nostre climat, sans rentrer toutesvo-
> yes en son trou sathanicque, une tres reverente dame, prudente, sage
> et de grant auctorité se mit aux champs pour visiter ce grief dommage
> et, entre les furieuses inhumanitez par elle mises a execution, trouva

une jeusne dame, selon la dicque d'une foriere, gisant comme pasmee, a demy morte et durement foullee, eschevellee et despoullie de ses nobles royaulx atours et auprés d'elle un petit enfant de l'eage de deux ans, criant angoisseusement, plongiet en lermes, oppressé de famine, querant les tetins de sa mere pour y trouver sa nouriture.

As soon as the rabid bitch had perpetrated this painful bondage through her minions, who called her Tyranny, with a following of arsonists, rioters, pirates, accomplices, ironmongers, rag-pickers, rascals, thieves, burglars, rogues, rakes, and ribalds, who made up the rear of her army to the great harm and devastation of these lands, and she had moved a little away from our climate without, however, returning into her Satanic hole, a most revered lady prudent, wise, and of great authority, set out to inspect this grievous damage and amid the horrible inhumanities it [the scourge] had committed, found a young woman lying against an embankment as if unconscious, half dead and severely trampled, dishevelled and despoiled of her noble regal adornments, and next to her a small two-year-old child, screaming with anxiety, bathed in tears, pressed by hunger, and seeking the breasts of his mother in quest of nourishment there.

What does prose achieve through such an operation, and with what success? If we follow the "actions" of the most revered lady, anthropomorphically moving about at this stage, very much like a character, we find that her actions do not contravene traditional narrative patterns: she discovers a young woman, and then we are given a description of the state of the young woman. The elements of a scene are given: the phenomenon seen and the character who sees. The problem that arises is a perceptual one: the young woman and her child are seen by the revered lady and by the reader simultaneously, and the distinction between the two perceptions is not thematized. Whether we call the revered lady our deixis, our subject or agent, our frame, or the anchor of the enunciative instance, the entity that fulfills the presentatory function is now a creature of the text.

The narration continues: "and next to her a small two-year-old child." The focusing angle of the gaze of the revered lady—our mode of cognition here—moves from the mother to the son, as one might expect, within the conventions of realistic discourse, to make out first the larger figure and then the smaller. All the while, however, the child is looking toward the mother, "seeking the breasts of his mother in quest of nourishment there." This barely noticeable perceptual shift is significant nonetheless because it disrupts the construction of the representation. We see the *reverente dame* seeing, and we also see what she is seeing. To this dual perspective is added a third perspective: the anthropomorphized intratextual *reverente dame* also sees what the infant is seeing. *She* now has a dual perspective. Our mode of cognition is involving perceptual positions that are at a further and further remove from the somatic and deictic possibilities of the opening "molinet." We are seeing things, but from where? Seeing through the sight of intratextual entities pushes certain levels of tolerance. How far do you go in letting them see for you? Such "second sight" adds depth, but it is also potentially destablizing. A jongleur always stayed close behind his seeing characters, always seconded, guaranteed their visions, saw with them and through them. Prose will not have to operate within such limits.

The representational system activated here is more in the three-dimensional realm of holography than in the two-dimensional one of photography. Instead of being disrupted, the representation paradoxically gains in credibility, and prose will use it to show that its own lack of somatic anchoring is all to its credit. It is a device that film will eventually use, although primarily in the comic mode: a character will be introduced in a scene of which he is not a part, and in which he has the capability to circulate around represented characters (who are unaware of his presence), pull their whiskers, mock their speech or facial expressions, et cetera. Because he is visibly the result of the layering of film images, he has a freedom of perception and action that is denied to a character inscribed in the representation, whose perceptual possibilities are determined by the known laws of optics as they constitute the realm of representation. This device, which is to be found primarily in children's documentaries (the man inside the body, etc.), clearly establishes this capability as having a *significant cognitive import*. In written representation, such shifts are common enough, and experienced readers of prose tend to accept them without analyzing the mechanism of their realization. However, to analyze prose is to confront the serious problem of their description, both synchronically and historically.

> Chose pitoyable et la plus douloureuse de jamais estoit a vëoir ceste desolee compaigne et n'y avoit tant riant œil qu'il ne fusist tourné en pleur. L'enfant moult haut crioit par destresse de faim, la mere se taisoit separ traveil inhumain, l'enfant queroit sa vie ou sain de sa nourice, la mere queroit mort et derrenier supplice, l'enfant plourant succhoit une wide mamelle et la mere enduroit plaine doleur mortelle.

> It was a pitiful and most heartrending thing to see this desolate assembly and there was no eye so mirthful that it would not turn to tears. The child cried loudly in the straits of hunger, the mother kept silent through inhuman duress, the child sought for life at the bosom of his nurse, the mother sought for death and last suffering, the child crying sucked at an empty breast and the mother endured completely mortal pain.

At its most literal, the first sentence is a comment on the problems that had just been offered to our perception. The statement functions more interpretively than as a witness. It cannot be attributed to the revered lady, whether as utterance or thought, for it would be most incongruous for her to have a "riant oeil" at such a time. The claim of this sentence is that no perceiver, no matter how joyful, could manage to hold back tears at such a spectacle. *Who* can make such a claim, and *why* is it made here?

Because the text is caught up in representing the revered lady as a character, this must originate in a "narrator." In spite of our reluctance to import this poetological entity, any faltering of the mediation provided by the lady invites us to fall back on such a knowing, if not downright omniscient, entity. But our haste in giving this answer to the first question ("who?") may eventually preclude our ability to answer the second one ("why here?").

By answering, "the narrator," we ought to recognize that we are adopting a substantialist point of view for which statements of any kind must emanate from either an actual human being or a represented one (i.e., mimetically or diegetically). We are falling back on the notion of a necessary presence as the guarantor of the integrity of the text.[11] There is no more a narrator here than there is a mirthful eye or, in the earlier interpretive sentence, a hearer. Vérité is no longer our mode of cognition, but we are not sure who is.

The second sentence is an *ekphrasis* (a description) of the "chose pitoyable a vëoir," that which a speaker lays out for a tearful eye to see. That it comes from performer or orator is clear: "To my left, the child; to my right, the mother; to my left, the child," and so on. It is full of rhythm, parallelism, and isocolon, endowing it with much of the sonorousness of verse with minor metrical variation: in all, high *Kunstprosa* with which the Rhétoriqueurs constantly experimented, but which, as we shall see, will not mark the future of prose.[12]

Et tantost la bonne dame qui premiere trouva ceste piteuse assamblee, regarda la patiente en face, et jassoit ce quelle fusist fort deffiguree, recognu par certain secret signe que celle estoit Justice, sa sœur germaine, et l'enfant estoit le petit peuple.

And then the good lady who found first this pitiful gathering looked the patient into the face and in spite of the fact that she was very disfigured recognized by some secret sign that it was Justice, her full-blooded sister, and that the child was Common Folk.

The lady looks at the "patient," in the sense of the "one who suffers," and recognizes her in spite of her disfigurement, thanks to a secret sign. She is Justice, her full-blooded sister, and the child is Common Folk. This scene of recognition calls for several remarks.

The presentation mechanism is the same as that for the other allegorical entity, Tyranny, except that Tyranny was recognizable by her attributes,[13] whereas neither Justice nor Common Folk seem, at this point, to correspond to theirs.[14] Thus, the revelation that the agent of devastation was Tyranny was not shocking, whereas the identity of the victim is.

Our second point is more difficult. Neither the reader nor a witness of the scene could have recognized Justice in the battered figure. She is too "disfigured." This term must be taken in both senses, that is, too physically altered—at the level of representation—for her *figure* (or face, and let us remember that the lady looks at her face-to-face) to be recognized, and too concretely depicted, at the level of textuality, for her figurality (her allegorical status) to be recognized. A rhetorical figure too concretely drawn is disfigured. Her figural status had been sacrificed to her status as a character, which is how we have been induced to read and visualize her. (Whereas we do not so read those in Tyranny's band: they are just named and no doubt named justly, instantly recognizable as Crudélité, Famine, Fraude, and so on.) Through scrutiny and secret signs, this character is revealed to be a personification allegory.

The revered lady, who does the looking, possesses uncanny powers of observation: she can tell the difference between a straightforward scene and an allegorical one. We can too, but only after the fact and owing to her intervention. But there is a clue concerning her cognitive powers: she is related to the victim,[15] and so it is a case of "It takes one to know one."

The text, although remaining faithful to allegorese, will not abandon the representational aspect of Justice. To be sure, we have seen that the discursive shift in the interpretive "chose pitoyable" sentence occurred to put an end to the representation of the rape of Justice. After all, the rape of Justice is a conceptual entity, not a visual one. The former does not gain from the inclusion of new prurient details in the depiction of the latter; quite the opposite. The text will carefully chart a course between an allegorical discourse and one that would have to confront the dangerous politics of the representation of Justice, one that through exposition and analysis would require that the state of Justice in "nostre climat" be examined. Such a path is ideologically far too dangerous. Allegorese is safer. And, in this instance, it can claim that although it is double, it is not duplicitous, for in truth (with a small *t* for another ten lines), the violence against a mother and child by Tyranny does represent a rape of Justice and Common Folk. The text will reach that conclusion itself, by making explicit this fact, changing it from "in truth" to "for Truth."

> . . . qui ambedeux par paresse, foiblesse ou male garde estoyent tresbuchiez ou parfont cavain de tirannique pestilence et lors, par pitié et compassion dont elle [la dame reverente] fut a cop navrée, esleva ung merveilleux cri farsy de pleurs, entrelardé de souspirs, baisa sa

soeur en la face, le couvri de son riche mantel, puis print l'enfanchon
en ses bras et de sa tres doulce alaine lui reschauffa les petites manottes,
en ce faisant comme celle qui ne redoubtoit ame synon Dieu, car Vérité
se fait appeller.

. . . both of whom through laziness, weakness, or lack of watchfulness
had fallen into the deep cave of tyrannic pestilence, and then the lady,
suddenly struck with pity and compassion, raised a marvelous cry filled
with tears and interlarded with sighs; she kissed her sister on the face,
covered her with her rich coat, then took the little child in her arms
and warmed his little hands with her most sweet breath, acting like
someone who fears no one but God, for she has herself called Truth.

Although now identified as allegorical constructs, Justice and Common Folk
retain their anthropomorphized status. In fact, and most curiously in the light
of the description of Tyranny's outburst and endemic proliferation, their pitiful condition is attributed to their laziness, weakness, and lack of watchfulness. The ideological position of the text becomes clearer.

It is in this passage that the revered lady is finally named as Truth. The
naming occurs in a curiously offhand manner, as if the text's tremendous
investment in having Truth here, which our reading has traced and measured,
was suddenly being down-played, treated as casual. Its immediate context
makes clear its importance: the revered lady has begun to vocalize, crying,
sighing, and warming up, and now she is about to speak. Her courage,
strangely displaced in the not particularly dangerous act of warming a child's
hands, is characterized as bowing only before God. Thus her authority is
reasserted, just in case we had forgotten it. We ought to note that this authority
is not invoked in what we could call her inaugural speech act: her naming.
She does not call herself Vérité. Nor does the text, or any enunciatory instance within it, take on that responsibility. It is merely said that she *has herself called Truth*. As in the famous paradox of the liar, of which the Middle
Ages are so fond, the questionable nature of the naming leads to a questionable nature of the truth-value function of the text's discourse. If she *is* Truth,
why does she not assert herself to be so, or why are we not monologically
told she is? Because there is no *one* to do so. At the very moment when,
both retrospectively and prophetically, she is about to speak and guarantee
the truth of the text, the truth of prose, she is revealed to be a creature of the
text. We will see that this is an example of the way in which prose controls,
contains within it, the authority that it uses for guaranteeing itself, author-
izing itself.

We ought to stress, however, that this deconstruction of Truth's authority
does not invalidate the text insofar as it had previously relied upon Truth's
authority, for this deconstruction has been deferred precisely until this point

at which prose is about to stage its own passing from the text. Prose brings us Vérité, as a mode of cognition, and is now going to give way to her speech, which is verse. She takes the floor. Before going on, let us remember that both to make irrelevant the truth-value function of Truth and to continue to maintain her as a figure of capable authority is a powerful matrix for any ideological discourse.

> Par ung ardant couroux qu'il luy monta au cœur, d'une vive voix tres agüe, sans riens celer, desgorgua son invective contre les recteurs de la chose publicque et dit en tel maniere:

> With a burning anger that rose to her heart and in a sharp voice, holding nothing back, she discharged her invective against the leaders of the republic and said in this way:

Truth is about to speak, presumably, the truth. But is that the case? Truth ought to state facts, state things as they are, conceal nothing, and speak dispassionately as befits one previously characterized as wise, prudent, revered, and authoritative. We expect, we have been led to expect, that, aside from the original *cri* of recognition, we would hear the cool voice of reason and wisdom, controlled, aware of its impact, and confident of its reach. Instead, the text tells us she will give shrill invective, regurgitated without restraint, and provoked by a sudden burst of fiery anger rising straight from the heart. Clearly, hers will not be the voice of reason; another will have to be sought. She, as sister of the victim and aunt of Common Folk, is much too involved (shall we say "personally" involved?) to remain . . . "true" to herself. Again, the duplicity of allegory is used for effect; but, if Truth cannot be true to herself, can she be true to the facts? It is time that she be invested with the power of the word. Indeed, she has said nothing so far. She will speak.

Prose ends. Vérité speaks, in verse, 18 eight-line decasyllabic stanzas. Contrary to what we had been led to expect, her statement is not a statement of facts but a rhetorically animated denunciation of the rulers of the republic ("la chose publicque") and a call for them to end their fratricidal war in order to unite under the pope's leadership to face the mounting Turkish menace. It is a political speech, nonpartisan in the sense that it does not side with any of the factions in the conflicts of the War of French Succession, an advocate's speech pleading the cause of peaceful resolution of the internal conflict to face the external enemy. Because our purpose here is to study prose, we will not examine this section of the text in detail. The reader should note, however, the exhaustion of paradigms and the sacrifice of semantic values.

A last ideological observation: Vérité's previously noted courage is at first apparent because she does not address Tyranny, who as far as we know was the perpetrator of the crimes, but "Princes puissans." How can Vérité get away with giving a nonallegorical reading, particularly when she is the one who can recognize allegories? For one thing, she is using a collective term, still refraining from naming the personages themselves. This is still on the way to a dangerous concreteness, but that is invalidated by the apostrophic status of her speech. She is making a demand of "Princes puissans," who are not there to hear it. Apostrophe is a figure structured in such a way that its illocutionary force is directed at those who are not part of the circumstances of utterance (the hearers), and those who *are* part of the circumstances of utterance are not recipients of the illocutionary force. Apostrophe is then a call to action, which is structurally designed to prevent the fulfillment of that action.

At the end of the speech, prose resumes, but under the rubric *Acteur*. What is this all about?

The end of Vérité's speech has presented the text with a major difficulty: how to continue? how to resume? In the beginning of the *Ressource,* the problem of its enunciative instance was handled by the presentatory discourse anchored in the assigned subject homonymic to "molinet." We have seen that this authorial presence was not sustained. Having jettisoned its "author," the text relies on a number of formal devices, which we have briefly noted, to author-ize itself. Near the end of lady Vérité's speech, the problem reasserts itself: who is in charge here? Vérité has spoken in too impassioned a manner to be able credibly to fill presentatory, witness, or interpretive functions anymore. Whereas Molinet is available, "he" would represent a step backward and a loss of representational capability. So "he" is permanently and gratefully left behind. In the *Ressource,* as in other works written by Molinet and by other writers of his period who faced a similar problem, the solution is "simple": *Acteur.* What does this term mean? Who is "he"?

Noël Dupire, the learned editor of Molinet, translates the term *acteur* as *auteur* (author).[16] His information is philologically correct. The issue cannot be resolved so quickly, however, for it involves more than an etymological and philological filiation. It involves changing conceptions of literary property and transformations in the social practice of writing, some of which are constitutive of prose's emergence.

The Latin *auctor,* from *augure,* to divine or foretell, yields the Old French *acteor* and *acteur.* At the same time, Latin *auctoritas* evolves into *authorité.* Great bodies of texts from the past that were considered authoritative were called *authorités.* Their authors, in turn, were called *auctors* and *autheurs.* Among these we find pagans like Ovid and Virgil, as well as later writers such as Priscian, Boethius, and Isidor of Seville. Not one of them writes in the vernacular.

The question of denomination for writers in the vernacular at this time is astonishingly obscure and is worth probing at some length. To begin with, the function of a writer qua writer does not exist: we have scribes who write, who copy or take dictation, but who may not even read. We have the ubiquitous jongleur. We do not know what Chrétien de Troyes or Marie de France called their profession, for example. Jean de Meung speaks of Guillaume de Lorris as *escriteor,* the ancestor of *écrivain,* writer, and refers to himself as *litterateur.* In addition, in a very important passage in the *Roman de la Rose,* a claim for authority in the sense of *auctoritas* is being made on behalf of Jean de Meung. At the moment of the text's inability to move beyond its entrapment in an unending siege, the god Amor says Jean de Meung will write a *Miroir aux Amoureux,* a speculum, the kind of book that can only be an authoritative one,[17] thus implying that here a vernacular *écrivain* accedes to the dignity of *auteur.*

Thus, after 1280, "authorship" as *auctoritas* is available to medieval writers, but it is generally not claimed. For one thing, writers of verse cultivate the lyric genres and receive either the title of poet or *chanters.* Prose writers are initially *dérimeurs* or become specialized: Froissart is a *hystoriographe,* Robert de Clari and Molinet are *chroniqueurs.* The title is drawn from the function, and the larger, more abstract term does not come into use.

But the thirteenth century also witnesses the birth of the medieval theater, for which the writer had to compose, sing, act, stage, and so on. In many ways, his activity is as varied as that of the jongleur; yet, obviously, the latter term is inappropriate because this individual is also backstage. The terms that come into use are that of the *maître de recors, maître de jeu,* or *fatiste,* one who rewrites and directs dramatic productions.

Molinet's own works are divided between his lengthy *Chronicles* (written in his capacity as *chroniqueur,* court historian) and the collection *Faictz et dictz.* In the latter, the *dictz* refers to pieces meant for oral rendition, whereas the *faictz* refers to all others including, presumably, *La Ressource du Petit Peuple.* Molinet would have been aware of the term *fatiste* because he is the author of at least one theatrical piece, a mystery play. But that term seems inappropriate to the context in which we find *Acteur* in the *Ressource.* The *fatiste,* who works offstage at least as much as on, could not be limited to a single function. What is needed in the *Ressource* at this point is an entity that can pick up from Vérité.

We need to consider two additional facts. The modern French word *acteur* is derived from *agere,* to act, and its Latin agent, *actor.* The term is known in the Middle Ages among the educated because the difference between active, passive, and deponent verbs is an important one. We can be sure that it was known to Molinet, who had a master of arts degree, for in one of his poems, addressed to King Louis XII, he describes his state of mind through the metaphorics of the Latin verb voice system.[18] Nevertheless, the term is a learned one, and it is believed that *agir* did not enter French until 1459. Before that time, the term for actor was most commonly *joueur* or *compaignon,* as the players in a *mystère* or *miracle* were in general not professionals.[19]

The passage on Jean de Meung's claim to authoritative authorship has received so little critical attention that one might well hesitate to invoke it in this instance. But invoke it we may, for Molinet was doubtless familiar with the claim because he was also a derhymer of the romance. His version is entitled *C'est le Romant de la Rose moralisé cler et net translaté de rime en prose par vostre humble Molinet.*[20]

This rapid historical inventory of the lexicological field of scription helps us delimit the meaning of *acteur.* We will review it by contrasting it to other terms in the field.

The *autheur* is one who has produced a body of work worthy of admiration, consultation, and imitation; he is a classic, an original creator within the framework of medieval poetics. He is an individual, considered from the point of view of his accomplishments. It is not at all certain that the term can be applied to anyone still living. The authority vested in his denomination requires the death or, more precisely (as the example of Jean de Meung demonstrates), the nonexistence (in his case, not-yet-existence) of the individual.

The *escriteor* is but a functionary. The activity is named at its most basic: he writes. It is not clear that the word had any intransitive meaning, so it appears with a genitive of purpose or ownership: "L'escriteor du *Roman de la Rose.*" It refers to a flesh-and-blood individual and it distinguishes him from other workers in the field of culture, to speak anachronistically. Like the allied term *litterateur, escriteor* names the activity on the basis of its material opposition to singing or reciting to the accompaniment of music.

The *jongleur* is a complete entertainer. In any case, by Molinet's time, his functions have been subdivided between musicians, dancers, animal trainers, court jesters, and a variety of word-crafters. Labor specialization has set in.

The *fatiste, conducteur,* or *maître du jeu* represents an instance of the adaptation of the jongleurian function. At a time, then, when all activities leading to a performance, as well as the performance itself, are no longer united in the person of the jongleur but subdivided among performers, the *fatiste* takes over, supervising all the preparations for the performance and directing it.

Which of these terms did Molinet apply to himself? In his professional capacity as court historian, he was a *chroniqueur.* As the author of a prose version of the *Roman de la Rose,* he was a *dérimeur.* He was a *fatiste* in his activity as dramatist. There is little doubt that, on the evidence of his bantering correspondence with other Rhétoriqueurs such as Cretin, he aspired to the title of *autheur*. As the author of *Dictz*, he was also a poet.

The terms we have examined are referential: they point to an individual, whether as the metonym for a body of works (*autheur*) or as the agent of a certain kind of activity (*escriteor*) or as the holder of a position (court chronicler). *Acteur* differs from all these in that it is a purely textual function: that from which a text is understood to be uttered.[21] From the point of view of a modern sensibility, which is steeped in prose to the point that it cannot imagine the world without it, the passages of *Ressource* or of the *Petit Jehan de Saintré,* which appear preceded by the notation *Acteur,* do not need such an *inquit*. They seem "natural" to us. We read them straightforwardly, without requiring further specification of the enunciative-scriptural instance at work.

This capacity of prose had nothing "natural" or obvious about it at the time of its emergence. Readers born and nurtured in an oral culture, a culture of performance, living in a society highly attentive to hierarchies and the privileges appertaining to them, would experience a sort of shock at encountering a segment of discourse that could not be marked by its provenance. Moving away from a literacy in written verse, which reads in the jongleur, a text will keep certain functions and discourses of the jongleur but will begin to jettison him as subject, flesh-and-blood or just "named." The jettisoning must be gradual, otherwise the discourses emitted could too quickly be questioned with respect to their means of evaluation. "It is no longer a jongleur or a Molinet, dear reader," we are being told with the use of *Acteur*, "but be not concerned, it *is* someone." Latin texts, both ancient and medieval, were capable of such discourse without any marks of status, but it is precisely because Latin was not implicated in the full range of social hierarchies that it could do so. Its territory was limited to the clerical class, which used *it,* Latin, as *its* distinctive trait. That is, its agency was institutional.

For the vernacular, a device was needed to inscribe a sort of degree-zero of enunciative markedness: "Yes, this is discourse," it states, "but it is a discourse that is neutral with respect to all forms of societal markedness." The hermeneutical rules it summons forth are classless, for it stands at a level that precedes the inscription of class. It marks no more than the enunciative-scriptural instance as such, prior to, and by opposition to, any further specification. At those points when all the attributable voices are gone, it is the "voice" of prose (prose, which is voiceless). It is obvious that the claim that this discourse is neutral, that this enunciative-scriptural instance is socially disinterested, is a sham, as is the pretense that prose has a voice. Prose is managed totally differently, it has a different economy, but, at those points when prose is compelled to disclose itself, as it is here, it covers itself with a mark, *Acteur*.

Acteur, then, as descendant of the *auctor,* the diviner, the foreteller, suffers the normal semantic loss of a long process of derivation. From foretelling, its function has shrunk to that of only for-telling or, more precisely, the function of marking the resumption of textual propulsion once it falls out of the responsibility of represented figures, such as, in our text, Molinet or Vérité. That is, it keeps the text going when everyone is disqualified. *Acteur* is background in a representation for which background is thought to be needed, functioning as a movie "extra" (what current French usage calls *un figurant*). It has no role and yet it is crucial to the textual economy, for it marks the binding that keeps together those discourses that *are* attributable. Later, even this mark will become unnecessary, as we learn to accept, and even believe, discourse with no, or uncertain, provenance.

In fact, *Acteur* is already unnecessary because the discourse it marks has already appeared without it. That discourse has been slipping *in* throughout the first prose section, or shall we say it is Molinet who has been slipping *out.* Disqualifications of the perceptual bounds of subjects have been happening (once Vérité sees what the infant sees, are we still to believe that Molinet is seeing it?), and we have been accepting those discourses without need for special *inquits.* It is just that at certain times, such as when Vérité stops talking, this written *parole* is understood to need attribution. In other words, there are times when a deictic expression is needed and times when it is not. The criterion is likely to be inconsistent during the emergence of a new signifying practice.

Inconsistent usage goes further than that. Works completely in prose, for example, *Le Petit Jehan de Saintré,* show the rubric *acteur* assuming the *parole* at certain times but have few or no other rubrics and do not mark when *l'Acteur* ceases to be the understood point of locution. That is, under its rubric other speakers are eventually introduced who are not rubricated but simply have an *inquit* in the text and who then speak directly; *Acteur* seems to slowly fade from consciousness only to be reinvoked, from time to time, with another rubric, *usually* after some character's speech. (Similar to its first appearance in *Ressource,* right at the point where another's speech ends.) In prose texts, then, there are signs that mark the beginning of an *acteur* utterance but none that, like the other rubrics here, mark its end. This is understandable because *Acteur* remains in the background whenever possible, to be not there. Notice how in this text Molinet presents himself, then presents Tyrannie and Justice; Vérité has herself presented, and she will soon introduce Conseil. *Acteur* is the only locutor who is not announced. (In fact, *Acteur* is mentioned only in rubrics, never in an *inquit,* for who is there, who could say that "*l'Acteur* says . . . "?) One final remark here: a more profound question underlying all this is the matter of why such rubrics, why *inquits* standing outside any kind of "narrative voice," are at all necessary in a versiprosa text or, for that matter, in an all-prose text. We will further discuss this subject in chapter 5.

Having established that the enunciative instance is a disembodied one, the text of prose is no longer ruled by perceptual requirements. *Acteur* is not to be read as one of the percipients, extra- or intratextual, who have their own somatic capabilities or interpretive possibilities, those of actual percipients, extra- or intratextual. The recourse to the unsubstantial *Acteur* marks prose's recognition that it does not need to formulate a claim to authority as such, that more is to be gained by leaving the determination of the source of authority suspended. By being "out of bounds," *Acteur,* whether named or unnamed, shows how prose can eliminate, when it is desired, the perceiver as intermediary and move directly to the different kinds of perspective that are specifically the readers'. These questions will be discussed more fully in chapter 6.

These are the words of *Acteur:*

> Les parolles de vérité estoyent tant haultaines, trenchans et vives qu'elles penetroyent les cœurs de tous ceulx qui les escoutoyent et fut a cop avironnee de gens de tous estas qui regarderent en pitié la miserable violence dont Justice estoit oppressee, ensamble le petit peuple, son enfant, tout affamé de longue jeusne, traveillié de criier et braire, qui n'estoit pas de prime face a rappaisier d'une hochette.

> Truth's words were so elevated, so sharp, and so animated that they entered the heart of all those who listened to them, and she was suddenly surrounded by people from all estates who looked with pity upon the miserable violence with which Justice was oppressed together with Common Folk, her child, starved from long fasting and exhausted from crying and bawling, and visibly beyond being pacified with a bauble.

How are these words to be understood? A kind of place, a textual place, has been carved out for the entity called *Acteur.* Shall we call it a "he"? He is not flesh-and-blood. He has heard the words of Truth, has even seen them penetrate the hearts of listeners, but he does not say that those words penetrated *his* heart: he does not have one. He is not there listening and seeing, like "ceulx qui . . . escoutoyent et . . . regarderent." Nor does he have a story about himself to tell. This is not Molinet. Were *Acteur* there, listening, were his heart throbbing, he would be just another feeling, sensing subject, to be read as all the others. What would be lost is the potential to escape perceptual requirements and to construct perspectival possibilities, in which, for example, although no *one* (no character, witness) could stand, a member of the audience or (much better) a reader might stand.[22] The textual difference between the perceptual and the perspectival might best be formulated as follows: perceptual concerns predominate when the representation being attempted is considered from the point of view of an agent, that is, someone of ontological status equal to that of the represented; perspectival concerns dominate when the point of view is that of a recipient of the representation, the audience. The difference drawn here between an agent's perceptual concerns and an audience's perspective is not one that can be decided cleanly and finally while one goes from one passage to another in a reading. (For one thing, a reader can always take as his or her perspective the perception of a represented agent such as it *is* represented and understood.) Such final judgments are products of an inquiry that is poetological, not part of a prosaics that sees such articulations and boundaries as that around which the text vitally operates. Perception and perspective are independent but are not necessarily mutually exclusive. Their relation is one of the things that a prose author suggests and a prose reader pursues.[23] With both perception and perspective, questions of verisimilitude arise, but they are of a radically different nature. For perception, verisimilitude requires that the mediator not adopt perceptual angles that exceed somatic capability. For perspective, the representation is constructed to conform verisimilarly to the perceptual angle of an audience. But how this is done is an effect of the text, a construction of the mediation. One either adopts the perceiving mediator wholesale—"If that's the way she sees it, that's the way I see it—or constructs or attends to a transparent mediator, one who has no immediacy. The invention of *Acteur* achieves just that: mediation without the immediacy of the mediator, representation as presentation. Thus the audience gains the impression that it is the recipient of an immediate, rather than mediated, semiotic matter.

In the preceding *lexie*, the *Acteur* could characterize the speech that Vérité has just concluded by providing a represented audience with which the reader can identify if he or she likes. Percipients are introduced to help the reader establish, but not be coerced into, the appropriate perspective. It should be noted that these are indeed percipients who have seen nothing that is new or different to us; they have *seen* only what has been *said,* nothing more (nothing has been written to imply otherwise); they have *seen* only what we have *read.*

The metalinguistic terminology available to us as critics, here and elsewhere in this study, is problematic; we can refer to *Acteur* as "he" although that term is merely a verbal operator. What sort of pronominal name do we give to a function that is not to be embodied? "It," perhaps, but an "it" that is less a pronoun than it is akin to the "it" of "it is possible that" or of "it is raining." That is an "it" that does not refer to anything but is a grammatical device without which the sentence could not occur.[24] *Acteur* does not refer to anyone but is a textual device without which it was believed that certain functions could not occur.

With the turn from a represented "he" or "she" to an only functional entity as addresser within the text, there coincides a change in the status of the textualized addressees, we the readers. Whom do we hear? What do we see? We will further explore this in chapter 6.

Entre plusieurs qui arriverent a ce tres douloureux spectacle, Vérité, qui moult estoit sage, choisy ung homme tout meur, assez grave, de reverend maintien, discret et bien moriginé, habitué de robe longue et d'ung bel chapperon foudré et, comme celle qui reclame au besoing son leal amy, Vérité s'escria vers luy a haulte voix et se print a dire:

Among the many who came upon this doleful spectacle, Truth, who was very wise, espied a mature man, rather serious, of reverent countenance, discrete and well behaved, dressed in a long gown and a beautiful blue hood; and like someone in need who calls out to a loyal friend, Truth raised high her voice and began to say:

Truth is seeking an interlocutor, to whom she will surrender her place. Let us examine the situation a little more precisely. The movement of the text's representation has been directed toward the scene of the ravaged mother and child. The apocalyptic eruption of Tyranny and her subsequent withdrawal were there to leave this scene as a remnant. In retrospect, we can see that Truth's central contribution was to stand in front of the pietà-like group and identify them for us, to see them as she knows them to be, giving the scene its true dimension. In addition, as befits an allegorical figure, she raised in her speech the tropological question: what is to be done? Having addressed the moment, Truth can address nothing more, and she is presently in the way. Before she leaves, however, she has to invest her authority in someone else.[25] She perceives and selects an individual in the audience, who, following the presentation custom in this text, is first described and only later named. Truth will speak to him and this will in turn give him the right to speak. The relay of utterance-making and authority (which is here in prose) is tightly controlled.

The description of the newcomer is worthy of some mention. He is a figure of authority—there is no doubt—but there is nothing in his person or demeanor that suggests the source of that authority. We may, for the sake of comparison, recall the descriptions of other figures of authority in older medieval texts: an authority always having as a direct measure physical stature and condition of the individual. Force, physical force, was what lay at the source of that individual's authority. Our protagonist has no physical presence except for a reverent demeanor. Moreover, he is not armed. His body, in fact, is covered by a long robe and his head by a fur hood, details that would tend to indicate a fear of physical realities. He is discrete, subdued. This is the beginning of a faceless authority. That such figures can be immedi-

ately associated with either the ecclesiastic or the jurisprudential confirms
the displacement of authority from the knightly class to the clerical in particular and to an anonymous, institutional power in general. And because such
a displacement is a controversial act, only Truth (who, we may recall, does
not fear anyone but God) may operate it.

Ha, Conseil, nostre bon amy, nostre bon amy, Conseil, se vous avez
en espargne quelque nombre de lermes procedant de la pitoyable fontaine de vostre cœur, sy les desployez a cop, car mieulx emploiier ne
les sçariez. Vecy Justice, vostre maistresse, ma desolee soeur et germaine a Prudence, vostre espeuze, nouvellement tombee en pamoison
et le petit peuple son enfant tirant a fin dure et mortele, se n'est par
vostre bon secours. Je cognoy par espreuve vostre science et proesse:
Conseil, nostre bon amy, vous avez sept ars sur le doy et le droit canon
en possesse et tant tiens je de vostre escolle que nul prince, tant soit
haultain, ne doibt chose ardue ou doulteuse encommencier sans vostre
advis. Quiconques vous prent en desdaing, ja n'ara bonne consequence: les nobles progeniteurs dont vous tirez naturele origine ont
suscité Justice en pluiseurs regnes, eslevé sceptres royaulx jusques aux
estoilles et entretenu jadis en glorieuse renommee Assiriiens, Italiiens,
Troyens, Cartagiiens, Belgiiens, Lacedemoniiens, Babiloniiens, Persans, Macedoniiens, Egiptiens et souverainement la triumphant monarchie des Romains, car, par la tres noble industrie d'armes ou ilz estoyent
habilitez, aveuc le cler engin, sens et praticque de vos samblables qui
lors ou senat flourissoyent, touttes les nations du monde, mansuetes
et barbaricques, se vindrent rendre tributaires en l'ombre de leur Capitole. Depuis ce temps, je suis certaine, nostre bon amy Conseil, que
la chose publique est grandement augmentée en vos mains en pluiseurs
provinces, palais, villes, chasteaulx, citez et cours et meismes de nostre
vivant en la tres clere et resplendissant maison de Bourgoigne. Qui esse
qui soubz la chevalereuse baniere du duc Philippe, prince de glorieuse
memoire, a debrisié les pointes des guerres apparantes, humilié les rebelles et nourri le petit peuple du fruit de paix, d'amour et de leesse?
Conseil. Qui esse qui soubz la tres flamboyant espee du tres illustre
duc Charles, que Dieu absoile, a soustenu Justice haultement auctorisie
en parlement honourable et en audience publicque, concordé le rice
et le povre? Conseil. Qui esse qui soubs la tres victorieuse main du
duc Maximilien peult susciter Justice en convalescence, corrigier les
delinquans, subvenir aux oppressez et conduire le petit peuple au bien
heuré temple de paix? Conseil. Conseil dont, nostre bon amy leal, en
qui flourit, croit et resplend noblesse, sens et preudhomie, aveuc la
tres recommandee science de medecine, tesmoingz grans et horribles
playes par vous sanees en pluiseurs bonnes villes, donnez soing a vostre
engin, regard a vostre œil et labeur a vostre main, sy reduisiez en estat
de prosperité Justice aveuc son petit peuple qui expirent devant vos yeulx.

Ah! Counsel, our good, good friend Counsel, if you have some tears to spare in the fountain of your heart, then spill them now for better use you could not find for them. Here is Justice, your lord, my devastated sister and the very sister of Prudence, your wife, who has fainted anew, and Common Folk, her child, about to meet a harsh and deadly end, unless you bring them succor. From experience I am aware of your knowledge and prowess: Counsel, good friend, you have the seven arts on your fingertips and canon law you have, and I hold your schooling so high that no prince, however exalted, should undertake any arduous or uncertain thing without your advice. Whoever disdains you will suffer the consequences: the noble progenitors from whom you descend have brought forth Justice in several realms, raised royal scepters to the stars, and once assured the flourishing fame of the Assyrians, the Italians, Trojans, Carthaginians, Belgians, Lacaedemonians, Babilonians, Persians, Macedonians, Egyptians, and above all the triumphant monarchy of the Romans, for through the noble art of fighting in which they were expert, the clear ingenuity, good sense, and practice of your counterparts who flourished then in the senate, all the nations of the world, civilized and barbaric, came to pay them tribute in the shadow of the Capitol. Since then, I am sure, the *res publica* has increased in your hands throughout provinces, palaces, cities, castles, strongholds, courts, and even in our day in the most noble and splendorous House of Burgundy. Who is it that, under the chivalrous banner of Duke Philip, a prince of glorious memory, blunted the points of the lances of emergent wars, humiliated the rebels, and nourished Common Folk with the fruit of peace, love, and happiness? Counsel. Who is it that, under the most flamboyant sword of the most illustrious Duke Charles, may God absolve him, upheld Justice with high authority in honorable parliament and in public hearings and brought accord among the rich and the poor? Counsel. Who is it that, under the most victorious arm of Duke Maximilian, can assure Justice of recovery, straighten the delinquents, relieve the oppressed, and lead Common Folk to the most happy temple of peace? Counsel. Counsel therefore, our good and loyal friend, in whom nobility, sense, and wisdom flourish, grow, and shine, in view of your most highly recommended knowledge of medicine and in light of the cures you have achieved of the great and horrible ills that had befallen several good cities, apply the care of your mind, the perspicacity of your eye, and the activity of your hand to bringing Justice and its Common Folk, who are dying in front of your eyes, to a state of prosperity.

The speech of Vérité is technically like an encomium, rhetorically articulated. But to call it such is both inappropriate and anachronistic. The encomium is originally Greek and is a form of discourse that occurs in the course of revels or celebrations in honor of an epic hero. By the time the

Latins take over the form, it is used not only in this formal context but in another: the paying of tribute to a departed hero. Old French oral literature treats the form in similar fashion. A tribute is paid, a eulogy is delivered on the passing of a hero whose death one mourns. Such a eulogy, formally constructed along the lines of the ancient encomium, is always in verse, for verse is the medium of commemoration—in the dual sense of remembering together (and thus collectively mourning the passing) and committing to memory, to collective memory.

The speech of Vérité bears all the formal marks of such a tribute: the appeal to the personal experience of the qualities of the subject ("je cognoie par espreuve"); the extent of his learning (the seven arts, canon law, and, a little later, medicine); the high lineage; the achievements of this lineage (from the Assyrians to the Romans); and the high feats of the hero (here limited to three and introduced by the anaphoric rhetorical question: "Who is it who . . . ?"), with the name Conseil recurring as the motif to be committed to memory. Even the final apostrophe to Conseil is within the rules of the form, for in the eulogy the departed is believed to be still capable of intervention, by virtue of his example, in the course of the affairs of those who are living.

Conseil is an unlikely hero, however; he is not even dead. Here we witness a new step in the conveyance of authority, into the hands of Conseil, and for this, the form of eulogy-tribute is exploited. At least as unlikely is the fact that the entire passage, 69 lines, is not in verse. Why is this in nonverse, and what does this (new) nonverse have to do with the (new) kind of authority invoked by the figure of Conseil?

This is Vérité's last speech. She must leave her interlocutor in full possession of any authority she had, and had for the giving. And at first glance, he seems to be qualified to assume that mantle. Like the other allegorical figures, he lacks any referential concreteness. Furthermore, we are told that he is related to the other figures by blood.[26] As an abstraction among other abstractions, he seems to possess the status shared by all. However, he is not an intellectual but a social abstraction. He is a representative of an inchoate social force. He can be represented by any sign that is a human being because he need not be anthropomorphized: he is already an *anthropos* but one whose function is conceived abstractly. He does not need to be personified: he begins as a person and is then de-individualized. Although associating with personification allegories, Conseil is more precisely a type.

In earlier literary models, there is no lack of characters possessing great knowledge by virtue of their experience and unusually venerable age, for example, the figure of Nestor in the *Iliad*. In the French tradition, the duke Naimes in *La Chanson de Roland* has long been recognized as possessing Nestorian characteristics. And, of course, the Arthurian material has given us in Merlin the quintessential incarnation of specialized knowledge at work. Other literary figures of this sort may be summoned. These figures, however, do not address the larger audience. Their roles are limited to purely intraplotted levels of storytelling—they are merely performing their functions. Nestor calls upon the Greeks to exercise caution; similarly, Naimes warns of the treachery of the Saracens. Their activity is apprehensible through an actantial narrative theory (à la Greimas) that would have no pain in describing how they got where they are. Such is not the case with Conseil.

His competency has not been established either through an accident of birth (Merlin) or as a result of the experience provided by longevity in a society in which life expectancy is short (Naimes, Nestor). The *specialty* of Conseil is to advise the mighty; he would appear next to the king or Duke Charles of Burgundy, telling them how to put an end to the trampling of Justice and Common Folk. He appears here, however, to address Justice and the audience that has gathered around Vérité since her outcry.s The introduction he gets suggests that his success in his own area of competency qualifies him for performance in this arena as well. He has become an expert, a mediator between a particular knowledge and society. We may tend to think that the rise of the expert is directly linked to the emergence of a technocratic society and therefore our invocation of this category for this figure's description in the context of the fifteenth century is anachronistic. But in inquests of the time, specialists of various kinds, especially doctors, were called upon to testify specifically as outside experts.

As an expert, Conseil fills a very practical function, as allegorical as he may seem. He does not come forward himself, like Tyranny or Vérité: he is not an initiator of action, which is the province of others. He is nothing until he is called upon, and he is called upon only when needed: his distinctness emerges when his function is necessary. He is to be unremarkable, disponible. When Vérité bids him to shed a tear, we can infer that he has not even been reacting to the scene at hand, he has not been part of the emoting throng. Like *Acteur*, or like a functionary, it is not as a person that he behaves but as an occupier of a position. He has no personal stake. He has no heart. Conseil is a professional.

At the end of Vérité's nonverse speech, *Acteur* picks up the utterance.

Adonc Conseil, vaincu par les prieres de Vérité, sans faire longue excuse pour la hastivité du cas, regarda en fac Justice, tasta son poulx, visita son urine et lui pria tres instamment, s'elle avoit esperit en elle, qu'elle monstrast signe de vie et, se possible lui estoit de parler, elle s'en mesist en paine pour plus a plain congnoistre la cause de sa doleance. Et lors la desolee patiente, Dieu scet a quel traveil de corps, leva ung petit le chief in hault et de une voix bassette et casse en faisant ses dures complaintes, complaindant ses griefves doleurs, dolousant ses piteux regrés, en regretant ses bons amis, proposa ces motz.

And thus Counsel, overcome by Truth's prayers, without making any excuses for the haste of the case, looked Justice in the face, felt her pulse, examined her urine, and asked her most insistently if there was life within her that she should give a sign of it and, if it was at all possible for her to talk, that she should do so in order for him to know the cause of her doleful condition. And then the devasted patient, with God only knows what bodily pain, raised her head a little and in a low voice intercut with heavy complaints of grievous suffering, pitiful regrets, and sorrow for good friends, said the following words.

First, the actions of Conseil are silent as he sets about his professional task. He performs diagnostic functions: examining Justice face-to-face, feeling her pulse, ascertaining the condition of her urine. Conseil's actions are drawn from the field of medicine, which, by virtue of its antiquity and preeminence as specialist practice, frequently serves as the metaphoric field of other specialist procedures (and is also, of course, a typed behavior). We are all familiar, in this context, which the metaphoric transference that authorizes us to speak of the "body politic", and the eventual emergence of social pathology, of which Conseil is obviously an early practitioner. *Acteur* then tells us that Conseil asks Justice to describe her state. We are not given Conseil's words: they are in indirect discourse.

This is the first instance of indirect discourse. It occurs only one other time, and again it is *Acteur* (he who does not "speak") who gives us the unspoken words of Conseil: Conseil "prit congé aus dames," says *Acteur*. Clearly, in the representational world of *Acteur* and Conseil, one can utter without "speaking" in quotes. (Of course there are also the words of Molinet: the prose that begins the story.) Note how, in the second sentence of the *lexie* we are examining ("Et lors . . . "), prose words frame, even elaborately, the act of speaking, but they stop short of coming out into the open themselves. Prose conserves its own silence and leaves the sonorousness to verse.[27] It is only Conseil's spoken words that admit of the silent treatment. This behavior tends to establish prose as that which is out of quotes, that which is not for attribution, that which frames but is not framed itself.

In response to the request of Conseil, Justice gives her first words, in verse. More than a functional communication with Conseil, it is, like Truth's earlier invective, addressed not to anyone in particular but to everyone. It stands as a statement. In verse, it takes its place and time. It is speech. To analyze this lengthy (144 lines) and rhetorically wellcrafted speech, interesting as it would be for Grands Rhétoriqueurs poetics, exceeds our needs in this chapter. From the point of view of the plot, little advance is made. Justice does not explain to what she owes her present condition. Whatever she does say seems sufficient for Conseil, who then, interrupted only briefly by a question from Justice, renders his verdict in 182 lines of prose. He is the first represented character who "talks" exclusively in prose, which we might well have guessed.

Justice replies briefly to Conseil, and to do so she speaks his language, switching to prose. She addresses him in particular, and she needs specific, practical information: how do I find Puissance? He has the information and furnishes it in the continuation of this now very prosaic exchange.

His speech is an exercise in reassurance, which we will summarize briefly: the wounds of Justice are not fatal, Common Folk is more exhausted by its own cries than by any *sévices* suffered. There is nothing in their condition that a little faith in the future, some further privations (this time voluntarily assumed), reliance upon the power of the Grandees (specifically the House of Burgundy and its new system of alliances alluded to through various conceits), much prayer, and a pilgrimage to the duke of Burgundy's court, will not alleviate or even cure. The message is clearly an ideological one: as bad as conditions are, they could have been worse; things are getting better, place your faith in those whose business it is to rule, endure a little more, and, in the meantime, pray and be meek. Conseil himself liberally disperses such clichés: "Take an ounce of joy against two pounds of sadness."

From the moment when medical metaphorics were introduced in the *Ressource,* we might have expected this sort of *attentiste* message. After all, the chief effect of the body-politic metaphor has always been to reformulate any social question into the authority patterns of pathological and curative medicine: ills are in those who suffer them, the patients (well-named) must cure themselves by following a regime(n) prescribed for them by people who know better about such things. Nevertheless, in the context of the beginning of the *Ressource,* such a message of passivity does seem somewhat surprising, and the overall impression produced is one of discordance. It remains to be seen whether the outcome could have been different, given the tasks and functions prose assumes.

Although full of the stylistic flights and flowerings associated with oratory and verse, this speech has chosen a different standing. In nonverse, the words do not comprise the marker of the occasion. It is less important—less a monument for all to hear—than the other speeches. Its authority, like the appearance of Conseil, is retiring, less incarnate; one for which the signifying practice of prose is appropriate. Conseil's contribution is not years of strength or wisdom; all do not readjust around him when he speaks; he does not cut a figure in the landscape; there is no crowd to react to *him*. His is a competency as such: a knowledge for application in specific instances. The face, the place, the time, the situation of the imparting of that knowledge, they are all secondary. Conseil is a forerunner of the functionaries of specialized knowledge and the specialized discourses they inspire, which—marking the inevitable fragmentation of *gemeinschaftlisch* discourse—necessarily create a new problem with new needs: communication. No less necessary is a vehicle, a medium, that which can contain both the specialist discourses in their dispersion and such remnants of the unifying discourse as remain available. The emergence of prose is linked to and determined by the emergence of specialist competencies, the fragmentation of discourse, and the need for and deployment of communication(s). The expert is one figure of this conjuncture.

In a change of signifying practice, there is, as we discussed in chapter 1, a generalized shift among functions and holders of functions. We have seen certain jongleurian functions be assumed by discourses. There is therein an abstracting-away of body. Here, by contrast, what is usually one aspect or function of a character—being in the confidence of the ruler—is abstracted away but is invested in another character made to the specific purpose. This character is now functional in a way not usually associated with "characters." He occupies a position. Prose's ability to approach all existing communicative situations formally, to abstract from them their mechanism without at the same time taking on the human agents in the process, and finally to appropriate the mechanism for itself under its own agency, is its most signal procedure, the very basis of its strength. It truly marks the beginning of a process of reification. Conseil shows that the evolving modern state is the social formation in which such functionaries have a constitutive part. They are the bearers, by virtue of their narrow confines, of an increasingly faceless authority. Prose is custom-made for the pros.

In the following nonverse of *Acteur,* we are told that Conseil leaves to prepare the reception of Justice at the house of Puissance. Justice travels more slowly (how did Conseil spirit himself away so quickly? Obviously a forerunner of the modern, faceless "advanceman": "pour avancer sa venue") and arrives at an abbey, where her last words in this text, a prayer to God, must clearly be in verse.

Here are the closing words of the text:

L'ACTEUR

Ainsy faisoit son oroison,
Au temple de Bonne Esperance,
Justice querant guerison
Et de joye la recouvrance;
Servant les sains de brance en brance,
Je le leissay devant l'autel
Et pour en faire remembrance,

Je retournay en mon hostel.

Ainsi que l'anee presente
Est dure et desplaisante a voir,
L'histoire que je vous presente
Ne peult guaires de mieulx avoir.
Puisque chascun pert son avoir,
Son heritage et son bien meuble,
Prions Dieu que nous puissons voir
La resource du petit peuple.

ACTEUR

And thus did Justice pray
In the temple of Good Hope,
Asking to be healed
And to recover joy.
Paying tribute to the saints one by one,
I left her at the altar
And returned to my hostel
To make a record of all of this.

Since the current year
is hard and unpleasant to see,
The story I present you with
Cannot be any better.
And since everyone is losing his possessions,
His inheritance, and his goods,
Let us pray God that we may see
The recovery of Common Folk.

The final words of *Acteur* are, as might be surprising, in verse. Why? And how can *Acteur* speak verse?

The verse prayer of justice marks the end of the action. (Obviously, all initiative is being put back in God's hands.) The text will end in an equivalent fashion, with a call to prayer. Prayers, in versiprosa texts, are, for reasons that should now be clear, in verse. But who will end the story? Justice cannot have that role; she is inside the story. There must be something at least apparently inside that also stands at enough of a distance, is outside enough, to embrace the story. *Acteur* is the obvious candidate.

But it must speak, and it must speak in verse. This is because notions of versiprosa closure are still so close to speech and performance that closure must consist in (the representation of) ceasing to speak by an utterer in a given place and at a given time. As prose tends to stop short of speaking (in the sense we have suggested), its writing and reading taking place at an indeterminate time and place, prose is not at this point the appropriate instrument with which to mark an ending. Texts of this kind will eventually be able to end in prose, but it will not be because prose changes (starts to speak, marks anew the enunciative instance). It will be because notions of what the totality of a text is will change, and thus notions of closure will change.[28]

Because *Acteur* has to mark the end, it has to stop speaking; however, it had never really started. Logically, then, it has to begin to speak. And its speech, to mark time and place as speech, must take its own time and place. Such a type of speech, as we have seen, is traditionally put forward in the signifying practice of verse.

And there is a second conundrum. To take one's place is to be "one," to have an "I." How can an "it," a grammatical, impersonal, textual entity, turn into an "I" and refer to itself, its deictic situation? In the face of this necessity, a deflection results: a subject is sought to which *Acteur* can be attached. There is Molinet, who had been left behind and at this stage in the text, could have been forgotten. We get him by default. So the "je," named *Acteur*, is associated with Molinet, summoned back because of local need, joining the call to prayer and returning to his "hostel."

It must be simpler than that, one might say. Molinet opened it, and so he closes it, a simple closural device. If that is so, however, why is not the rubric *Molinet*? Because, although he was there before, he was never an *inquit*, was never presented as a speaker, so he cannot return as one. Molinet opened this versiprosa text in a fashion that easily moves into the signifying practice of prose: an outsider, an observer, who can contain, say what *he* sees, and then what *is* seen, even while his own presence is slowly being effaced, and who ends up no place. We modern readers are totally at home with this. But a transitional text like this, a text of emerging prose, cannot go the whole distance. It finds itself ineluctably dealing in speech and agency, restraining prose from containing freestanding speech, which here must still be freestanding verse, and thus falling into an economy of verses and prose based on alternatiosn and of speech and agency and authority based on relay. And so the somewhat phantomlike Molinet, who almost in spite of himself gives the *impetus*, sets the wheel turning (Molinet who, we must remember, opens the story stating his emptiness, with no grist for his millstone, no stories to tell, nothing to *say*), has no place of his own in this story. He cannot be called upon "in person" to speak the closure. He has been replaced, for better and worse, by *Acteur*.

As we said earlier, *Acteur* will soon become unnecessary. All the better too, for then we will not be entangled, as we are here, in its presence, not on the plane of representation but as "locutorial" marker in the text. Even that is a presence that can be undesirable.

Chapter 5
Chantefable

The crisis of authority that results from the fall of the signifying practice of performance (and written verse) is going to be solved in favor of prose. From historical hindsight, this is clearly the case. However, we are not in any position to write a simple linear history of this development, much less acquire any *understanding* of the steps through which prose became predominant to the point of appearing "natural." To anyone who has even casually thought about this problem, *Aucassin et Nicolette,* an anonymous thirteenth-century work divided into 41 sections in which verse and prose alternate, imposes itself as a major object of inquiry. It chronologically precedes the derhymed *Bérinus* and the versiprosa *Ressource,* but we have left it until this point because of its peculiarities.

It is the story of two lovers forcibly separated from each other and then reunited. Aucassin is a young valet who, too much in love with the fair Nicolette, does not want to be a knight and defend the lands of his father, the count of Beaucaire. His father will not allow him to see Nicolette, on the grounds that (having been brought from Saracen lands and merely adopted by the neighboring viscount) she is not a fitting match for him. The viscount, at the plea of Aucassin's father, locks up Nicolette in a tower. The count Bougars de Valence mounts a stiff attack against Beaucaire, who urges his son to take up arms and defend their lands. The son consents to do so only on condition that, upon his safe return, his father will let him see and kiss Nicolette. The father reluctantly consents.

Preoccupied by thoughts of Nicolette, however, Aucassin loses control of his horse and is captured, until he realizes that death would eliminate any possibility of seeing her again, at which time he battles furiously, captures Bougars de Valence, and leads him literally by the nose to his father. His father refuses to keep his end of the bargain, so Aucassin sets Bougars free on condition that Bougars continue to attack his father. Aucassin is then imprisoned by his father. One night, Nicolette escapes from her tower, finds a crack in the wall of Aucassin's prison, and they secretly exchange vows of devotion before she is forced to flee the dawn. She escapes the town in unladylike fashion, by jumping into the surrounding ditch, preferring the dangers of the unknown outside the town to persecution within. She sleeps in the forest and the next morning meets some shepherds whom she induces to tell Aucassin that there is a priceless beast that he should pursue. She then goes more deeply into the forest and makes a shelter.

Nicolette's disappearance prompts Aucassin's father to let him go, and a nameless knight suggests to him that a trip to the forest would be beneficial to him. There he discovers the shepherds, who are gaily singing a song about a lovely and generous blond they have met. He asks for the song to be repeated, and after some difficulties, he is given the message that induces him to go farther into the forest in search of his love. He meets a rustic cowherd, ugly and miserable, who states that he has just lost his best ox, Roget. Aucassin gives him some money and then finds Nicolette. Together at last, they decide to go off together.

They come to a seashore and get on a boat. A storm brings them to the kingdom of Torelore, where, they are surprised to learn, the king is abed with child and the queen is fighting a war. Aucassin goes to the king's chambers and threatens to beat him unless the latter admits that men do not give birth. The king consents and then they both go, without Nicolette, to the place where the queen is waging war with rotten apples, mushrooms, eggs, and cheeses as weapons. Aucassin offers to do vengeance on the enemy and starts to kill them right and left until the king stops him, for killing is not the usual way of waging war there. Saracens attack the castle, take the two of them away in separate boats, and the one holding Aucassin arrives at Beaucaire. His parents are now dead (three years have passed), so Aucassin becomes lord. Nicolette is brought back to Carthage, which she recognizes from her childhood. She learns that she is the daughter of the king of Carthage, and plans are made to marry her to another pagan king. She decides to train herself to play the *viole*, disguises herself as a male jongleur, and gets aboard a boat that takes her back to Provence and eventually to Beaucaire. She approaches Aucassin in disguise and sings to him of the love of "Aucassin" and "Nicolette" and tells him that "Nicolette" is now in Carthage, recognized as noble herself, but imprisoned for refusing any husband other than her long-lost Aucassin. At the real Aucassin's ecstatic response, she pledges to bring "Nicolette" back to him. She then returns to her lodgings, from which she emerges a few days later as her former beautiful self.

The text concludes;

> Or a sa joie Aucassins
> et Nicholete autresi:
> no chantefable prent fin,
>   n'en sai plus dire.
>
> (XLI)[1]
>
> Now Aucassin has found his joy
> and Nicolette as well;
> our chantefable comes to an end,
>   I know no more to say.

The name it calls itself, which is unique to this text (of which we have only one manuscript copy), is chantefable, song-story. Presumably, the prose sections were meant to be recited and the verse sections sung. In fact, we have the musical couplet to which the verse (which is in heptasyllabic assonanced couplets with an "orphan-verse" at the end) was sung. The regular interplay of verse and prose passages has mystified scholars from their earliest encounter with the text. They both contain direct dialogue and both narrate action, and what is recounted in one section is occasionally said differently in the next.

Some very general observations can be made about the verse-prose distinction. For example, there tend to be more "lyric" moments in the verse than in the prose sections, and more monologues in the verse, more dialogues in the prose.   J. Trotin has shown that the verse portions are not only indispensable from the point of view of information but are also invaluable for the pivotal character decisions they assert, such as Nicolette's decision to escape.[2] Further study of the text has inspired many ingenious explanations for the distribution of verse and prose, like the statistical analysis of lexical items done by Monsonégo,[3] but none has achieved broad consensus. What is not addressed is how these passages are articulated, that is, the matter of the textual economy, the matter of how the whole thing "holds together." Such attempts as have been made in this area have become mired in difficulty, and thus we must reexamine Aucassin et Nicolette after having gained a surer footing, as far as the future of prose is concerned, in our examination of a dérimage and a versiprosa text.

The text tantalizingly articulates the passages with its famous inquits, that is, in the rubrics that precede all but the first segment. All the verse passages (except the first one) are preceded by the notation "Or se cante" (Now it is sung) and the prose passages by "Or dient et content et fabloient" (Now they say and recount and tell the story). The triple designation that stands as the rubric of the prose segments has proven to be quite mystifying. Why three terms instead of one, as in the verse? Why a plural subject, whereas the verse has a perfectly serviceable reflexive singular? Is this difference significant? Do they refer to the same agent(s)? Is this performed by one, two, or many subjects? What differences of meaning, if any, are intended by the three terms? There is no need to rehearse here the somewhat tedious discussions of the philologists, who, for the most part, have considered the resolution of these questions as the answer to the puzzle of the generic identity of the text. Their enterprise was taxonomic, part of the poetological project to draw clear distinctions between verbal forms. But we know this text to be historically part of a movement in which a consciousness of such distinctions begins to emerge, and there is shifting going on.

The terms of the *inquits,* at least most of them, do not refer to preestablished entities whose inner configurations and rules of textual articulation and insertion are known beforehand. Rather, they attempt to constitute such entities in accordance with novel demands. For example, the use of *dire* admits of special explication. Although used in the rubrics only to preface nonsung portions, it is used in the text to also mean the singing of songs. Aucassin, after having heard the shepherds *chant,* makes the following request: "Bel enfant, fait il, redites le cancun que vos disies ore!" (Child fair, says he, repeat the song you were singing now!) Which earns him the following reply: "Nous n'i dirons, fait cil qui plus fu enparlés des autres. Dehait ore qui por vous i cantera, biax sire!" (We won't sing it, said the one who was more outspoken than the others. Let him be damned who will sing for you, good lord!) And when the shepherd recounts, in nonverse, the encounter with Nicolette and the message she entrusted to him and his companions, Aucassin uses the same term in thanking him: "Bel enfant, fait Aucassin, asses en avés dit, et Dix le me laist trover" (Fair child, says Aucassin, you have sung me enough, and may God let me find her). Within the verse containing the shepherds' song, the song itself is introduced with the *inquit:* "Li uns dist." Thus *dire,* at least outside the *inquit* seen as formula, is not strictly opposed to *chanter.* There are asymmetries here that require some further examination on our part.

Since our concern is text-economic and not one of taxonomy or poetics, we need not delve into the nature of these individual and problematic terms. We may begin instead by noting that whoever wrote the *inquits* did not think that the prose passages could be properly labeled by a single term. And so we have three terms, all in the plural. These multiple plurals are an indication of an awareness that something irreducible to any singularity is at work in these passages. And although these prose segments contain a large variety of what we call discourses (e.g., monologues, descriptions of action, notations of feelings, dialogues, invocations, etc.), a fact that would suggest a variety of *inquits*, there are just as many in the singly labeled verse segments. To be sure, the word prose does not enter the language until 1265, but the absence of the term, or, rather, the fact that it was not "borrowed" (as philologists put it) from Latin earlier, is not the whole story. For one thing, *chanter, conter, dire,* and *fabloier* are all verbs; prose was not a verb, was not seen as an action, did not bespeak an agent. That the *inquits* are both passive and active, singular and plural, indicate an instability of agency and a disruption of "subjecthood," which we can recognize as a symptom, if not more, of a configuration of signifying practices in which prose is to emerge.

The problem of the definitive denomination of that which is not verse becomes clearer if we briefly consider the semiotics of the medieval denomination of verbal forms. The fundamental terms are drawn from performance: *chanson,* which can then be specified as a *chanson de geste,* or, if unspecified, means (as Zumthor has made very clear) courtly song. Subgenres of *chanson* can receive the name of the dance step that their music follows: *ballade, rondeau, virelai,* et cetera. Other terms, of which the *Vies de saint* would be a good example, draw their name from the object of their concern. They are referential in that sense, and the object dictates the nature of the interdiscursive play that is characteristic of them. The problem for *prose* was that the term did not correspond to any identifiable form of active performance, nor was it referential inasmuch as it did not have any object that was proper to it.

To go from the terms of the *inquits* to their functions is no less controversial. Grace Frank's reading of the unique manuscript suggests to her that these are not rubrics, whose addressee would be the reader alone, but cues, recited by the performers to signal either the end of a recitation so that a song could begin or the end of a song so that a recitation could begin. "'Or se cante' occurs without hiatus of any sort after the last word of the prose portion (usually on the same line with it), and . . . the words 'Or dient et content et fabloient' are regularly compressed into a small space at the end of the musical staff containing the words and melody of the refrain, to which indeed they appear to form a sort of conclusion."[4] This fact, together with the fact that there is no prefatory "Or se cante" prior to the first section, and other minor observations, leads her to the conclusion that

> these words serve as cues, that beginning with the first prose section and continuing throughout the rest of the piece, the person entrusted with the recitation indicated to his companion, the singer, when the moment to begin had come by saying "Or se cante" and that the singer in his turn told the reciter when he was to perform by pronouncing the words "Or dient et content et fabloient." It would follow, if this view

is correct, that *Aucassin et Nicolette* was destined for performance by two persons and that the plural pronoun in the next to the last line (*no chantefable*) is to be taken literally.

However, we must ask why such cues were suddenly necessary when there was nothing like it at the time, and for good reason: endings are the easiest thing to note nonverbally,[5] particularly the ends of songs, and especially the songs of *Aucassin et Nicolette,* which mark their ending by a four-syllable not a seven-syllable verse and have a different melody for that ending line. So, as occurs quite frequently in these kinds of studies, new information is valuable but only restates the problem: where did these come from? Frank's observations still do not deny that this was a manuscript that tried to put performance in writing, albeit somewhat clumsily. The *inquits* are discourse out of frame, even if (improbably) not out of recitation, and discourse that is in any sense to be understood as out of frame, as recited but "not really," becomes problematical. This is nothing more than the *acteur* problem, and we will return to it.

To be sure, there are signs in *Aucassin* that the prose attempts to establish its own hegemony. For example, it demonstrates that it has the capacity to refer to what happens in verse: more than a half-dozen prose segments begin with "Si que vos aves oi et entendu" (As you have just heard), referring to the verse that immediately preceded it; verse segments do not so refer to prose segments. This is first a gesture toward an appropriation and containment of the verse, which prose will eventually show itself capable of citing, something the verse can never do with respect to prose, because of its formal constraints. In other words, if we were to remove the numbers and the rubrics, we could conceive of this work as a work of prose that cites verse but not the other way around. However, this is precisely the kind of remark that would have been uncalled-for then, making no sense. In any case, in *Aucassin et Nicolette* the prose is stymied in this process because the chantefable contains not only verse but also *song.* (The shepherds' rejoicing is even represented as a song.) We have the music, which the prose cannot cite. This barrier is paradigmatic of the prose in this text, possessing incipient and formal powers of hegemony but unable to extend them beyond the boundaries of its segment. Furthermore, although the verse does not refer to the prose, it still claims the position of both that which is heard and sung *and* that which contains it, such as the "Li uns dist" in the shepherds song previously mentioned, and:

> Dementer si se prist
> *si con vos porrés oïr:*
> "Nicolete, flors de lis."
>   (XI)

Par devant lui s'arestit,
si parla; *oés que dist:*
"Di va!"

(XXIX)

He began to deny,
as you will be able to hear:
"Nicolette, fleur-de-lis."
In front of him [her] he stopped
and spoke; *listen to what he said:*
"Pray tell!"

Verse will also be that which contains.

Neither rhymed nor unrhymed has predominance; each pretends to hold the whole. In other words, song is still there to hold song, that role is not ceded to nonsong. Having both verse and nonverse in its performance or transcription of performance, the text runs into a complex of other problems that are no doubt interlocking: singular versus plural subject, active versus passive subject, oral versus written, writing that is subordinate to the oral versus writing that bespeaks the oral, and that which is contained and framed versus that which is containing and directive. It would be easy if we could segregate, if we could make these pairs into two paradigms, of which the set of all terms on the left constitutes one signifying practice and that of all terms on the right constitutes another, but that is not the way it is: it is rather a mixture of new and "archaic" uses[6] and a general jockeying for position. The various dichotomies are used collectively to hold change in check: a move in one direction with one pair of dichotomies will be balanced by a move in the opposite direction with the next. What we can say with certainty is that *Aucassin et Nicolette* has a double character both performed and written, verse and prose; it is caught in an irresolution, and we might well have expected it to be a hapax, that is, one of a kind, with no successors.

In our examination of *dérimage* and versiprosa, we have spoken of the emergence of nonverse in writing, a writing that has among its ancestors a performed verse. *Aucassin et Nicolette* can be seen as the first transcription of performance that marks the incursion of nonverse *in performance*. As such, it shares with other early "theater" the questions of where nonverse fits in performance, how the rest of performance fits within it, and what kind of performance could fit around it. Dating from around the same time of *Aucassin et Nicolette* is Rutebeuf's *Dit de l'Erberie* (1250), the parodical harangue of a charlatan claiming to have been all over the world and then enumerating the precious materials he has for sale, lauding their miraculous properties. The first half is in verse and the second in prose. "Dits," considered only for performance, were included in a genre defined by scholars of the late nineteenth century as dramatic monologue or "mime." They are made up mostly of parodical sermons, the spiels of charlatans, and various kinds of braggadocio *matamoros*). They are virtually all in verse, the "dit" of Rutebeuf being exceptional (like *Aucassin*) until the sixteenth century.

The emergence of nonverse in performance brings its own set of problems: scholars ask whether these works *are* really "performance" or "dramatic" or "theater." Monologues are qualified as "dramatic" if they are acted out rather than recounted, spoken by a *joueur* rather than a *conteur*. Of course, we are not often in a position to know who they were spoken by or how they were spoken. The only evidence we have of this is written documents, so we are to a great extent barred from making final judgments. *Aucassin et Nicolette* raises the question, which we cannot resolve but can recognize, and what there is to recognize is only instability and nonfinality. The debate over the rubrics, over the marking of the beginning and ending of speech and song, may never be resolved as to how exactly they participate "verbally" in the performance, for how can we talk about verbal actions outside writing (i.e., "dramatics") when virtually all we have is the writing? The distinction between what is and what is not "dramatic" is a distinction of a *written* culture faced with the necessity of defining some writing as "dramatic" and some not. This opens the door to extensive hairsplitting,[7] as scholars, probing for more evidence, apply a microscope of higher and higher power to the same words, a procedure that we both sympathize with and apply ourselves from time to time but which has the undeniable limit that whereas it is reading the performance, it is armed only with a literacy of script. The paradox is as follows: insofar as documents of performance are transcriptions of verbal content only (of only what in the performance is to be recited), such a transcription can tell us, in some sense, the *least* about so-called "dramatic" qualities of the performance.

This is not just a problem for us; it was clearly a problem for them. If we wonder about *Aucassin et Nicolette's* stage directions, said or unsaid, we might look at the *Courtois d'Arras* of the early thirteenth century, which is an all-rhymed dialogue of characters, except that interposed between their speeches at a few points are "stage" directions, *which are also rhymed*. Were they "said" as well, making this, then, a monologue that had narration as well as speech? If they were performed by many characters, rather than a *conteur*, would these directions have been suppressed? Even when prose is not at issue, strictly speaking, we can see how signifying practices become implicated: if it is writing, rhymed narrative is fine; if it is theater, who says the narrative? Where does it come from?

We have the mystery play *La Passion d'Autun* in two different manuscripts: *La Passion de Biard* and *La Passion de Roman* (fifteenth century),[8] both of which are probably drawn from an earlier, nonsurviving original. The *Roman* is "dramatique" (just the locutors' names and their words) and seems, from information gathered from related manuscripts, to have abridged the original, but the *Biard* has intercalated passages of narrative, so that *within* the speech of a character are narrative phrases that describe the action of that character. Note the following pairs of corresponding passages:

La Passion de Roman

Or parle L'OSTE a Jhesus
Tous ceulx que meneront ta vie
Auront de paradis la vie.
Or parle L'OSTE a seint Pierre
Pierre, festes soyre ces gens.
Et je seray vostre servant.

(Lines 82-85)

La Passion de Biard

Or parle L'OSTE a Jhesucrist.
Et tous ceulx qui tiendront ta voye
Arons de paradis la joye.
Et puis se tourna vers saint Pierre
Et ly dy: Amys debonnayre,
Faites seoir toutes ses gent.
Quar je sera vostre servant.

(Lines 96-101)

La Passion de Roman

Or parle PYLAS.
Barons, je sçay bien que a grant tort
Jhesus volés delivrés ad mort.
Sans droyture et sant reyson
Luy fecsiés soffrir passion.
Droyture est que decharge.
Or parle UNG DES JUIS a Pylas.
Se nous volons, qu'i soit
Sur nous et sur nostre enfans,
Et que nous gant en soit culpés,
Puisque de mors vous ecytés.
[Pylas]
Prenés le et le jugés.
Or sa, je veulx lavés mes mains,
Car checung doit savoir
Que je n'en ay culpe de ssa mort:
Bien sçay que serax a tort.

(Lines 478-91)

La Passion de Biard

    Respont PYLAS es Juifz.
Seigneurs, sachés que nous avons grant tort.
De le ainsy mectre a mort.
De cecy je me descharge
Et vous trestout en encharge.
Et pour mieulx a eulx le cueur detourner,
Ilec fit de l'eaulx appourter;
Et puis en lava ses mains,
Affin que depuis le plus grand Juif qu'au moins
Chascum puisse sçavoir et entendre,
Contre luy mal ne vouloit entreprandre,
Aussy que n'eusse culpe en sa mort,
Quar sçavoit bien que avoent tort.

                          (Lines 853-64)

The Passion of Romans

    The HOST speaks to Jesus now.
All those who lead your life.
Will have life in heaven.
    The HOST speaks to Saint Peter now.
Peter, sit these people down
And I shall be your servant.

The Passion of Biard

    The HOST speaks to Jesus-Christ now.
And all of those who will hold to your way
Will have the joy of heaven.
And then he turned to Saint Peter
And told him: good friend,
Sit all these people down.
For I shall be your servant.

The Passion of Romans

    PILATE speaks now.
Barons, I know full well that you are wrong
In wanting to deliver Jesus to death.
Without right or reason
You are making him suffer the passion.
It is right that I should free him.
    Now ONE OF THE JEWS speaks to Pilate.
We want it, and let it be
Upon us and our children,
And let the guilt be upon our people
Since you are hesitant to apply death.

[Pilate]
Take him and judge him.
And now I want to wash my hands,
For everyone must know
That I bear no guilt for his death:
I know full well that it will be wrong.

The Passion of Biard

PILATE answers the Jews.
Lords, know that we are very wrong
To put him to death thus.
I discharge myself from this
And make it entirely your burden.
And to better turn their heart around
He had water brought right there;
And washed his hands,
So that from the highest Jew to the least
Everyone would know and understand
That he did not want to undertake any bad thing against him
And that he had no guilt in his death
For he knew full well that they were wrong.

Just as *dérimeurs* would fall back into writing the verse of performance, dramatic playwrights fall back into jongleurian *diegesis*. These narrative phrases are rhymed. Who recites them? A facetious answer would be: "A verse *acteur*." This is clearly a time when what needs to be written (stage directions) may also need to be said, then need to be rhymed, then . . . the question must be asked: "who" or "what" says it and "how" is it said? Hidden here is the desire to have utterances not said, even though they are in verse, but how does one draw verse away from voice?

Some narrative lines seem to be résumés of dramatic lines of other versions. Sometimes they replace the rubrics of other texts, and often the rubrics remain. As the first example illustrates, these narrative octosyllables enter into the rhyme scheme of the dialogue. At other times the rhyme perfectly meshes the two kinds of discourse, and at other times narrative rhyme is faulty or poor. In any case, although what they recount is often the kind of narrative that other plays have as stage directions, these cannot be easily suppressed or, say, detached to a reciter on the sidelines, as such lines can in the *Courtois d'Arras,* because they are too interwoven, often sharing a couplet with a line of dialogue.

So *La Passion de Biard* is not a mystery play. It seems clear that this is the work of some *fatiste* or *remanieur* or *arrangeur*, transforming a dramatic play into a narrative poem for recitation or reading. At the time, many villages took known Passions and retained such a craftsman to adapt them to a particular occasion. This was an era of *rifacimento* and reprocessing: new agents got into the action but in an oblique and almost invisible role.[9] This is a time when works of performance were negotiating between dialogue and narrative, most of the time maximizing the first and minimizing the second but unable to always stabilize the distinction. So that, in *Biard* for example, there are two kinds of "stage directions": rubrics outside recitation, nonrhymed, with verbs in the present; and speeches, inside, rhymed and in the preterit. In a jongleurian communicative framework, the latter is perfectly called for. It is in moving to theater, that which does not present an embracing voice, that they seem freakish.

There is an unmanageability to the whole question of the identity of the uttering subject and the bounds of the utterance: anthologies of dramatic monologues constantly debate whether the document at hand is in fact a monologue or a dialogue, whether it might be a "réponse" to another document, and whether it was in fact meant to be performed by only one person.[10] Questions of subjecthood and integrity of the whole work are entangled. How to be literate with respect to the margins of the works? What is extrinsic and what intrinsic, what container and what contained? And how is it that the transcription of only that which is presumably *in* (e.g., words spoken) begins to in-clude what was held to be extrinsic or excluded and consequently to redraw all the lines and start new processes of occlusion and occultation? Even in these all-verse documents (except for the rubrics) in which there is no prose per se, we see the kind of uncertainty that betrays the fact that *parole* is being divided between the "said" and something that has a problematic adjacency to the "said," that signifying practices cannot defend their borders (particularly as writing is now applied to these kinds of utterances), and that prose is emerging. And the need for something like prose must have been sorely felt. We have only to look at *Entrées,* descriptions of parades announcing the entry of the king into Paris, an incredible polysemiosis coming down the street (with people on stages, in costumes, carrying signs containing the first letters of the poems that are being recited, etc.) combined with a constant shifting of the means of recounting, from citation to narrative verse, to freestanding acrostic poems, to nonverse, and even with the rubric *acteur* thrown in from time to time, as some sort of framer of the words to follow. The phenomenon is entirely akin to a three-ring circus or, better, the halftime show of a major football game, another collective practice addressed to a collectivity, a practice whose polysemiotic nature can find no single place from which the multiplicity of perceptions, even in their partiality, can be "told".

We can see the chantefable as one result of the strains being brought to bear on the performance of the spoken word. How can words be couched otherwise, how can they be unspoken? Perhaps the unspoken word should just be excluded. Our quandary is not fundamentally different from that of the thirteenth and fourteenth centuries: the medieval transcriber or reworker wonders whether and how to include some words as part of the work at hand, and then, if he does so, the modern philologist wonders whether or not to recognize that inclusion as part of the same voice or work. In the case of verse and prose, this becomes particularly circular: if one dogmatically accepts that performance is in verse, then prose cannot be in performance, which allows for two ways in which to account for the presence of prose in such textual environments: first, the text would have to be something other than performance once prose is within it. For example, Julleville judged that the *Dit de l'Erberie* is not a dramatic work because of the part in prose.[11] And second, the prose portion is judged as not inside the work but outside it and so becomes an extrinsic and expendable factor. In either case, rather than redefining preexisting boundaries, one uses them as the justification for exclusion.

The second case is illustrated in the frequent exclusion of the prose portions of medieval texts, as if they were extraneous. Prose has been more frequent than it appears. (There is no adequate anthology of the occurrence of early prose. Early prose cannot be anthologized because it comes in on the margins, it never presents itself as just prose.) There are many cases where the medieval scribe has included prose portions in an otherwise verse work (although not in alternation), but today's scholars of the Middle Ages have been spared this knowledge by the modern editors of these texts who, applying concepts derived from the nineteenth century, have ensured the valued homogeneity by lopping off the offending prose passages.

To show how pervasive this phenomenon may be, let us cite the case of the *Vie de Saint Alexis,* a text generally taken to be the third oldest verse in the language (after the *Séquence de Sainte Eulalie* and the *Vie de Saint Léger*). It comes to us in the authoritative editions *all in verse.* Yet its manuscript "L," the so-called Hildesheim MS, generally dated at 1123 and believed to be based on an "original," which has disappeared, dating back to 1040, has a prologue in prose, written in the same hand as the verse. This 30-line prose prologue is written in alternating lines of red and black ink, which Lausberg believes to have a moral value, with red standing for Christ, and black for Satan.[12] Then comes the verse. From its oldest monuments, then, the interplay between prose and verse is to be found, but the prose is "exceptional," in the pejorative sense. We could have played this game and excluded *Aucassin et Nicolette* from this book on the grounds that it is not really a prose work but "just performance."

Such heterogeneity of signifying practices is but an instance of a more pervasive type of heterogeneity to which medieval scholarship has perhaps not been sufficiently attentive and which may help us in determining more precisely the conditions of the emergence of prose and its workings. Because we have just alluded to the *Vie de Saint Alexis,* hagiography may provide an illustration of this broader type of heterogeneity.

As one of the earlier textual forms of the vernacular, the Saint's Life finds itself in a situation of dependency vis-à-vis Latin textual models. Already in Latin, translations of the Bible, especially of the New Testament, forced a crossing of the boundaries set up by Latin rhetoric because the Christian ethos introduced topics of humility, poverty, and social difference that would not be contained within the classical oratorical divisions:

> In attempting to place chronological limits around the [move from classical to vulgar Latin], attention has naturally shifted to the Late Latin period, that is, roughly between A.D. 200 and 600. The first boundary corresponds to the age of Tertullian and the early martyrologies, which, Löfstedt persuasively argues, are as useful an indicator of linguistic shifts as the death of Tacitus around A.D. 117, the event normally taken to signal the end of the classical age. More importantly, the third century also saw the introduction of a new cursive which by 1367 had become the "common script" everywhere except the imperial chancery. This *scripta latina rustica* took its vocabulary from popular usage; it absorbed morphology and syntax, as well as traces of phonology; and it adopted new graphic signs to express the sounds actually spoken. Many factors influenced the linguistic and scribal changes: the interplay of social classes and levels of education, migration from the countryside to the towns and from the peripheries of the contracting empire to the metropolis; the conflict of different generations, ethnic groups and religions, through which the vulgarisms of one period became the fashionable styles of the next; and above all political considerations like the *constitutio Antoniniana* of 212, which bestowed Roman citizenship on all inhabitants of the empire regardless of origin.
>
> Among all the forces contributing to the growth of popular Latin in the later empire a special place is reserved for Christianity. Members of the new faith constituted virtually a "third race" after Romans and Jews, no less marked than the latter by their refusal to participate in official cults and by their sense of exclusiveness. One of the clearest ways to delineate boundaries was through the spoken or written word. What was created was "not quite a new language, but certainly new forms of expression" [Löfstedt, *Late Latin* (Oslo, 1959)]. Whether in everyday, literary or liturgical Latin, Christians introduced words and phrases drawn from ordinary speech and occasionally from Greek. The novelty arose both in language and style. The Old Latin versions of the Bible, which drew heavily on colloquial usage, influenced speech patterns among Christian communities, and this linguistic phenomenon, reflecting in turn the often low social origins of the converts, allowed

a measure of freedom within the restrictions of the literary language. Notions of genre were similarly affected. Christian "literature," Auerbach observed, that is, stories from the Bible, dealt by and large with topics that did not fit into the classical oratorical divisions. Their forms of expression were "humble" but their matter "sublime." New canons of taste were obviously at work. The Bible, or its translations, attempted to make God's word accessible to all, no matter what the level of education. It intermingled high and low in both audience and inner message: the complexity depended not on rhetorical figures—although these, Augustine showed, were found in abundance—but in the desire of the faithful for spiritual enlightenment. The blending of classical stylistics and biblical themes greatly influenced the development of medieval Latin and Romance languages. The gradual abandonment of the classical curriculum in the schools after Justinian could not but promote the acceptance of spoken Latin, whose rhythms were now not far from those of the translated Bible itself.[13]

In the vernacular now, Saints' Lives, introducing as they do a new conception of the life of an individual, are forced to forge discourses appropriate to this new object, and to reconfigure the ordering of discourses in the Latin model, that is, reinscribe their mutual boundaries and thus design new constellations within the discursive realm. Specifically, hagiography as textual form (for it is that) includes such discourses as: "historical" account, panegyric, (auto)biography, martyrology, funeral oration, Christian apology, legend, parabola, exemplum, set piece of juridical rhetoric (as in the almost obligatory trial scenes in which the saint appears in front of a pagan judge), and ultimately liturgical insert. Moreover, the fact that this takes place in the vernacular accelerates the reworking because the vernacular will not have been subjected to prior rhetorical regulation and poetological specification. Thus, rather than consider hagiography as just a genre among others, a perspective which in effect pigeonholes it, we should see a broad process of cultural transmutation occurring within it, by means of its discourses, which it subjects to a type of labor, in the Freudian sense of the term.

In particular, hagiography, like the biblical texts preceding it, allows a humble style to find a place in great works. Saint Augustine admits having found the Bible lowly in style, at a time when he could not see how "sublime" it was. It is only after his conversion that he sees the Bible's strength to reside precisely in such low style.

> Sancta Scriptura parvulis congruens, nullius generis rerum verba vitavit, ex quibus quasi gradatim ad divina atque sublimia noster intellectus velut nutritus assurgeret.

Holy Writ, adapting itself to babes, has not been afraid to use expressions taken from any kind of thing, from which, as though drawing food from it, our understanding may rise gradually to things lofty and sublime.[14]

Augustine's initial disdain for this kind of writing had come from a tradition of ancient, Ciceronian rhetoric that treated style as part of a concern for pragmatics, of language in action, a concern that present-day approaches tend to neglect (as poetics looks to an analysis of the inner structure of discourse) and which also differs from medieval approaches, as we shall see.

Ancient rhetoric, and the poetics that was, in a sense, its adjunct, was a form of speculation and regulation of language as a communicative means between speakers or speaking subjects conceived of as free and as equal to each other inasmuch as they could be substituted for each other. These are the fundamental concepts of ancient democracy. One would read in vain all the ancient treatises of rhetoric to see if matters of *social* differentiation are addressed in discursive or linguistic terms. Women, slaves, children are all disenfranchised, as are foreigners. Those who accede to discursive status are thought of as constituting a homogeneous group within which the only differentiations that could occur are of an individual nature. Such was the ideological position of Greek democracy and of the Roman republic.

By contrast, medieval speculation on matters of linguistic communication occurs in a society that is stratifying itself in those aggregates that will be known as estates. The feudal order presupposes such forms of social differentiation with their ideological underpinnings. But, in contrast to democracy, or more precisely, to the ideological presentation of the latter, which presents the image of an all-encompassing whole, the feudal order must face the problem of the relative definition of the limits between the estates and the even more vexing problem of their porosity, especially because the feudal order, although long-lived, proved to be the ground upon which the class society of the future would develop by breaking up the limits of the estates.

The best way to illustrate this emergent consciousness of the function of language as a means of social differentiation is, as Vance has pointed out,[15] to see the treatment afforded by medieval rhetoricians to Cicero's distinction between the three forms of style. Cicero, it will be recalled, distinguished a high, a middle, and a low style—a distinction that the medievals preserve but articulate in a way that is completely different from Cicero's. The latter's distinction followed the Aristotelian approach; it was based on an inquiry into the ends of these styles. Cicero recognized three ends: to move, to teach, and to delight, and it is these three ends that he classed as high, middle, and low. But among the medievals, there is a shift away from the ontological question of ends to the sociopragmatic question of decorum. The three styles are reinterpreted in terms of three different levels of social standing suited to the speakers in the communication. Geoffroi de Vainsauf makes it clear: "When one treats of great people or things, then the style is grandiloquent; when of humble people, humble; when of middle-class people, middle."[16] John of Garland further theorizes this area and formulates the term *ydioma* to designate the relationship that must prevail between social status and speech decorum.[17] Identification of the *ydioma* applying to differing social groups inevitably moves one's linguistic conceptions away from a single, universal magisterial word and toward a diversity of utterance that we recognize as *sermo*, familiar discourse, conversation, the speech of a particular group, the words and expressions that are *idoneus*, appropriate to each. John of Garland defines the term *sermocinatio* as the assignment of discourse to characters in accordance with their station in society.[18] The boundaries of such *ydioma* induce us to take another look at *Aucassin et Nicolette*.

Aucassin et Nicolette is a text that has puzzled and charmed several generations of medieval scholars. The routine orthodox questions of medieval scholarship remain without answer: questions of origin, of authorship, of generic classification, and of "sources." As its most recent editor, Jean Dufournet, puts it: it is the sole example of the chantefable, a literary genre known only by the isolable occurrence of its name at the end of *Aucassin et Nicolette*. "Is it a unique work in all the senses of the term or did others disappear without leaving a trace?" In addition, there is but one manuscript of this text. "Must one conclude that this masterpiece, universally admired for decades, found no success in its own time?"[19] Must one adhere to Jean-Charles Payen's belief that other copies were deliberately destroyed because the text "offends the cultural comfort of the medieval audience . . . upsets too many commonplaces even though the provocation hides behind an innocent exterior"?[20] Or must one follow the reluctant conclusion of Mario Roques, the editor of the authoritative Classiques Français du Moyen Age edition, who, after having reviewed all the proposals, suggestions, and theories of scholarship to his day, sees the only real agreement among critics of *Aucassin et Nicolette* to be that its characters and its author were all "naïve,"? Since then much scholarly analysis has shown that the author is at least a learned parodist who is thoroughly familiar with the epic traditidon, the Tristan texts, and the works of Chrétien de Troyes.[21]

The two types of codes that are parodied the most in *Aucassin et Nicolette*, according to Dufournet, are the epic and the courtly. It is very clear that the eponymous heroes of the text are creatures of the courtly code, and it would not be incorrect to say that the text explores what happens to such heroes when they circulate in a world of other sociolects, no longer bound exclusively by the discourses and rules of that code.

Let us consider a brief example in which elements of the courtly code are not automatically functional and are being recast in other terms. Count Garin de Beaucaire, Aucassin's father, presents himself as an upholder of chivalric values. As such, for example, he refuses to contemplate the possibility of his son's mésalliance with Nicolette. But he finds these values severely tested when his own son determines that he will fulfill normal and ordinary obligations of war-making under both the epic and the courtly code only if his father enters into a bargain concerning his relationship with Nicolette. The fact that the father does not ultimately abide by the terms of the agreement may be seen as his deeper commitment to the older codes or, conversely, as the aporetic situation of a man who no longer knows how to apportion honor between the older code that requires him to ignore the bargain and the newer one that requires him to uphold it. This conflict remains unresolved.

In the same episode, Aucassin behaves in a manner that under the older codes would be termed that of a miscreant, that is, of one who is unfaithful to the code that ought to govern his life. If he decides to battle Bougar on the side of his father, it is merely to obtain leverage against his father. In the battle itself, which he approaches without any of the appetite that ought to be characteristic of a knight going into battle, he is rapidly made prisoner, and he decides to defend himself only by means of the logical deduction that his impending death will interfere with his social life. This is surely not where the motivation of an epic hero or courtly knight conventionally lies. And when he does fight, it is without any regard for the decorum of battle but in strictly utilitarian fashion, driving Bougar's head into his helmet and leading his prisoner back by the noseguard. The whole incident is not the occasion for the display of uncommon valor or heroism: it is simply the material means for the exaction of the bargain. It has become an element in a world of exchange. In the behavior of both the son and the father, one can see that the older codes no longer hold exclusive sway. We have changing conceptions of honor, of value, of valor, of what motivates human beings (rationality vs. instinct), and the intrusion of utilitarian considerations, as opposed to behavior worthy of one's standing.

Two parallel passages will show how the two lovers, caught up in their *ydiom*, will fare in the world that now surrounds them. In the first, Nicolette, having escaped from prison and communicated with her lover in two extended episodes marked by a clear observance of the codes of courtly literature (with references to *Piramus et Thisbé* and the *Chevalier de la Charette*), sets out for the forest. The forest is here a dual semiotic object. For urban aristocrats, the forest has become a mythical place; it is a locus of passion, in which one can experience marvels and adventures. But to the shepherds, who are also city dwellers, the forest is a different semiotic entity. They do not expect to find passion or marvels or adventures there; it is simply where they earn their living. Nicolette heads into a courtly forest, but the shepherds she encounters are in a forest of their own, more material *ydioma,* and they are not, most emphatically, pastoral (or courtly) shepherds themselves.

In segment XVIII, the confrontation is staged, and the conflict, or rather the rupture of the hitherto apparently seamless world of courtly romance, is thematized. Nicolette, having entered the forest at night, wakes up in the world of pastoral, with its shepherds, bubbling spring, and singing birds. She addresses the shepherds in the condescending tone of the aristocrat, calling them children, and engages in a rather complex conversation with one of them, described as "the most outspoken." She wants them to convey a message to Aucassin: "Dites li qu'il a une beste en ceste forest et qu'i le veigne cacier, et s'il li peuit prendre, il n'en donroit mie un menbre por cent mars d'or, non por cinc cens, ne por nul avoir" (XVIII) (Tell him that there is an animal in this forest and that he should hunt for it, and if he can take it, he would not sell a leg of it for a hundred gold marks, nor for five hundred, not for any amount).

This message is *ydiomatic* of Nicolette, of Aucassin, and of the forest as the locus of pastoral. It is a request and an invitation, in the sociolect of the courtly. It is couched in highly artificial and figurative language, cast in a style known as *ornatus difficilis* (characterized by an abundance of tropes and *figures de pensée*). There is nothing innovative or startling in the message or its form, by the standards of the courtly or of the pastoral: the aristocratic pastime of the hunt for a prized animal provides the vehicle for an extended metaphor, the tenor of which is the erotic quest. Both elements are common to romance (cf. the hunt for the white stag in *Erec et Enide* or in *Guigemar*). But the shepherds addressed here are not the shepherds of romance. Refusing to acknowledge the message, they assert its semantic unacceptability:

Je li dirai? fait cil qui plus fu enparlés des autres; dehait ait qui ja en parlera, ne qui ja li dira! C'est fantosmes que vos dites, qu'il n'a si ciere beste en ceste forest, ne cerf, ne lion, ne sengler, dont uns des menbres vaille plus de dex deniers u de trois au plus, et vos parlés de si grant avoir! Ma dehait qui vos en croit, ne qui ja li dira! Vos estes fee, si n'avons cure de vo conpaignie, mais tenés vostre voie.

"I should tell him!" said the more outspoken of them; "Let him be damned who will speak of it, let alone tell him! You are talking of phantasms: there is no animal of such value in this forest, be it deer, lion, wild boar; one of their legs is not worth more than two farthings, three at most, and you are speaking of such large sums! Damned be whoever believes you, let alone tells him! You are a fairy, and we care little for your company; keep to your own way."

The message speaks of relationships of value that do not make sense to them.

The speaker is a dangerous fairy with whom one should not associate; to the devil with her! The message is rejected. What we have here is a failure to communicate.

One could conceive of a solution in which Nicolette would suddenly become aware of the lack of understanding and translate her message into terms the shepherds could understand or at least find acceptable. This kind of solution would be a modern one, for it presupposes that the *ornatus difficilis* and the discursive conventions of the courtly code are somehow secondary elaborations upon some basic ground of communicability. But the very existence of such a ground is what is being questioned in this passage.

Translation presupposes a shared code, and shared discourses that are part of it, but what if it really does not exist? What if each interlocutor can speak only in his or her own appropriate manner and does not know how to cross over? The discourses of courtly code have stepped into a world that radically rejects its claim to the universality it enjoyed so much in the world of romances. Its extension is being restricted. Nicolette can only repeat herself, but she can avoid being rejected: she will offer money along with her message. The message may be meaningless to the shepherds, but it is not valueless to them. Its meaning will suffice to Aucassin who has the *ydiomatic* capability to decode it.

> Ha! bel enfant, fait ele, si ferés. Le beste a tel mecine que Aucassins ert garis de son mehaing; et j'ai ci cinc sous en me borse: tenés, se li dites; et dedens trois jors li covient cacier, et se il dens trois jors ne le trove, ja mais n'iert garis de son mehaig.
> Par foi, fait il, les deniers prenderons nos, et s'il vient ci nos li dirons, mais nos ne l'irons ja quere.

> "Ah! fair child," says she, "you will do it. The animal has such a medicine that Aucassin will be cured of his wound, and I have five shillings in my purse, take them and tell him the message. He must hunt it within three days, and if he does not find it within three days, he will never be cured of his wound."
> "Faith," he answers, "the pennies we will take, and if he comes this way we will tell him, but we will not go looking for him."

Note that the language of monetary exchange not only permits the circulation of meaning across regions of incomprehension—to negotiate its passage—but also provides a model of translation. Nicolette says: "J'ai ci cinc *sous* en me borse." The shepherds, accepting the money (and the message), say: "Par foi . . . les *deniers* prenderons nos." In the incipient monetary economy of the Middle Ages, most lower-class individuals would count only in the lower coinage, *deniers* or even in *mailles,* half a *denier*), whereas the richer aristocrats would use the higher denomination of *sous,* and only very large financial transactions between estates or political entities would be discussed in *livres* or *marcs* (hence the incredulity of the shepherds at the mention of the five hundred gold *marcs* as the value of the limb of the fantastic hunted animal). The shepherds reply *ydiomatically* in *deniers* to Nicolette's *ydiomatic* offer of *sous*, but the world of currency, that is, financial transactions, provides value-equivalents, thus permitting exchange across difference. And the institution that sets the value of the currency (i.e., the incipient state) will be the ultimate arbiter of all exchange and of all translation.

Even with the money in hand, the shepherds insist upon striking the deal on their own terms: they will retain the message and make it available to its *destinateur,* but they will not seek him out. The shepherds will amend the proposed exchange so as to delineate clearly that they can be induced to act only so far. They have limits that are, properly speaking, not negotiable.

An almost symmetrical encounter is then staged between the shepherds and Aucassin. Aucassin, freed from imprisonment by his father, owing to the circulation of a rumor that the escaped Nicolette is dead, is advised by a friendly knight to seek the diversion of the forest, with its *Natureingänglische* flowers, herbs, and singing birds, as an escape from his grief. Drawing on his own experience, the knight intimates that Aucassin may even hear an encouraging word there. Aucassin sets out and soon encounters the shepherds, whose workday routine has brought them back to the spring, so that all the features of the morning's encounter with Nicolette are reproduced. But this time the shepherds are in a playful mood. They are celebrating the acquisition of Nicolette's money[22] with a song that not only names Aucassin and alludes to Nicolette but also lists all the objects they will now purchase.

> Or s'asanlent pastouret,
> Esmerés et Martinés,
> Früelins et Johanés,
> Robeçoris et Aubriés.
> Li uns dist. ''Bel conpaignet,
> Dix ait Aucasinet,
> voire a foi! le bel vallet;
> et le mescine au corset
> qui avoit le poil blondet,
> cler le vis et l'oeul vairet,
> ki nos dons denerés
> dont acatrons gastelés,
> gaïnes et coutelés,
> flaüsteles et cornés,
> maçüeles et pipés,
>   Dix le garisse!
>   (XXI)

> The shepherds then get together,
> Aimery and Martin,
> Frederick and John,
> Robert and Aubrey.
> One of them says, "Fair friends,
> May God help Aucassin,
> a truly fair knight!
> as well as a young lady in a corset
> who has such blond hair
> clear face and blue-gray eyes
> and who has given us money
> with which we will buy cakes,
> sheaths and knives,
> flutes and cornets,
> drum hammers and recorders,
>   May God help them!"

What is this song? It is a love song and it is sung by shepherds. The temptation is great—indeed irresistible to many scholars— to call it a *pastourelle,* especially because the diction (lexical items, overuse of diminutives, rhythm, etc.) is that of the *pastourelle.* But there are some notable differences. First, the love story, so briefly alluded to, is not the traditional one (a triangle involving a shepherdess, her intended, who is another shepherd, and an importuning knight attempting to exercise the privileges of his social status) because there are only two lovers and they both belong to the same social sphere, the nobility. Second, the song is hardly concerned with any love plot: divine blessings are wished upon the two lovers, to be sure, but in the context of the more immediate material rewards that the love has produced for the shepherds, namely, the money they obtained from Nicolette with which they will purchase sundry objects for work and pleasure. Third, the composition of the singing group is wrong: it is an all-male group, whereas the *pastourelle* requires either an all-female group or at least a mixed group. The song may look, or rather sound, like a *pastourelle,* but it is not one. It is perhaps a parody of a *pastourelle,* but it would probably be safer to say that it is playing with the constitutive subcodes of one. Such playfulness has nothing obvious about it, given the social status of the individuals who engage in it. To what extent can the shepherds of an aristocratic fiction (the *pastourelle*) play with the rules of that fiction? These are no longer courtly love shepherds. By playing with one of the genres of the courtly code, they establish that they are not courtly themselves (according to that code, they never were) and, even more strongly, that they do not acknowledge the courtly code's hegemony over them. They are not only not courtly but not *of* the courtly.

Aucassin, who *is* of the courtly, although his courtliness leaves something to be desired, fails to notice this shift in the status of the shepherds. The text again thematizes the tearing-asunder of the hegemonic claims to universality of the courtly code. And so, when Aucassin finds the shepherds, he recognizes neither their game-playing nor the fundamental shift in discursive and social status that such game-playing implies. He simply assumes that they are what the overt signs of their discourse—their diction—seems to convey they are: stock characters from the courtly code. He concludes from the song, which he has imperfectly heard, that Nicolette has been in the vicinity and, to obtain additional clues as to her whereabouts, he asks that the shepherds repeat the song. His request is met with refusal, and, although he pleads and reveals his identity as their lord's son, he cannot budge them until he too offers money.

What is being staged at this juncture of the text, and thematized in the play of request and refusal, is the nonnaturalness and, therefore, societal-conventional basis, of forms of verbal interaction. Aucassin, hearing the diction of the shepherds' song, automatically assumes that he is its proper recipient: after all, (1) his fellow knight had suggested that the forest may hold messages for him, (2) *pastourelles* are sung for the members of the knightly class, and (3) he is the only knight around. By all the rights and regulations of the courtly code, although *they* sing it, this is *his* song. Its very performance presupposes his presence. His request for its reiteration is thus perfectly natural within the set of assumptions of the courtly code. It will be noted that Aucassin does not ask any of the obvious questions that we, less attentive as we are to *sermocinatio* and discursive protocols, might have thought of asking: why are you singing about me? Who is the young blond? Which way did she go? For him to do so would be tantamount to acknowledging that the shepherds have access to the meaning of what they sing, that is, that they know the hermeneutical rules of a mode of signification that properly belongs to another social group. Only a member of the knightly class possesses the discernment necessary to divine the meaning of the song. The shepherds can be no more than the vessels for the preservation of the message (which, by the way, was the conclusion of the encounter with Nicolette).

As a creature of the courtly code, Aucassin expects a message, and he expects this message to reach him, and to signify to him, by indirection. So all he is asking for is repetition. The message that he will eventually get from the shepherds, comprising Nicolette's conceit of the prized hunt, would delight any courtly lover's appetite for indirection. Meaning and the hermeneutical rules for its establishment continue to be governed by intracode conventions. But the delivery and circulation of messages is now an intercode process, across the boundaries of *ydioma*. Hence the shepherds' rather remarkable directness in their negotiation of the delivery of the message with Aucassin.

Bel enfant, si ferés, je vos en pri.

Os, por le cuerbé! fait cil; por quoi canteroie je
por vos s'il ne me seoit, quant il n'a si rice home en cest
païs, sans le cors le conte Garin, s'il trovoit mé bués
ne mes vaces ne mes brebis en ses pres n'en sen forment,
qu'il fust mie tant herdis por les ex a crever qu'il les en
ossast cacier? Et por quoi canteroie je por vos, s'il ne
me seoit?

Se Dix vos aït, bel enfant, si ferés; et tenés dis
sous que j'ai ci en une bourse.

Sire, les deniers prenderons nos, mais ce ne vos
canterai mie, car j'en ai juré; mais je le vos
conterai, se vos volés.

De par Diu, fait Aucassins, encor aim je mix conter
que nient.

(XXIII; our emphasis)

"Fair child, you will do it, I beg you."

"Sblood!" he replied, "why should I sing for you if it does not suit me,
when there isn't a man rich enough in this country, except for Count
Garin, who if he found my oxen or my cows or my ewes in his
meadows or in his wheat field would be so obviously bold as to dare
hunt them? So why should I sing for you when it does not suit me to
do so?

"If God helps you, fair child, you will do it; and here are ten shillings
that I have in a purse."

"Sir, the pennies we will take, but I will never *sing* for you, for I
have sworn it, but I will *tell* it to you if you want."

"By God," says Aucassin, "I would rather have you tell than nothing."

Their refusal is thus motivated by more than greed, and it is very specifically
focused, so specifically in fact that Aucassin, who has only courtly code
modes of discrimination, is blind to the distinction the shepherds are drawing.
They will not sing, no matter how, or indeed by whom, they are entreated
to do so. They are the masters of their own discourse. Aucassin's money will
be accepted, and the message *will be* transmitted (with rather astounding
fidelity) but not in song, not in the mode of signification of which Aucassin
believes himself to be the master. They will deliver it in another mode, one
of their own choosing. Note that it is the shepherds who set the terms, and
Aucassin must accept: it is the best he can get.

In refusing to *canter* for Aucassin but consenting to *conter,* the shepherds
effect a rather novel distinction concerning the nature of messages: they propose to distinguish between the form and content of the message on the one
hand, and its mode of transmission on the other. This is not an instance of

translation, then, but something much more akin to the *dérimage* that is beginning to happen contemporaneously to the writing of this text: the semantic content of the message and its rhetorical form are preserved, but they are transmitted in another medium. Aucassin, defined by the courtly code, is unaware that such a possibility even exists; he learns it here, and of course he must pay for the lesson.

If we now compare the two encounters between the shepherds and the lovers, we can begin to formulate some conclusions about what has been staged and thematized in them.

First, major cultural codes, such as the courtly one, govern behavior, meaning-formation, textual organization, et cetera, and hold sway in a hegemonic way, which permits them to operate as if they were at once organic and universal entities: organic in that they do not admit of any internal subdivision, and universal in that they have exclusive rights of dominion. The *community* of persons is reflected in a commonly understood code and a communal set of discourses, a communal *ydioma*. What is staged in this text is a cultural revolution in which these codes are forced to acknowledge their limitations of extension, thus losing their claim to universality, and to effect internal distinctions that reveal their constructed nature and deny their claim of organicity.

Second, codes retain something that we could call internal autonomy, that is, they continue to articulate and govern such meaning as is still within their purview, even though they have lost exclusive control over the transmission of this meaning. This is the sense of the shepherds' acceptance of a message that they do not understand, an acceptance that demonstrates the functioning not of a community but of a successful *communication*.

And third, verse and prose become implicated in the move from community to communication.

No longer under the hegemony of a universal code, other codes become unregulated, can erupt anarchically, take on a centrifugal force of their own, and lead to chaos. What can govern the articulation of the codes among themselves? What can establish boundaries and territoriality? How are these codes contained an d managed? Once one has *ydioma*, which differentiate among social groups to integrate those individuals who use and understand them and to exclude those who do not, the novel problem arises of how one mediates between them, whether through translation from one to the other or through a third, presumably more neutral or common instance.

There is some evidence that the medievals thought of prose as a sort of style, or at least that they attempted to apprehend it through that category of their conceptual machinery. Cotgrave, usually quite conservative in such matters, confirms this by defining prose as "any stile which is not Verse, or Meetre."[23] But we must remember that for John of Garland, style refers not to a manner of treatment (*modus dicendi*) but to the social status of the subject or the object of the utterance. Here must have resided the conceptual puzzle of prose. Of what was *it* the *ydioma*? It is clear that this was the question that mystified the medievals for a very long time, and although *Aucassin et Nicolette* will stage *ydiomatic* exchanges, as we shall see, it is a question that is unresolved in that text.

To ask what the prose passages are *ydiomatic of* in this chantefable is also to ask that question of the verse passages. And there the answer is much more obvious: the verse is the *ydioma* of the aristocratic class, as our previous discussion of the courtly code confirms. (The only time the shepherds use verse is when they are singing their "courtly" song.) This is a class that then enjoys considerable political hegemony and cultural prestige, even though, as we have seen, its discursive correlative is under some pressure. It is also clear that in the social sphere, the pressure is not going to come from any other class—not for quite a while anyway—and yet there is *some* pressure on it, originating in Christian heterogeneity straining the textual economy of Latinity, of which the prosaic functioning of the text provides evidence and which the eventual selection of the term prose for the phenomenon confirms.

This term is borrowed from Latin but not from rhetoric. It is borrowed rather from the designation of the style of the papal chancery, a set of writing styles that, from the reign of Henry I in England and Philippe Auguste in France, is being adopted by the bureaucracies of the nascent states of Europe, states that will progressively usurp the customary powers of the aristocracy and concentrate it in the central apparatus of the monarchy. Prose looks like the *ydioma* of the state. In its emergence, it is a *signe avant-coureur* of that political entity, which will emerge as the arbiter of a conflictual social sphere, the guarantor of the rights of the third estate against the excesses of the nobility, the protector of the church (the first estate). The state, then, will act as something transcendental to the social sphere, yet, through its apparatus, it will be quite immanent to it. Prose will fulfill similar functions in texts. But not in this one. Here, the situation is one of stalemate. The courtly and aristocratic hegemony has been challenged, it has been ruptured, but it will not give way.

This is a problem for the text and for the society. The text must find a way of ensuring not only that the codes continue to function as meaning-producers and -organizers within their newly defined domains but also that meaning obtain at the boundaries of their interaction and indeed throughout the text. The text's mode of signification is no longer isomorphic or coextensive with that of any one code. What do you call something that articulates codes?

Once again, we are dealing with a text that poised on the cusp between two rather different universes of discourse and signification. The old order of a hegemonic courtly code will no longer hold, but the new order is barely discernible. In fact, from the perspective of the old order (and we need to bear in mind that this is the only perspective tenable and textually construable in *Aucassin and Nicolette*), it is not at all clear that what is emerging *is* an order. It may well be chaos or, at the very least, the negation of order. A perspective grounded in the hegemonic order will always take itself to be given, natural, ordained, and it will not easily grant the possibility that there may be other perspectives with equal, if not greater, legitimacy. To move even a little in that direction is to jeopardize, with untold consequences, the unspoken and perhaps even unreflected acceptance of the existing order as the only possible one. There is thus built in a powerful structural resistance against any consideration of other perspectives, especially if they are grounded in alternative orders. The text of *Aucassin et Nicolette* gives ample evidence of such resistance; yet it has already traveled too far down the road to the unknown not to acknowledge that other perspectives exist.

At this juncture, it faces two tasks: first, how to represent this fearful otherness, and second, how to determine what means to put forward for its reduction to a reassuring sameness. These problems are not unique to *Aucassin et Nicolette,* nor should we expect them to be: much of medieval literature is constructed around the opposition of the same and the other, with the latter to be reduced to the former through the heroic feats of the main protagonist, who sets everything straight. The representation of otherness haunts medieval texts from the *Song of Roland* to the harrowing of hell or ascension into heaven. It has long been observed that this otherness is represented as a negatively or at least as a differently marked variant of the existing order, so that, for example, in the *Song of Roland,* the Saracens, rather astonishingly in the light of the uncompromising monotheism of Islam, are depicted as worshiping a trinity made up, for *les besoins de la cause,* of Allah, Muhammed, and Apollo. It is indeed in these representations of otherness that the imaginary gives us a glimpse of the society's self-understanding as it makes explicit the boundaries of what it will consider an "unthinkable," although formulatable, alternative to itself. Similarly, in the necessary elaboration of the means by which the otherness is absorbed, it gives us an idea of how it perceives, however dimly, the direction of change and what may prevail once change has been effected. Such is certainly the case in *Aucassin et Nicolette.*

We are of course referring to the famous episode of the castle of Torelore. The two lovers are reunited in the forest; they sail away, get lost in a storm, and wind up in the distant kingdom of Torelore. When Aucassin inquires about the king, he is told the latter is resting after childbirth, while his wife is leading the armies into battle against the hereditary enemies of the kingdom. Aucassin ascertains the veracity of this information and reacts rather uncharacteristically, considering his previous reluctance to uphold any of the obligations incumbent on the courtly knight unless he could use them as bargaining chips with his father in securing Nicolette's hand in marriage. Here, without any prompting and quite spontaneously, Aucassin attacks the king with a club when he indeed finds him recoveiring from a recent childbirth. He exacts from him the promise that this custom of men lying-in will henceforth be abandoned throughout the kingdom. He then rides out to the battlefield with the king, only to discover, to his astonishment and mirth, that the conflict is fought with rotten apples and unripened cheese. Aucassin plunges into the fray with his far more lethal weapons and begins to pile up an impressive number of slain enemies, but the king reins him in, telling him that it is not the local custom to kill, or indeed harm, one's enemies. The people of the country are even more vociferous in their rejection of Aucassin's ways, calling upon the king to expel him from the kingdom altogether, while keeping Nicolette as a bride for his own son, a turn of events that Nicolette is able to forestall.

Torelore is not a disorderly society, then; it is simply governed by a different order. Internally, this order enjoys a double legitimacy: tradition, and the consent of the governed. The weight of custom is twice invoked—in the case of the lying-in and in the nature of combat—and the people's rising against Aucassin indicates their preference for local ways. Such internal legitimacy is characteristic of otherness, but it is not, as a result, acceptable, especially because it is inevitably seen as a perversion of the sanctioned order prevailing within the realm of the same. The role reversal among genders is particularly striking in this respect, as in the perversion of the very idea of armed conflict when the weapons are calculated to inflict no harm. Against an order grounded in perversion, there is a moral obligation to rise up, and this is what propels Aucassin. Of course, in so doing, he seeks to impose the moral and ideological universe of the courtly code, thereby confirming that Torelore is a noncourtly, if not an anticourtly entity. From within the courtly code, it is the "unthinkable" other. The text cannot leave this other in place, but, unlike the world of the romances, it cannot reduce it to its self-sameness. In this respect it is interesting to note a curious role reversal between the two protagonists.

All readers of this text have observed that Nicolette is the far more active character of the two protagonists. She takes nearly all initiatives, whereas Aucassin is consistently described as passive, unable to see his way out of the predicaments in which he finds himself. A case in point is the very ending of the story, when Aucassin, once again separated from Nicolette following a Saracen raid, passively sits in Beaucaire as its new ruler not knowing what his next step ought to be. Nicolette, meanwhile, has recovered her rightful identity as a princess and is in active pursuit of the man she loves. The means by which she rejoins him are telling: she learns how to play the *viole*, disguises herself as a jongleur, gets on a boat, and makes her way to Beaucaire, where she sings the story of her love for Aucassin. Aucassin hears this "male" jongleur, finds himself serenaded, and inquires about the provenance of the story, eventually being reunited with Nicolette. This makes explicit what all readers feel: Nicolette is a sign-maker. She is indeed jongleurlike in that she is the performer within this text. By contrast, Aucassin is not even a very good sign-reader: he fails to recognize Nicolette in her disguise, which must be undone for the final reunion to occur.

In the Torelore episode, however, this opposition is curiously reversed, as part of the broader play of reversals. We have seen Aucassin act spontaneously, without any prompting on anyone's part. In the meantime, Nicolette has been uncharacteristically unenterprising and silent, retiring into the queen's chambers, for example, when Aucassin sets out to do battle. Even more interesting in this respect is her only intervention in Torelore: when the local people threaten Aucassin with expulsion, she addresses the king to describe the pleasure she has in being embraced by Aucassin, a pleasure that finds her "grasse et male" (soft and moist) and which she values above that procured by the dances and instruments that are characteristic of the jongleur. In other words, Nicolette prefers the passivity of lovemaking to the agency she enjoys as a jongleurlike figure.

The king is clearly swayed by this argument because he allows the lovers to remain, and remain they do for three years, until Torelore is raided by the Saracens. What happens during these three years? We do not know. The text has nothing to say beyond the fact that Aucassin had "grant aise et grant deduit" (great satisfaction and great pleasure) in being there. This bears thinking about, for, unlike the initial encounter with Torelore, when it was the topsy-turvy version of the world of the courtly code, there is now a *de facto* order that the text does not describe but which we can discern. Aucassin has the king's word that men will no longer lie-in after childbirth, thus the perversion of gender reversal is ended and the presumed "natural" basis of the social order is respected. In return, Aucassin supposedly refrains from the exercise of his warlike instincts. Thus the courtly code does not triumph; in fact, it is stymied on two fronts: Aucassin remains at the court because he surrenders to the pleasures of the flesh rather than to the martial obligations of the code, and Nicolette also surrenders to sensual pleasure rather than to that of a jongleurian acting-out. The courtly code is being contained. From the hegemonic position it occupied in the public sphere, it finds itself relegated to the private, it becomes courtly *love* and nothing but that. And for this new condition, the text has no words. Nor does it have any for the broader situation. It is silent, as it again will fall silent when the two lovers are reunited at the end of the text.

Silent Torelore is what is of interest to us. It is, after all, a society in which rule prevails, a king reigns. This is not an imperious king who seeks to impose his will. Rather, he listens to contending parties, one of which is constituted by the people (*gens*). This is not a heroic ruler or a courtly ruler seeking to impose a set of values so compelling that they require their implementation and extension everywhere. He adjudicates between contending values and, for him, the courtly is but one contender among others. In this representation, the king occupies the structural position that the state and prose respectively occupy in the social and in the textual realms. Within *Aucassin et Nicolette*, such a position is unspeakable; the king has no name, only silence can cover it. Yet others will act and speak, just as the people and Nicolette do here. But the king's mode of intervention is not of the same order as theirs: he decides between their claims. Unlike a hegemonic code such as the courtly, which needs to be proffered, this new order is to be judged on its operations, on how it manages voiced claims.

The skills attendant to the proper use of the code such as the courtly one are not thereby rendered obsolete, for the courtly code continues to operate, although in a much more restricted fashion. But there is a need for new skills that will recognize a broader arena of contending codes. A new signifying practice is coming into being, and it cannot be verbalized in the terms of the older practices. It calls for a new literacy, one appropriate to it, which, like all literacies, will contain instructions on how to handle, henceforth, the verbal, as well as all the relevant nonverbal elements.

Once again, then, we see the unique position of the chantefable. It stages for us the world of topsy-turvy reversals, destined to great fortune in fifteenth- and sixteenth-century writing as part of what Bakhtin has called the carnivalesque. It does not yet function in that carnivalesque way. It is a vision of a possible future rather than of a phantasm.

PART III

Chapter 6
Prose Literacy

Archaeologists have approached the artifact to a great extent through a poetics: how did the artifact come into being, how can it be classed with others, what is its morphology, and how do pieces of artifacts fit together? Alongside this kind of inquiry is a wonderment about how these artifacts were used; what was their role—male or female? sacred or profane? public or private? The anthropological archaeologist asks what other factors were involved in the use of this artifact, what were its pragmatics, what was the practice that it defines and in which it was allowed to have meaning? This kind of archaeologist knows that artifacts alone do not reveal much.

As analysts of prose, we start with what we take to be a verbal artifact. We accept that a signifying practice cannot be defined merely by its artifacts or a poetics of its artifacts, and that any utterance must henceforth be understood as consisting of its verbal elements plus that large and open class of elements most conveniently labeled the "nonverbal," which surround the verbal elements, situate them, and are understood as being real with respect to them.[1] This is the same as having to know the deixis of a verbal string, the pragmatic indexes, the necessary elements of the here and now of its utterance, to understand it. Among these elements, some may be manifest and some assumed. And there is a relation of linkage, conjunction, dependence, coincidence, intersection (the term is not important for the moment), which may be either manifest or implicit. That relation is what one understands when one understands a signifying practice. Prose, then, is not just a verbal artifact—the writing on the page. Such writing is the verbal and

written element of the signifying practice called prose. As such, the writing
is not freestanding, and its functioning is not a totally internalized one. This
distinction is the one made earlier about deixis: one must be able to understand the relevant aspects of its "outside," one must be able to "assign its
position."

There are compelling reasons, at certain times in the development of a
culture, to attempt to bring that position inside, to make it a formal position,
abstracted from any particular individual or class of individuals and inhabitable by anyone.

> Take the example of the mathematical treatise. . . . [I]f in the main
> body of the treatise, one meets a proposition like 'Two quantities equal
> to a third quantity are equal to each other', the subject of the statement
> is the absolutely neutral position, indifferent to time, space, and circum-
> stances, identical in any linguistic system, and in any code of writing
> or symbolization, that any individual may occupy when affirming such
> a proposition.[2]

Foucault's use of the mathematical example is telling because mathematical
discourses themselves elaborate ordering procedures by which one can conjoin units within them, by which the new, the different, or the unknown can
be placed within the already known. One might also wonder to what extent
the position assigned in mathematics is really "absolutely neutral and indifferent": such positions can in fact be laden with ideology, are not neutral;
we are talking here, however, about a know-how of reading, a literacy in a
mathematics dependent on an understanding of mathematics as conveying
truths that are context-free. Also, it is clear that there are eras, or occasions,
when a culture can have such an "absolutely neutral position" available for
assignment, and other eras, or occasions, when it cannot.

Furthermore, there are instances of communication in which discourses
heterogeneous to each other are used without there being any combinatorial
rules apparent. Certain types of writing, in particular what is commonly
known as exposition, attempt to establish a combinatorial order whereby
an effect of neutrality of subject position is produced. They do so by combining and intersecting those discourses by means of conjunctions or conjunctive strategies that appear "natural," so that, for example, in a description
of the diverse economic influences impinging on the behavior of members
of a society, the reader would come away with the impression that these
influences are aligned in an inexorable "logic" of forces. As the text unfolds,
then, the discourses conjoin as if by themselves, leading the reader to interpret this as emanating from a position of neutrality. In this sense, it is apo-
deictic: instead of each needing grounding independently of the others, each
mixes easily with the others, each seems to be held in a state of chemical

suspension produced by all of them. It has a concinnity; "it holds together," we would say. This is how the reader makes sense of it or locates its authority (here, the authority of neutrality, at a time when neutrality would be considered legitimate as authority), an authority established not by seeing a single and consistent discursive strategy at work but by deploying literacy in the larger sense we have been using it, that is, positing the position that would hold these different discourses together as the reader comes to believe they are held together.

The era under examination is one in which there appears a profusion of compilations, generally defined as those writings in which there is no author or to which an author lends nothing of his own. Saint Bonaventura said:

> Quadruplex est modus faciendi librum. Aliquis enim scribit aliena, nihil addendo vel mutando; et este mere dicitur scriptor. Aliquis scribit aliena addendo, sed non de suo; et iste compilator dicitur. Aliquis scribit et aliena et sua, sed aliena tamquam principalia, et sua tamquam annexa ad evidentiam; et este dicitur commentator non auctor. Aliquis scribit et sua et aliena, sed sua tamquam principalia, aliena tamquam annexa ad confirmationem et debet dici auctor.

> There are four ways of making a book. A man might write the work of others, adding and changing nothing, in which case he is simply called a "scribe" (*scriptor*). Another writes the work of others with additions which are not his own; and he is called a "compiler" (*compilator*). Another writes both others' work and his own, but with others' work in principal place, adding his own for purposes of explanation; and he is called a "commentator" (*commentator*) . . . Another writes both his own work and others' but with his own work in principal place adding others' for purposes of confirmation; and such a man should be called an "author" (*auctor*).[3]

The less the compiler adds, the more the compilation unproblematically takes on the authority of its sources. What compilation does add is a new *ordinatio*, a more condensed or convenient form.[4] The *compilator* is one who knows how to arrange given materials so that they are most useful to a reader. The removal of the uttering subject ideally creates an apparently seamless text in which each *auctor* is put in the service of the others.

Last, there are instances (be they epochs among others, or certain occasions within epochs) when "reality" is so construed as to call for a heterogeneity of discourses that purposefully do not permit an easy fitting, one within the other. They are constitutively immiscible, like oil and water. In this case, traditionally, only an outside position of subject will do. *Aucassin et Nicolette* contains that kind of heterogeneity but clearly is not opting for an outside subject, a unique deixis, a master discourse. In its clear limitations, however, the chantefable suggests the need for an alternative.

The question is, how is the unknown coherently brought into the known when heterogeneous discourses must be articulated vis-à-vis each other in ways that are not internally provided by them and in the absence of something that frames that articulation? Writing is a kind of communication in absence (in the absence of the addresser, in which we are given only traces of actions), and it is that quality of writing that prose exploits in particular. The necessity of establishing a stable position is less important for prose than the *process,* the know-how, which the *absence* of an identifiable subject forces on a reader. The strategy is not to establish a neutral *position* as if internally but to use the reading *process* by which such positions are assigned (the literacy we have just briefly developed) to other ends. In emerging prose, when faced with reading a text of heterogeneous discourses, one can assign a position without that position being single, neutral, or absolute. The reader must come to terms with *positionality,* that is, the assignment of different, multiple, and short-term positions. Instead of overcoming the loss of a subject by the establishment of such a single, neutral, and absolute position, readers of prose move from discourse to discourse to gradually establish a sense of relative position. Such is the literacy of prose.[5]

Literacy is not an abstract property of individuals but the relationship between an individual and a signifying practice. In this book we are inquiring into a prose literacy, but it should be made clear that this literacy is only one among many. In relation to each signifying practice, there are several possible literacies, one within the other, and the use of each of them can be totally legitimate, even if it differs from the one that is the hallmark of the embracing signifying practice. In fact, the barest kind of understanding and coherence depends on one's having recourse to certain of these inner literacies. This is a central problem at a time of the emergence of a new signifying practice. It is also a prominent aspect of artistic practice and reception, as artists explore the boundaries of signifying practices and seek to establish or transgress them.[6] Complex readings frequently involve the ability to call upon literacies of various kinds simultaneously or in rapid succession in non-exclusive ways. This is not a new insight or recent discovery: medieval biblical exegesis recognized the necessity of applying a set of different literacies, four "levels," to one text: the literal, the tropological, the allegorical, and the anagogical. This recognition functioned as much to legitimate each in the face of the other as to provide an institutional backing for some and to exclude any others as yet unsanctioned.[7]

A signifying practice contains other signifying practices within it, and each of those must be understood. For example, after Roland speaks to Charlemagne and the other vassals in the *Chanson de Roland,*

Li emperere en tint sun chef enbrunc,
Si duist sa barba, afaitad sun gernun,
Ne ben ne mal ne respunt sun nevuld.
Franceis se taisent, ne mais que Guenelon.
En piez se drecet, si vint devant Carlun,
Mult fierement cumencet sa raisun
E dist al rei: "Ja mar crerez bricun . . .

The emperor lowers his head,
he strokes his beard, arranges his moustache,
does not answer his nephew favorably or unfavorably.
The French say nothing, except Ganelon.
He stands up on his feet and comes before Charles,
very proudly he starts his speech
and says to the king: "Misfortune if you believe a rascal . . .

$$(15.40.214-20)^8$$

To understand this, we must know how a formal speech works as a free-standing signifying practice, what the deixis of formal speech is understood to be. We have to understand Ganelon's speech as given in front of his audience, as well as Ganelon's speech as recited by the jongleur for *his* audience. It must be understood as its own signifying practice, "inside," and from "outside" in the jongleurian performance of which it is a part. We readers today may not have a first-hand experience of the setting for Ganelon's kind of speech; it may have already been presented to us only in literature or movies, that is, among the discourses of succeeding signifying practices. In the case of the *Roland,* discourses can speak of the "coming to speak," of the prideful tone of the speaker, of the lowered head, and of other pensive, nonverbal behavior of the king. Moreover, and more impressively, they can "speak" of the silence. "Franceis se taisent."

To be literate with respect to outside signifying practice is to know how that signifying practice situates and orders its contained discourses and signifying practices. To see literacy from the point of view of the outside signifying practice amounts to putting everything which that practice contains in "quotes," as one might be tempted (say, in some kind of analysis) to frame by quotes each role or enunciative modality of the jongleurian performance.[9]

Like performance, novels contain other signifying practices, such as formal speeches, given by one character, heard by another. At the day of the Comices, the agriculture fair at Yonville, Emma Bovary and Rodolphe go to the second floor of the Town Hall and observe from the window.

Il y eut une agitation sur l'estrade, de longs chuchotements, des pourparlers. Enfin, M. le Conseiller se leva. On savait maintenant qu'il s'appelait Lieuvain, et l'on se répétait son nom l'un à l'autre, dans la foule.

Quand il eut donc collationné quelques feuilles et appliqué dessus son oeil pour y mieux voir, il commença:

"Messieurs,

"Qu'il me soit permis d'abord (avant de vous entretenir de l'objet de cette réunion d'aujourd'hui, et ce sentiment, j'en suis sûr, sera partagé par vous tous), qu'il me soit permis, dis-je de . . ."

There was commotion on the platform, long whisperings, much parleying. At last the Councillor got up. They knew now that his name was Lieuvain, and in the crowd the name was passed from one to the other. After he had collated a few pages and bent over to see better, he began:

"Gentlemen,

"May I be permitted first of all (before addressing you of the object of our meeting today, and this sentiment will, I am sure, be shared by you all), may I be permitted, I say, to . . ."[10]

One must take the words of the speech as meaningful within the signifying practice of formal speech, even though the speech is itself situated not non-verbally, as such a speech would be, but verbally, by other discourses (the murmurings of voices, the revelation of the identity of the speaker, the shuffling of papers) that are not part of the verbal string of such formal speech but are necessary to understand the verbal string as the signifying practice of speech. The speech should be taken "on its own terms," as well as through the perception of Rodolphe and Emma (and in other possible ways). As with Ganelon, many such early signifying practices exist for us only as contained in later ones. Today our knowledge of certain kinds of formal speeches probably does not come from having been present at such speeches but only from having read them as they exist in texts (in quotes), whose deixis is itself a set of discourses.

Once we have these contained signifying practices, with their attendant literacies, we can stop there, continuing to read for particular ones and not attending to others or to the practice that holds them all. Or we can move to the outer signifying practice. Part of the literacy of performance, which gives a represented "speech," is to be able to interweave the literacy of a "speech" with that of the larger signifying practice. That ability to be Ganelon and also one who listens to him and also one who sees those who listen to him, the ability to go in and out of discourses, in and out of quotes, is the jongleur's, and we depend on him. As a member of the audience of performance, if I step out from each of these discourses and discursively created situations (speech, *planctus,* biography, witness), I step into the jongleur because he too can step out, at the end of the speech, and still be materially there, always within his established, although implicit, parameters. Like the deixis of which he is such a basic constituent, he is a condition of meaning.

I also have the rest of the audience with me: I share my experience with them, who are always there.[11] When I became a *reader* of written verse (as opposed to a member of an audience), although still literate with respect to performance, my stepping-out from each of these discourses and discursively created situations enables me to locate myself in a position where I know the jongleur and fellow members of the audience are meant to be. I read it through a jongleur. He is part of the literacy; he need not be actualized out there. My literacy has made him an inner property; the position I assign is his. To step *out* from the "speech" of a character, or to step out from the page, is also to come back *in*, to an unquestionable attribution and grounding. The jongleur would be that which can frame but remain unframed, that which can put quotes around but escape quotes itself. Therein lies his dimension as ground.

As we said earlier, there would be no *one* to put the jongleur into quotes. It is not so much that one cannot do so—it would be easy—but to put him into quotes would necessitate "assigning" a position to the remaining utterance that is out of quotes, and what kind of position would it be? This may strike one as strange: there *is* a discourse for it, one can simply add the *inquit* and say, "The jongleur got up and said" (just as the jongleur can say, "Ganelon proudly starts his speech), and one can assign a position to that which is out of quotes, but at this historical point, there is something unstable about *that* position—that position will not remain an outer, final, grounding one. The reader's position is the only one that remains outside, but that is an unspecified, unsituable, disponible position.

The use of *Acteur* in the *Ressource* shows the fragile ontological status of a subject meant to be given as out of quotes in this sense, which is not meant to be "Vérité or "Justice" or even "molinet," just *there*. *Acteur* is a stand-in and is to be taken as such. The introduction of that entity and his subsequent scuttling[12] shows that his status as a grounding subject is a tentative one, the result of manipulations of the textual economy of prose: finding a subject when necessary for local grounding, when other subjects are exhausted, and dismissing it when another subject can be recalled. As we gradually approach modern prose, *acteur*like discourses will find their deixis in, and be interpreted in terms of, other discourses in the signifying practice. They will be more appropriately taken as the articulator of a particular perspective, the origin of a specific point of view, such as an explicit or implicit narrator. *Acteur* will also, then, be unfinal, susceptible of being put in quotes and in context.

As signifying practice changes, and particularly within the larger signifying practice of prose, all utterances are susceptible of being reassigned, recontextualized. In the absence of the jongleur, prose does this by burdening one discourse with the additional function of having the discursive situation (deixis) of that discourse serve temporarily as the deixis of another. Like a recipe, the ingredients are all knowns, but prose is more than the sum of the ingredients. Prose is the process part of the recipe, working with the ingredients, producing an emulsion that keeps things together and suspended in its particular way.[13] In this sense, prose is not an ingredient, it is not identical to any discourse or signifying practice it contains. It does not participate, does not get its hands dirty, cannot be put into quotes. Among all the discourses it contains, it takes the position that it is just holding them together, it is just what there is. The prose of the world.

Signifying practices construct deictic positions sufficient to bind the discourses they use.[14] To be literate in a practice is to have the capacity to recognize such deixis and positioning as is specific to that practice. In performance, the jongleur stands as the site of, inhabits the contained discourses.[15] These positions are negotiated by the jongleur, using, among other things, relative locations in his own physical space of representation. The process is capped by his physical presence as final deictic instance.

Prose has no grounding in the nonverbal, it does not stand, it does not inhabit. It has a textual space in which it holds together its discourses by referring one discourse to another, by positing deictic relationships between them, each legitimizing and reciprocally legitimatized, attributing and attributed, out of quotes and in. Not capped by an "outside," prose will anchor one discourse in another in the fashion in which discourses were anchored in the nonverbal.[16] This process is not prose-specific: it happens all the time in various kinds of speech, for example, where discourses are folded one within the other. In the excerpt from *Madame Bovary*, even when the speaker begins to talk he uses a discourse that is meant to situate subsequent discourses.[17] For prose, however, the process, far from being an internal step in the face of some larger grounding instance, is *the* way prose establishes its fundamental deixis. The literacy of prose is the ability to read by means of these inner deictic operations.

Each discourse brings with it a subject, a position. It does not yield ideal or abstract knowledge of an object but such knowledge as is available at that location and from that perspective. A signifying practice does not bring with it a subject or position. There is no perspective to a signifying practice as such. A signifying practice brings knowledge as a set of perspectives that it makes coherent, a Weltanschauung. But a new signifying practice redefines what coherence means, provides new ways in which the unknown can be included in the known, new possibilities for cognition, new fields of emergence. They are not always fully exploited, nor are they meant to be. New signifying practices embrace, comprehend earlier signifying practices, not only, as one might expect, to fill up what may have been discovered as areas of emptiness in earlier practices but also to set higher levels of tolerance for other kinds of emptiness. Emerging prose will retain many already existing signifying practices and their constituent and attendant discourses and possibilities, and it will make room for others—for perspectives and positions inhabitable by a reader alone. A reader is literate in prose to the extent that he or she can inhabit such positions. What follows will examine this and other aspects of prose literacy.

If we look at two stages in early nonverse, we can see how in the emergence of prose a reader's position is acknowledged and put to use.

Our text is two versions of the oldest short story in French, La Fille du Conte de Pontieu.[18] One version dates from the early thirteenth century and the other from the first half of the fifteenth century. It is the story of Thibaut, who, after five years of a childless marriage to the daughter of the count of Pontieu, plans to set off to Saint Jacques de Compostelle to make vows and ask that his marriage be graced with a child. His wife insists on joining him. As they traverse a wood, they stray from the appropriate route and wander onto a path set up by robbers to trap unwary travelers. They are surrounded by eight robbers, one of whom immediately attacks Thibaut. Thibaut, albeit unarmed, succeeds in killing three robbers but is made prisoner by the other five, tied up, and thrown into a bush of thorns. The robbers then undress his wife, rape her, and leave both their victims. Thibaut asks his wife to free him, but she, approaching with a sword to cut his bonds, attempts to kill him instead. She succeeds only in cutting his bonds and wounding him. The pilgrimage is then abandoned and they return home. Much of the rest of the story concerns the motives for this attempt: the destruction of the one who witnessed the woman's shame, and her possible plan to kill herself subsequently.[19]

The passage we will study is the pivotal one, from the point where the robbers tie up Thibaut and throw him into the bushes to the immediate aftermath of the rape.

Thirteenth-century version

Et quant il eurent cou fait, il vinrent a la dame, si li tolirent son palefroi et sa rebe dusc'a la chemise. Et elle estoit molt bele, et nepourquant si plouroit elle molt durement. L'un des larons l'esgarda et dist: "Seigneur, j'ai mon frere perdu, si voel avoir ceste dame en restor." Li autres dist: "Ausi ai jo men cousin germain, autant i clain jou comme vous." Et autel dist li tiers, et li quars. Et li quins leur dist: "Segneur, en li retenir n'arons nous mis grant preu, mais menon le en ceste forest et faisons de li nos volentés, puis le remetons a voie le et lasons aler." Ensi le fisent, et le remenerent a le voie.

Et mesire T. le vit et dist li: "Dame, pour Diu, desliés me, car ces ronses me grievent molt."

Thirteenth-century version

And when they had done this, they came to the lady and they took her horse and her clothing down to her shirt. And she was very beautiful in spite of the fact that she was crying very heavily. *One of the thieves looked at her and said:* "Lords, I have lost my brother, I want to have this lady in return." Another said: "And I lost my first cousin, I have as much of a claim to her as you." And as much was said by the third and the fourth of them. And the fifth said: "Lords, we will not get a large prize by holding her; let us take her into these woods and have our will with her and then put her back on the road and let her go." And so they did, and they brought her back upon the road.

And Milord T. saw her and told her: "Milady, by God, untie me for these thorns are hurting me a great deal."

Fifteenth-century version

O comme est marrie sa belle dame quand elle se voit mise a telz fins! Elle ne scet son sens, ains crie la mort, bat sa poictrine, desaffuble son chief, et par trop habondant destresse derompt et detire sez cheveux plus de chent fois, chiet pasmee, et a brief dire, elle ne scet qu'elle face, tant trespasse son angoesse lez termez de tritresse. Et fut en cest estat grand temps sans savoir ou elle estoit, jesant toute estandue sus la terre comme demy morte.

COMMENT CHASCUN DES LARRONS VOULOIT AVOIR LA DICTE DAME
POUR SON PLAISIR ACOMPLIR.

Tandis que ceste desconfortee dame estoit en ce pitoiable pleur, se mut ung grant estrif entre lez larrons, chascun pour sa part la vouloit avoir, disans l'un: "J'ay en ceste bataille perdu mon frere et, pour ce, elle sera mienne," et lez autrez disans aussy qu'il y avoient perdu leur oncle ou cousin, ou qu'ilz avoient droit sur elle, et ja se fussent par grant discord entretués se l'un n'eust trouvé ce moyen. Par l'enhortement d'icellui, ilz la chargerent, sy dolousee qu'elle estoit, et le porterent en la forest, ou chascun l'un apres l'auetre en fist sa voulenté. O que criminel ouvrage, lait et puant a souffrir! Ou estoit Phebus, et que n'environnoit il de sez rais le corps de ceste dame tant que les rapvisseurs ne l'eussent peu regarder? Ou estoit Solus, et que ne le faisoit il emporter dez mains d'yceulz larrons par ung tourbillon de vent? Ou estoit Morpheus, et que ne faisoit il endormir et songier cez felons tirans quand ilz toucherent la bonne dame? Ou estoit Octeanus, et que ne faisoit il par une onde de la mer transgloutir et noyer iceulx maldis larrons, villains et inhumains? Et ou estoit la verge de justice et la vengeance divine, quant ilz veoient commettre et perpetrer si obscurci et vil mesfait, qu'ilz ne se monstroient sur ceulx qui plus detestable office faisoient que bestez insensiblez ou cuers de lyons, non obstant leur crudelité, ne daigneroient faire? Lesquelz larrons aians fait leur plaisir d'elle, ilz la laisserent et le mirent devant la face de son seigneur, puis tirerent en la forest et s'esvanuyrent.

COMMENT MESSIRE THYBAULD, LUY ESTANT LOYÉ,
VEY ET OUY LEZ PITEUSEZ LAMENTACIONS DE SA FEMME,
ET COMMENT ELLE VAUT OCCIRRE SON MARY PAR DESESPERANCE.

Dieux scet que *Thybauld ne veoit pas* ce qu'il serchoit quand sez yeulx regardoient ceulz qui rapvissoient sa dame, quand sez oÿes oÿrent la lassee voix de sa souveraine joye par pammoisons defaillir d'eloquence et de son, quand il entendoit le cuer de sa bien amee redonder et envoyer souspirs et sougloux en grant habondance, quand il consideroit la chasteté de sa dame impetueusement, oultre son gré et a force corrompue. Hellas! quel est le cuer d'homme qui souffriroit veoir tant grant meschief sans habondant effusion de larmez? Quel est la pansee d'homme qui aiant cuer trespercié de mille larmez, corps pertransy d'aspre couroux, face tainte et obscurcie de pleurs, chief anuyé et bany de toute joye, chevelure detorse, voix afoibloyee, robbe deschiree, voire, et demenant la plus amere douleur qu'onquez fist dame imfortunee? *Thibauld la voit* et assés excuse son inconvenient, l'aimant autant qu'il fist onques. *Si luy prit a dire:* "O fenme esplouree, qui laboures en trop desesperé pleur, passe le plus beau que tu peulz ceste pestilence qui malgré toy t'est advenue, car maintenant tu me fais le cuer fondre, tu redoublez ma misere et la chetivité en quoy Fortune m'a renversé. Esdrece toy et haulce la face, contemple et regarde ma char sanglante, et acours vers moy, trés chetif homme, si me desloye et pense de mettre fin a ton triste maintieng, ou tu surcroisteras de tant grand peine mon engressé cuer que mourir le fauldra sans aultre moyen."

Fifteenth-century version

Oh, how distraught is his beautiful lady when she sees herself reduced to such extremity! She no longer has her senses, she cries to death, beats her breast, undoes her headdress, and in overwhelming distress breaks up and pulls her hair over a hundred times; she collapses in faint and, to make it short, does not know what she should do as anguish adds itself to her sadness. And she was in this condition for a long time without knowing where she was, lying on the ground as if half-dead.

HOW EACH ONE OF THE THIEVES WANTED THE AFORESAID LADY
IN ORDER TO HAVE HIS PLEASURE

While this distraught lady was in such pitiful cries, a great strife broke out among the thieves; each one wanted her for himself, one of them saying: "I have lost my brother in this battle, and because of this she will be mine," and the others saying that they also had lost their uncle or their cousin, or that they had rights upon her, and in their great discord they were on the point of killing each other if one of them had not found the following means. At his instigation, they picked her up,

as doleful as she was, and carried her into the forest where one after
the other they had their will with her. Oh, what criminal act, ugly and
stinking to suffer! Where was Phoebus, and why did he not surround
the body of this lady so that her ravishers could not look at her? Where
was Solus, and why did he not have her carried away from the hands
of these thieves by a whirlwind? Where was Morpheus, and why did
he not plunge these tyrannic felons into sleep and dream when they
touched the good lady? Where was Oceanus, and why did he not swal-
low and drown in a wave these accursed, inhuman and vile thieves?
And where were the staff of justice and divine vengeance when they
saw such a dark and vile misdeed committed and perpetrated, that they
did not show themselves unto those who were engaged in a more dastardly act than senseless beasts with lion's hearts would deign undertake in spite of their cruelty? And these thieves, having had their pleasure with her, left her; they put her in front of her lord, then fled into
the forest where they vanished.

HOW MILORD THIBAULT, BEING TIED UP, SAW AND HEARD
THE PITEOUS LAMENTATIONS OF HIS WIFE AND HOW SHE WANTED
TO KILL HER HUSBAND OUT OF DESPAIR.

God knows that *Thibault did not see* what he looked for when his eyes
looked at those who were ravishing his lady, when his ears heard the
tired voice of her supreme joy fail in a faint of eloquence and sound,
when he heard the heart of his beloved fill with, and expell, sighs and
cries in large quantity, as he considered the chastity of his lady cor-
rupted violently, against her will and through force. Alas! What man's
heart could suffer to see such mischief without a large outpouring of
tears? What can a man think having a heart pierced by a thousand tears,
a body surrendered to corrosive anger, a face washed and darkened
with crying, a head bothered and removed from all joy, hair disheveled,
a voice weakened, dress torn, and the most bitter pain ever shown by
an importuned lady? *Thibault sees her* and certainly excuses her lack
of decorum, loving her as much as he ever did. *And so he began to
tell her:* "O tearful woman who labors too much in desperate cries,
get as soon as you can over the pestilence that has befallen you in spite
of yourself, for now as you are breaking my heart, you are doubling
my misery and the destitution into which Fortune has thrown me. Raise
yourself and lift up your face, look and consider my bleeding flesh,
hurry to me, poorest of men, untie me and think of putting an end to
your sad countenance or you will so increase the pain in my heart that
it will have to die without recourse."

Our first look is at the move from the state of the lady to the action of the
robbers:

Thirteenth-century version

L'un des larons l'esgarda et dist: "Seigneur, . . . "

Fifteenth-century version

Tandis que ceste desconfortee dame estoit en ce pitoiable pleur, se mut ung grant estrif entre lez larrons, chascun pour sa part la vouloit avoir, disans l'un: "J'ay . . . "

In the early version, the sight of the lady is given to the robber: he "sees the lady and says." If we ask what he sees when he sees *her,* all we know is what was previously said of "her," a woman "molt bele mais pleurant durement." Such, as said, is also what we as readers have seen. We call this the seeing-saying pivot. It is unproblematic, successful apprehension; indeed, a particular kind of referential transparency, a king of anaphora. The seeing is what has been said; it is a conjoining device.

The seeing-saying pivot is a mainstay of early narrative, which ensures its cognitive efficacy by constructing cognition as a content to be relayed in a chain from one consciousness to another. Much of it works as follows: *X* occurred. *A* saw *X* (cognized it) and then acted. *B* heard about *A's* act and then said ———. When *C* understood what *B* said, she ———. Here is a portion of text by Robert de Clari.

Quant *li pelerin* furent tot asanle en Venice et il *virrent* le rike navie qui faite estoit, les rikes nes, les grans dromons et les uissiers a mener chevax et les galies, si s'en merveillierent molt et de le grant riqueche que il troverent en le vile. *Quant il virrent qu'*il ne se pooient mie tout herbegir en le vile, si se conseillierent entr-aus qu'il s'iroient logier en l'isle Saint Nicholai, qui tote estoit enclose de mer, qui estoit a une liwe de Venice. La s'en alerent li pelerin, et drechierent leur tentes et se logierent au miex qu'il peurent.

Quant *li dux de Venice vit que* tot li pelerin furent venu, si manda tous chiaus de se terre de Venice. Et quant il furent tout venu, si kemanda li dux que le motie d'aus s'atornaissent et aparellaissent a aler en l'estoire avec les pelerins. *Quand li Venicien oirent chou,* si s'esjoirent li un, li autre disent qu'il n'i pooient aler; ne ne se pooient acorder ensanle comment le moitie d'aus y peust aler.

When the pilgrims were all together in Venice and they *saw* the rich fleet that was being assembled, the rich ships, the large galleys, and the attendants leading horses and galley-rowers, they were very much amazed by it all and by the riches that they found in the city. *When they saw* that they could not all find lodging in the city, they counselled among themselves and decided that they would house themselves in St. Nicholas island, which was all surrounded by sea and was but a league away from Venice. And so that is where the pilgrims went, and they put up their tents and housed themselves as best they could.

When the duke of Venice saw that all the pilgrims had come, he called on all in his lands in Venice. And when they had come [we feel like asking here: who noticed?], the duke asked that half of them ready and equip themselves to join the pilgrims in the estuary. *When the Venicians heard this,* some were overjoyed and others said they could not go; they could not agree together how half of them could go there.

These chains, in their coordination, tend to make states of consciousness as unambiguous as overt action. Such coordination accounts for a modern reader's impression of them as "flat."[20] What was seen, or what was said to have been seen, is handed over, relayed to characters, with no loss, no friction, but also with no gain: we know who knows and we know exactly what they know, insofar as it is what was previously said and shared by characters and reader. In the early version, there is at this point no construal of the lady other than that subsequently adopted by the characters.

The pivot and other such conjunctive strategies are a way of negotiating the boundary between the said and the not-yet-said, the old and the new, the known and the as-yet-unknown. We know we are all cognitively conservative, and the tendency is to introduce the unknown in small doses and always by reference to the known, thereby making it known in a way that gives it the same standing, the same integrity as the already known: admitting it to membership in a homogeneous kind of knowledge. Devoid of any scars it might carry from any accidents of its origin, it can be handled by all, interchangeable currency.[21] In Isuch la fashion, the new is always whole, not fragmentary or incomplete, oblique or merely suggestive.

The later version "says" the lady, refers to her state, but it does not state that the robber apprehends her in that way. So the lady is not explicitly apprehended by any represented consciousness. The lady will have to be apprehended in the only consciousness that is constantly available: that of the readerly instance.[22]

The question is one of significance: how are we to understand what is going on? If there are conditions that enhance such understanding, the later version will state them irrespective of characters. Rather than orienting these conditions one-to-the-other, the later version orients them to the reader alone, who then has the option of "seeing" things differently from the characters. The "said" of the lady is not to be noted and conveyed but to be independently retained. The durative "tandis que" keeps the state of the lady separate from the robber's perception while at the same time linking them. The reader has no problem here because the reader is not limited by somatic and perceptual constraints that may bear upon characters. Now, in fact, given any text, a real reader can move from character to character[23] and never be limited by the constraints bearing upon characters. The possibility of readings beyond character, or subject, or place, readings that can "see" things differently, is inherent in all reading, but it is not necessary to, and may even be subversive of, the literacy of certain signifying practices. A reading expressly *attentive* to this incredible possibility of readings is the most subversive kind because it resists any ideologizing or reading in the service of God, humanism, the status quo, and so on. It is the fifteenth-century text that draws on that possibility and will ultimately depend on it as the mechanism to bind discourses that have less and less internal capability to smoothly conjoin with each other.

Readings in the High Middle Ages were not intended to be attentive to new possibilities. Monastic reading, as one example, was a process of reproducing the utterance in the reader, drawing the reader's body and soul into the repetition of the act of utterance. Done with the lips and ears as well as with the eyes, and engaging the whole body, reading was considered such a physical activity that when Peter the Venerable, suffering from catarrh, was no longer able to speak in public, he could no longer perform his *lectio.* Perspectival options were hardly the question: the monastic *lectio* was akin to a *ruminatio* or *meditatio,* which

> implies thinking of a thing with the intent to do it; in other words, to prepare oneself for it, to prefigure it in the mind, to desire it, in a way, to do it in advance, briefly, to practice it. To practice a thing by thinking of it, is to fix it in the memory, to learn it. All these shades of meaning [of *meditatio*] are encountered in the language of the Christians: but they generally use the word in referring to a text.
>
> For the ancients, to meditate is to read a text and to learn it "by heart" in the fullest sense of this expression, that is, with one's whole being: with the body, since the mouth pronounced it, with the memory which fixes it, with the intelligence which understands its meaning and with the will which desires to put in [*sic*] into practice.[24]

Scholastic reading, by contrast, was more tentative because it was more ratiocinative.

The reader has a quite different role in the later version of our story. The early text conflates "the lady" into "the robber('s cognition)"; it conjoins on the level of represented and representable cognition. The later text will leave them disjoined. The space in between may be unconnected, unembraced by the robber, merely nothing; but that space is inhabitable and embraceable by a reader, and in this way something is made out of nothing, something more than has been or can be said, something new but drawn from the "already." This is surely why the reader believes in the creative power of the writer. The reader can see the lady as the robber does not see her and can see the robber as not seeing the lady: these are perspectival possibilities that a reader is given, not that a jongleur or other subject assumes or pursues. A place has been made for the reader to circulate in between the state and knowledge of these two characters, a space uninhabited by either.

The thirteenth century uses a system of relays (or, more precisely, capacitors, which ensure uniformity of signal, i.e., parataxis[25]); it depends on positive cognition, of character and of final utterer, for its conjunction, because the seeing-saying pivot brings to the reader only that knowledge relayed, *and related,* by see-ers. Prose, as it emerges, begins to abandon that system; written texts refuse to give readers only one thing to read.

From a strictly syntactic perspective, "tandis que" functions as a *conjunction,* but its syntactic function does not tell the whole story. "Almost by definition, conjunctions cannot be fully dealt with within syntax, since they are not really part of the structure of syntactic units. They have rather a sequencing function of relating syntactic units and fitting them into a textual or discourse context."[26] The "tandis que," as it occurs in the evolution of nonverse from the thirteenth century- to the fifteenth-century version, functions as a *disjunction:* it disjoins what was formerly taken as conjoined conjunction.[27] Conjunction and disjunction work formally together: they are both seams. In a text, no disjunction ever functions as a final disjunction without also functioning as a conjunction. Similarly, conjunctions must have disjunctive potential. One way a signifying practice manages how one moves among its varied systems of representation is by neutralizing these potentials at some points and activating them at others. Disjunctions can be found everywhere. In fact, performance contains many disjunctions: the jongleur continually changes representative and discursive attitudes and modes. But his presence, and that of the characters he gives us, confirms a cognition of the seeable and audible and its conjunction with the sayable. What is more, such is his stock-in-trade: he is a purveyor of the visible and audible. Actually, the fact that what is said is seen and what is seen is said, the copula of seeing and saying, is emblematic of one conception of cognition itself. It is as if one way of representing knowing is by breaking it down into the halves of seeing and saying. And the site of this bond, the seat of this pivot (it pivots as it unfolds) is inhabited by a consciousness, be it character or jongleur. Where knowing is available, there is someone there to know it, to see it, and to say it.

Prose will emerge as perspectives and discourses need not be linked, conjoined, or unified through persons, consciousnesses, or knowers. There are perspectives that can be established, there is a knowledge that can be drawn, through the disjunction between perspectives, between discourses . . . if the reader is equipped with the proper literacy. Such a literacy is not meant to bring with it a particular reader's perspective or position. Rather, the reader is to unmoor himself or herself from single or singular perspectives and travel the roads of positionality. In moving from the thirteenth to the fifteenth century, the sight (or knowledge) of the state of the lady is, by means of the "tandis que," unmoored, disjoined from the sight of those who were around to see her. She can thereby be seen by the reader, if the reader understands that he or she is the conjunction that is complementary to the disjunction. That which may be uncertain or incomplete has cognitive value to those who have learned in this signifying practice how to vary their positionality.

In this way, the unknown is brought within the purview of the known, while still retaining its quality of being unknown. Henceforth, the distinction between known and unknown is not a final opposition between inside and outside but a division internal to the known. It is an unknown that is not as threatening, not an absolute, but is tolerated; a place where one can circulate around the border between known and unknown, glance over, venture across that border, have the opportunity to break through it for a moment and then withdraw, and thereby have the possibility of pushing it outward from time to time. This situation is fundamentally different from that in which a *sortie* outside the known is a move into the wilderness, at the total mercy of the unknown. With the emergence of prose, virgin territory becomes that which can be explored. The unseen can be seen if the reader is willing to venture onto uninhabited ground, ground that prose shows to be habitable but only by a reader. This is how a reader reads prose as prose.

Not all perceptions or perspectives need discourses fitted to them; they do not all need to be said. One can find new perspectives between existing ones, simply by refusing to conjoin existing ones in their own terms. For such cognitive value to be realized, then, there must be inconcinnity, disjunctions, boundaries, margins, immiscible discourses. (A single discourse or a set of homogeneous discourses reconstruct only the opposition of outside and inside.) Obviously there must also be something that can contain them all.

In a represented universe of seeing and saying, everything seeable can be said, shared, visually and verbally, by all: if not by all the characters, then by the jongleur and audience. In such a universe, the more a character may be blind or speechless, the more the jongleur will see and say. All can be put in quotes. In such a case, however, quotes are unselective, not marking breaks in the chain of cognition, not important deictically, not to be attended to as explicit framing devices. Characters in quotes say and see what non-character utterances, out of quotes, say and see: we can read the seen for the said, and vice versa. In prose, by contrast, what is in and what is out of quotes is important, not because of which discourse happens at one point to be in or out but because of the disjunction, because what is sayable or seeable from one position or perspective is not necessarily so from another.

We can now see that even with respect to traditional signifying practices whose literacies have recourse to outside positions, there can arise a significant confusion in making a final determination of what is outside and what is inside. The sibyl is authorized by the divine voice, which is an outside to her inside, but is not the sibyl, once authorized, an authorizer herself, an outside to the voice that issues forth from within her? Is the jongleur really just an outside constant presence when so much of what he does involves a manipulation of his own identity, in and out of presence, and a great deal of inconstancy and self-effacement? The variability of position (what we have referred to as positionality) exists in signifying practices before prose, and it is more precisely a property not of certain signifying practices as opposed to others but of deixis as such: in speech, the speaker's outside situation determines, bespeaks, implies, and conditions his or her words, but these words can determine, bespeak, imply, and condition his or her outside situation and even make it explicit.[28] (Indeed, by specifying the relevant aspects of the speaker's outside situation, his or her utterance can enact a kind of decoupage that can serve as an analysis of what deictic conditions are.) By virtue of deictic expressions, language can refer and even partially stand in the place of that which is not it and meant to be outside it. Operating with deixis gives one possibilities of substitution, and signifying practices vary to the extent that they allow certain deictic *expressions* to function subsequently as substitute *conditions*. Earlier signifying practices depend for their comprehension on an ultimate stabilization of positionality, a finally invariant deixis. That is how they are to be read. Prose is different in that it can live with the instability of the properties of deixis, it can allow substitution to go unchecked. Prose, the great container, will not fail under such conditions (as other signifying practices might) because it can locate a semblance of stability in the reader, but only a reader literate in prose, a literacy that calls for the reader to vary his or her own positionality, seeing himself or herself as not finally inside or outside but able to be drawn in among established, suggested, and discoverable perspectives.

Once a reader is armed with that kind of literacy, conjoinings can occur that go further, beyond questions of what discourses of "consciousnesses" provide for. All the resources of language can be mobilized to effect these sorts of conjoinings, including the most basic ones, having to do with recurrencies, whether straightforward or contrastive, at the level of the signifier (what we have come to know as "the play of the signifier"). In other words, there is a kind of cognition that truly is only in the reader's sphere, at least in the first instance. For the reader can pick up and collect signifiers, group or regroup them independently of their discursive origins, and turn them into *signs* of something. Detectable *across* the discourses, these signs articulate what is called a "theme." Here is another kind of prose literacy, one that is headed for a considerable future.

If we look at the next piece of text, up to the point where Thibaut asks to be untied, we see that the thirteenth-century seeing-saying pivot, now around Thibaut rather than the robber, is again broken in the fifteenth century. In both versions, we know that the lady is available for view and therefore for saying by Thibaut. In the thirteenth century, he is where a perception and knowledge of her is located in the text. "Ensi le fisent, et le remenerent a le voie. . . . *Et mesire T. le vit et dist li: '. . .' .*" In the fifteenth century, that does not immediately occur. First, his seeing and saying is deferred by a break in the sequence of action and reaction before the lady is returned to the road: an oratorical discourse, "O que criminel ouvrage," is introduced, which does not look at the rape per se but averts its gaze and asks where the gods were when all this happened.

The lady is put back in front of Thibaut, for him then to presumably see and say, but here we are told how problematic his seeing is, and consequently any saying of his is deferred by comments about his seeing, his other senses, and his state of mind. First, there is God who *sees* all and knows all but who never *says* anything (except under extraordinary circumstances), and then there is Thibaut, who is described as *not* seeing . . . what he was looking for: his perception comes into conflict with his desire. (Note the similarity with the fatal wound in *Bérinus:* rhymed, Aigres sees the situation; unrhymed, Aigres does not see the situation.) With the recounting of his perception, however, we are told what his eyes saw, what his ears heard, and so on. We see him as getting information in fragmentary ways, from his incomplete view and from each of his senses in its single limitation.[29] Thibaut, in this instance, does not just see; what is there is not simply seen. The opacity around the lady and reactors to her is such that a readerly instance is invited, in the formal rhetorics of oratory speech, to speculate on what a witness must be thinking.

With all this disjunction of seeing and saying, there is a good deal of indirect recounting of the state of the lady and of the rape. The oratorical discourse deploys five rhetorical questions paralleling the five rapes, and its invocations ("hands," "touching," "beasts") lend a concreteness to the act itself. Also, by describing what Thibaut's senses take in and by speculating about what he must be thinking, a picture begins to be drawn of the event about which so little has been "said" but which the reader, as well as Thibaut, is putting together.

The focus continues to shift from the lady to Thibaut, with rhetorical questions that indirectly, and even tortuously tell us of the state of the lady, as in the ungrammatical sentence[30] in which the "qui" begins by referring to the subject, Thibaut, attempting to conceive of the object, the lady, but in which that which is syntactically linked to "qui" (heart, body, face, head, hair, voice, dress) begin to apply more to the lady than to Thibaut.[31] Certainly the lady is not the only one violated by the robbers. Thibaut will finally see and say what he sees, although what he proffers with his saying is more the sight of himself than of her.

There is a break in the lady's behavior between before the abduction—faithful companion to her husband, insisting upon accompanying him on the pilgrimage—and after, when she attempts to kill him. Questions of motivation immediately arise; and their acuity is greater because her state has barely been reported as the result of any direct sight. The reader must intervene and elaborate some hypothesis of her state with respect to her subsequent action. Clearly there is a cognitive disarray at this point: what is happening?

Had this work been in performance, which the early text seems akin to,[32] the cognitive disarray would have been shared by the rest of the audience and made legitimate. There is also the nonverbal reaction of the jongleur to his own depiction, a reaction very probably meant to mirror the reaction felt by all. In performance, the state of the lady would not be meant to be experienced individually.[33] The later text, instead of a seeing and saying, provides other discourses that first defer such a seeing and saying and then put in doubt the possibility of having it. The fifteenth century text senses a gap and perpetuates it even while it may be trying to fill it with diverse discourses and perspectival stances: a position that averts its gaze and looks to the heavens ("Où est Phoebus?"), a See-er who is silent, and speculation about what an incapacitated witness-husband must see and think, appealing, through rhetorical questions, as much to the reader's experience as to Thibaut's. The addressee of the later text has been recognized as a lone reader, who is drawn in, involved, and experiences the tension of functioning as the conjurer of a scene that is never said.

In the different descriptions of the lady prior to the rape, there is preparation for the cognitive work that the reader must do to go further than the "said":

Thirteenth-century version

Et quant il eurent cou fait, il vinrent a la dame, si li tolirent son palefroi et sa rebe dusc's la chemise. Et elle estoit molt bele, et nepourquant si plouroit elle molt durement.

Fifteenth-century version

O comme est marrie sa belle dame quand *elle se voit* mise a telz fins! *Elle ne scet son sens,* ains crie la mort, bat sa poictrine, desaffuble son chief, et par trop habondant destresse derompt et detire sez cheveux plus de chent fois, chiet pasmee, et a brief dire, *elle ne scet qu'elle face,* tant trestasse son angoesse lez termez de tritresse. Et fut en cest

estat grand temps *sans savoir ou elle estoit,* jesant toute estandue sus
la terre comme demy morte. (Our emphasis)

The thirteenth century does not describe her distress but simply states that she
is crying very heavily. The fifteenth century deploys a discourse of extreme
mental anguish, and thus her being "beside herself" can be presented as such.

How is the lady to be comprehended? She is no longer her husband's.
She is not given as in the robber's perceptual sphere. She is radically dis-
possessed. How can this be said? There is a discourse—possession by
grief—and that is what the text will use. Now, such a discourse is well attested
in the tradition of performance and provides a great gestural resource as
well.[34] Here, however, as well as being a discourse of possession—she is
possessed by grief—it is also an *attempt* to possess (by a "said" from some-
where) that which is beginning to escape, and an attempt to prepare us for
the fact that anything can happen. It is to be read in a larger strategy that
unseats a final knowing: the robbers do not know her (they will not contemplate her), Thibaut cannot know her (his senses will be too fragmented and
stressed), even she does not know herself. She sees herself, we are told, but
we are also told she does not know her senses, her actions, her *place*. And
that is all the reader is given to know. That, however, is the appropriate kind
of knowledge here. The fifteenth-century version shows cognition at its margins, where it can go no further. Cognition will continue, but elsewhere, with
a reader who goes beyond reading the seen for the said and the said for the
seen.

We can now turn back and ask ourselves about the robber's sight. If in
the later version the robber *had* just "seen" her, would he have just seen
"her" as she is presented here or as she is given in the earlier version? That
is, in seeing her would he have seen how little she sees? Perhaps there is a
good reason that the robber does not look at her in the fifteenth-century version. As that version describes her, there is perhaps too much for him to see.
On the other hand, there may not be enough. Vérité sees the infant seeing
the mother's breast, but what do you see when you see someone who does
not see? (You see Aigres, in the derhymed version, not seeing the fatal wound.)
In *La Fille du Comte de Pontieu,* the lady's inability to know what she sees
extends to other actual and potential cognizers, within and without the text,
and leaves cognition to be both more and less than seeable. Indeed, this
story is about a woman's act, *both blind and blinding*. At least that is how
a modern reader would tend to read it. The extent to which the thirteenth-
century version comes to grips with that blindness, draws its readers toward
it, is uncertain. But it seems clear that the fifteenth-century version, by penetrating into and then withdrawing from the unseen (even if by means of discourses whose provenance is performance), can do justice to that very blind-

ness. The fifteenth century does read the thirteenth-century story as an act of the unknown.[35]

The new reading strategy calls for a somewhat nuanced conception of the "indirection" taken by the description of the rape in the later version. Indirection is more than a grammatical operator, systematically adjustable into a kind of direction.[36] In this signifying practice, it is of interest as underlining a cognitive perspectivalism and fragmentariness. It is indirection as, at least in part, a certain stigma on direction, an *oratio obliqua* wherein are recognized the limitations incumbent upon perspectives and discourses. Prose finds cognitive value, even possibilities of transcendence, by operating at these margins rather than by creating a master subject or master discourse that stands in a *position* of transcendence, and for this reason the reader cannot stand in a position of transcendence either but must travel along the fragmentary discursive perspectives both furnished and implied in the text.

Much more can be said about these two versions of *La Fille du Comte de Pontieu* in terms of (1) the figures and the discourses that fall between the seeing and saying in the later version (they are rhetorical strategies, neither verse- nor prose-specific), (2) the rubrics that subdivide the later version (the later version drawing the margins of what is now a textual space, according to its reading of the action), and (3) the shift away from the lady as focus of attention and toward Thibaut (at that time, a woman's rape was a grave insult to the male members of her family). We bring this story to the attention of our readers because it shows the kinds of concerns that are raised when performance, as the signifying practice of record, is more and more definitively put aside. Note that even after all the breaks and disjunctions in the later version, Thibaut finally "sees her and says." Here is a step back, a recouping and regrouping. Cognitive links have tightened again.

But before Thibaut has seen, there is a space for a looking without seeing, a suspension of knowing, made possible, at this time and place and for these purposes, only by the absence of the jongleur, who in his own communicational framework is understood to be saying what he has seen or heard; and the audience is to see what he is saying, which he also has the ability and responsibility to make visible. The jongleur is always there before. One of the consequences of the signifying practice of performance is that the jongleur cannot present anything to the audience that the audience is the very first to see.

In this pair of texts, the fifteenth-century version is much longer. We know that derhymings are in general longer, but not consistently so, and this is surprising because one of their most popular, professed grounds of justification at the time was to reduce the "wordiness," the excess of a verse "moult longue." Maybe epics were derhymed because verse was considered to "say" and display too much. In the sense we have suggested, prose, although sometimes using more words, can be seen as "saying" less, showing less, but not losing any cognitive ground to verse: on the contrary, it guides us to infer more. It is full of holes, but they are the kind of holes that carry meaning-making opportunities. This is what prose has to offer and why it is successful.

Although there are no words, expressions, discourses in the later text that cannot be used in performance and its transcription, the absence of the jongleur as deictic has moved that version from a seeing and saying to that which is only said: it will all be discourse, as far as the reader is concerned, and can then be read for such things as "theme." More precisely, the reader's powers of sight will extend to the unsaid, to simply the written. Note how Louis Aragon describes how as a child he refused to learn how to write:

> Enfin on y renonça, ma mère disait que c'était affreux, un enfant qui ne saurait jamais écrire. Moi, je m'en passais. Je dictais ce qui me traversait la tête à ces deux tantes que j'avais, et je constatais qu'après, leurs gribouilles restituaient pour d'autres yeux ce que j'avais dit, très exactement. Si bien que la parole dite me paraissait fort suffisante.
>
> Quand on eut renoncé à me voir écrire, cela me donna de longues heures pour moi tout seul, dans le mépris où l'on m'abandonnait avec quelque tristesse. J'en profitai pour réfléchir, et dire à voix haute ce que je pensais, quand personne n'était à portée de m'entendre. Il m'en souvient, je m'en émerveillais, remarquant l'identité de ce que j'avais voulu dire et de ce que je disais, et cela me rendait encore plus dédaigneux d'écrire. Tout de même, à me parler ainsi, je pris l'habitude de me poser des questions et d'y donner des réponses. Parfois bizarres, et je pris goût à leur bizarrerie. Parce que, je vous le demande, pourquoi se répondre ce qu'on savait avant de le dire? C'est ainsi que me vint l'idée d'*inventer* mes réponses, de toute pièce. Je pouvais bien avoir six ans, ou pas encore.
>
> Ainsi que me vint aussi à l'esprit un certain mépris de mes tantes pour leur fidélité à reproduire ce que je leur disais, au lieu d'écrire d'autre chose, comme je l'aurais sûrement fait à leur place, si j'avais su écrire. Par exemple, si je leur dictais que ce matin-là on avait perdu le petit châle blanc de ma grand'mère, ces sotte n'auraient jamais imaginé d'écrire *le petit châle rouge* ou *le grand châle vert* . . . non, elles ne voyaient pas plus loin que le bout de ma langue. Un beau jour, l'idée me vint que, si je savais écrire, je pourrais dire autre chose que ce que je pensais, et je me mis à essayer de le faire des syllabes, des mots. Si bien que je fis en très peu de temps de grands progrès, parce qu'on ne me tenait plus la main, que j'employais mon crayon à ce qui me passait par la cervelle, intercalant des bonshommes entres les lettres, ou des poissons, des cerfs-volants tenus au bout des mots par un grand fil zigzagant. Evidemment si de tels exercises étaient tombés sous les yeux de quelqu'un, de mes tantes, ça leur aurait fait hausser les épaules,

on n'aurait pas *su me lire,* et j'en éprouvais, non pas du dépit, mais, au contraire, de la fierté. Peu à peu, je me mis à me persuader que l'écriture n'avait pas du tout été inventée pour ce que les grandes personnes prétendaient, à quoi parler suffit, mais pour fixer, bien plutôt que des idées pour les autres, des choses pour soi. Des secrets. Le jour où cela me vint à l'esprit, j'en fus si frappé que je me mis à tenter d'écrire, en cachette, sur n'importe quoi, le papier, les murs, avec une passion violente. On m'en tira les oreilles, on m'en flanqua des gifles, rien n'y fit. Et quand on me demandait: "Mais enfin, qu'est-ce que ces gribouillages, dont tu salis tout, les nappes, les cabinets qu'on vient de repeindre, l'intérieur des placards, enfin c'est infernal!" Moi, je continuais de plus belle. *Je jouais aux secrets,* voilà ce que personne ne pouvait savoir. Et c'était un jeu qui m'enflammait, d'abord parce qu'il me forçait à avoir des secrets. Puis à leur donner forme, comme si j'avais un correspondant, un ami, qui seul pouvait les comprendre, mes griffouillis. Qui, seul, aurait pu me répondre, par ce même moyen. Enfin, c'est pour cet ami-là que je me pris à faire des progrès dans l'art de tracer des signes, que je montrais aux miroirs, où un autre moi-même faisait semblant de les lire. Un beau jour, mon oncle, que je détestais à cause de ses moustaches, me chipa un papier que j'avais noirci et s'écria: "Mais cet enfant écrit! Quand a-t-il appris à le faire?" . . . J'écris comme cela des romans.[37]

They finally gave up, my mother saying that it was scandalous, a child who would never know how to read. As for me, I did without. I would dictate what would go through my head to those two aunts of mine and I confirmed that afterwards, their scribblings restored for other eyes what I had said, very precisely. So well that the spoken word seemed to be quite sufficient.

When they gave up on seeing me write, that gave me long hours to myself, in the disdain where I was abandoned with some sadness. I took advantage of the time to do some thinking, and to say out loud what I was thinking, at times when no one was within earshot. I remember, I marveled at this, noticing the identity of what I had wanted to say [what I had meant] and what I would say, and that made me even more disdainful of writing. All the same, talking to myself this way, I got into the habit of asking questions and of giving answers. Sometimes strange ones, and I got a kick out of their strangeness. Because, I ask you, why answer what one knows before saying it? That is how the idea came to me of *inventing* my answers, out of whole cloth. I was probably around six years old, or a little younger.

There came to mind a certain disdain of my aunts for the faithfulness with which they reproduced what I would say to them, instead of writing something else, which I surely would have done had I been them, and had I known how to write. For example, if I would dictate to them that on that particular morning the little white shawl of my grandmother had been misplaced, these silly old ladies would never have imagined writing *the little red shawl* or *the big green shawl* . . . no, they could not see any farther than the tip of my tongue. One day, the idea came to me that if I knew how to write I could say something other than what I thought, and I set out to try to do that with syllables, with words. To the point that I made big progress in a small amount of time, because no one was holding my hand, because I used my pencil for what went through my brain, sticking in little men between the letters, or fish, kites held to the end of words by a long zigzagging string. Obviously if such exercises were to fall under the gaze of someone, of my aunts, that would have made them shrug their shoulders, they would not have *known how to read me*, and I felt, not resentment, but on the contrary, pride. Little by little, I began to be persuaded that writing had not been invented at all for what adults said it was, for which speaking sufficed, but in order to fix, rather than ideas for others, things for oneself. Secrets. The day when that occurred to me, I was so struck by it that I began to try to write, secretly, on anything, paper, walls, with a violent passion. They pulled me by the ear, they slapped me, nothing worked. And when I was asked: "What are these scribblings, with which you dirty everything, tablecloths, freshly painted rooms, the insides of closets, it's devilish!" Me, I kept on going. *I played secrets,* that is what no one could know. And it was a game that excited me, first because it forced me to have secrets. Then to give them form, as if I had a correspondent, a friend, who alone could understand them, these scribblings. Who alone could have answered me, by the same method. Finally it is for that friend that I began to make progress in the art of tracing signs, which I held in front of the mirror, where another myself pretended to read them. One day, my uncle, whom I detested because of his moustache, grabbed away from me a paper that I had blackened and cried: "But this child writes! When did he learn it?" . . . That is how I write novels.

To disjoin the known from the knower is to limit the knower, put the knower in a kind of quotes, that is, always a product of prose's deictic ground, not a source thereof. What is said in prose, whether attributed speech (*parole*) or not, is to be taken as grounded locally, as if in quotes, not finally. Quotes are among the more obvious marks of discursive shift. They are conjunctive or disjunctive depending on the signifying practice. So the question can be, for each signifying practice, where are the quotes? We know just from the way literary criticism is written that an exposition of a particular interpretation of a work involves drawing quotes around some things and not others (as we did with the *Ressource*). For example, thematic studies put different parts of a text in quotes and then reassemble them into a new whole. Cerquiglini shows that certain grammatical particles, like *mar* in Old French,

function to signal shifts of *parole,* quotation marks. Quotation marks delineate other textual divisions: (1) the editor of the *Pontieu,* Brunel, sees paragraphing as based on quotes,[38] (2) in dialogue paragraphing occurs at the
quotes, when the utterer changes (probably with the introduction of printing),
and (3) plays are similarly divided into scenes by change of speaker, soma,
presence.

Talk of quotation marks as marking the enclosing of speech vis-à-vis non-
speech obliges us to discuss, if only in brief, the subject of punctuation as
it relates to other developments. Most ancient manuscripts seem to have been
written in *scriptura continua,* without punctuation, even without spaces between sentences and between words. Latin added points between words,
and gradually different kinds of points and other diacritical marks were introduced. The usual debate with respect to the development of punctuation is
whether it has to do with elocution, grammar, or sense. Although these are
all closely related, early punctuation seems to serve mainly to control breathing and mark pauses when reading aloud: it is a system of graded pauses.[39]
The grades of pauses (of a colon, of a period) then become associated with
different kinds of meaning, distinguishing *sententiae* and *sensus,* and move
away from a primarily elocutorial role to one as a reader's aid in interpretation, the way a reader, reading aloud or otherwise, could bring out the sense
for himself or herself.[40] Our discussions about rubrics in chapters 4 and 5
suggest another dimension of punctuation: layout. The earliest codices used
layout to indicate the major divisions of a text, be it verse or prose. Today
we recognize as one implicit distinction between verse and prose that, paragraphs and chapters aside (a significant exception), layout is not used to articulate divisions of prose as it is for verse.[41]

Modern punctuation is primarily influenced by the new practices of French
and Italian printers of the fifteenth and sixteenth centuries, and we mentioned
in chapter 2 that it was through them that quotation marks were introduced.
The printer Wechsel, publishing Ramus's *Dialectique* (1555), distinguished
citations of verse (translated from Latin) from the rest of the vernacular text
through typographical means, by printing the verse in italics, and distinguished Ciceronian prose citations by putting an inverted comma in the
margin at the lines where the citation begins and ends and two inverted
commas next to each line in between.[42] We must recognize the rise of quotation marks as acknowledging operations of reading that are fundamentally
different from monoplanar pauses: they are a recognition that certain discourses differ in status from the rest of the text and yet exist within the text.
In this sense they are the functional equivalent of parentheses, which also
did not make their appearance until the fifteenth century.

If changes in signifying practices involve changing relations in the status
of discourses with respect to one another, then quotes, parentheses, punctua-

tion, and all kinds of markers and articulations can be activated to put forward such distinctions. In a moment of broad speculation, we could pose the question: what would happen to a text if all the quotation marks were reversed? If the said became the unsaid, and vice versa? Certain forms of very sophisticated prose, for example, modern novels, might survive such a transformation very successfully. Faulkner in particular comes to mind, as he will at one point have dialogue in italics while the surrounding *inquit* and deictic expressions are in roman type, and then, a few pages later, he will reverse this arrangement. It is worthy of note here that the French guillemets have been reversed by the Germans, who enclose dialogue thusly: >>———<<. No doubt someone had the impression that speech in a text is the one kind of discourse that does *not* have to be "set off." It is everything else that should occupy a special place.

A modern prose reader understands that what is in and what is out can be treated as variables, that the writer can place his or her quotes in one way, with a kind of posited ground that is "out of quotes," but that the utterances can be read differently. For example, if what is taken as a "narrative voice" seems to have a particularity to it, an unreliableness or instability, without the transcendence that one likes to attribute to or feels one needs of a "narrator," the reader might try reading that in quotes, as if it is a character talking. The converse for a character, supposedly one among any in a novel, upon whom a reader happens to increasingly depend to hold things together: the reader might try reading that character without quotes. Once writing introduces quotes, then, in a pseudomorphic move, readers can even "speak" in them.[43] In *A la recherche du temps perdu*, when Marcel tells Swann that his parents do not allow him to go to the theater, Swann's reply is as follows:

> C'est malheureux. Vous devriez leur demander. La Berma dans *Phèdre*, dans *le Cid*, ce n'est qu'une actrice si vous voulez, mais vous savez, je ne crois pas beaucoup à la <<*hiérarchie!*>> des arts; (et je remarquai, comme cela m'avait souvent frappé dans ses conversations avec les soeurs de ma grand'mère, que quand il parlait de choses sérieuses, quand il employait une expression qui semblait impliquer une opinion sur un sujet important, il avait soin de l'isoler dans une intonation spéciale, machinale et ironique, comme s'il l'avait mise entre guillemets, semblant ne pas vouloir la prendre à son compte, et dire: <<la *hiérarchie*, vous savez, comme disent les gens ridicules>>. Mais alors, si c'était un ridicule, pourquoi disait-il la hiérarchie?).[44]

> That's a pity. You should insist. Berma in *Phèdre*, in the *Cid;* she's only an actress, if you like, but you know I don't believe very much in the *"hierarchy"* of the arts. (As he spoke I noticed, what had often struck me before in his conversations with my grandmother's sisters, that when-

ever he spoke of serious matters, whenever he used an expression which seemed to imply a definite opinion upon some important subject, he would take care to isolate, to sterilise it by using a special intonation, mechanical and ironic, as though he had put the phrase or word between inverted commas, and was anxious to disclaim any personal responsibility for it; as who should say "the 'hierarchy', don't you know, as silly people call it." But then, if it was so absurd, why did he use the word?)[45]

Marcel is directing us to the kind of literacy he needs (and we need, to stick with him or to "read" Swann ourselves) to understand the way Swann speaks.[46] Prose writers, as they situate discourses deictically with respect to one another, indicate various literacies through which readings can be sought. As a final example of speech within the signifying practice of prose but interpreted in terms of a particular literacy, we read in *Absalom Absalom!* of Sutpin's proposal of marriage to Rosa Caulfield, the younger sister of his deceased wife. The words are those of Rosa telling the story to Quentin.

"And then before the fire in Judith's bedroom [Judith, Clytie and I] sat as we always did until he came in the door and looked at us and said, 'Judith, you and Clytie—' and ceased, still entering, then said 'No, never mind. Rosa will not mind if you both hear it too, since we are short for time and busy with what we have of it' and came and stopped and put his hand on my head and (I do not know what he looked at while he spoke, save that by the sound of his voice it was not at us nor at anything in that room) said, 'You may think I made your sister Ellen no very good husband. You probably do think so. But even if you will not discount the fact that I am older now, I believe I can promise that I shall do no worse at least for you.'

"That was my courtship. That minute's exchanged look in a kitchen garden, that hand upon my head in his daughter's bedroom; a ukase, a decree, a serene and florid boast like a sentence (ay, and delivered in the same attitude) not to be spoken and heard but to be read carved in the bland stone which pediments a forgotten and nameless effigy."[47]

In chapter 2 we spoke of the impossibility of putting the jongleur into quotes. Quotes are the margins between discourses, but the jongleur is embracing. He plays at the margin between discourses, but there is no play at his margin. As long as he is present, or understood to be present, he has deictic power, can point anywhere and draw anything in for his purposes: he has no margin. If his words, in a written text, were put in one embracing set of quotes—we pose the question again—would what remains out of quotes be a jongleurian, found voice? Although that outcome is certainly possible, a "founding voice," at the time and place we are examining, is no longer seen to be the appropriate means of deixis for certain messages.

What is called for is discourses, positionable vis-à-vis one another. What would the utterance out of quotes be, then? It would not be voice, nor would that which was contained within the quotes be a jongleurian founding voice any longer. They would both be "voice," that is, able to be put into quotes, just another discourse, one way of seeing and saying things, among many, valuable because perspectival and oblique, seeing some things, saying some things, but deaf, blind, and speechless with respect to other things that nonetheless deserve a reader's attention. Quotation marks, in this differential sense, tend to be inserted during the shift of signifying practice from performance to prose.[48] In any change of signifying practice, all signifying behavior, verbal or nonverbal, is *susceptible* of being revoiced or reattributed, devoiced or de-attributed. This is particularly true of prose as signifying practice, which explicitly or implicitly uses all articulating and framing devices at its disposal to process its utterances and make them unfinal, ready-to-hand.

Discourses can have margins, be assigned subjects, be positioned. But signifying practices, as they deal in deixis, have no margins. Prose, like the *real* jongleur *there then,* is connected everywhere. But if the jongleur has no margins, it is because of his own presence, his implicit and explicit contact with his addressee and all aspects of his situation: all the links, extensive and potentially unending, of deixis. How can writing duplicate that? How can writing have no margins? It cannot: writing is only a *tekhne,* and inscriptions do have margins, are within books, and do not extend into the world. But a signifying practice that uses writing can compete for, and beyond, the deictic power of the jongleur. Prose sees position not as dependent on presence but as the result of a process. It abstracts the process and can thereby put it all on paper. It can contain all margins and manipulate them but is itself untouched by them. As we learn in elementary school, prose differs from verse in that it has no margins.

The question is: how does one embrace all this without having an outside in which to stand? That question was asked by the person whom we consider to be the founder of the problematics of deixis, Archimedes. He had the mechanics but needed something more: "Give me a place to stand on and I will move the earth." For prose as signifying practice, the task is not to move the earth but (at least as challenging) to hold it in its movement. And to do so one does not need another place to stand: one needs only to know how to harness the forces already at work inside.

The era was one of technologies aimed less at finding new sources of power than at probing the nature of perpetual motion and impetus[49] and at harnessing the forces already discovered: flowing water and wind, expanding gases and vapors. The later Middle Ages developed, with astounding rapidity, what Lynn White, Jr., has called "an arsenal of technical means for grasping, guiding and utilizing such energies."[50] White notes the fact that whereas the expansive force of heated vapor had been noted for 1000 years, it is the thirteenth century that picks up the invention of the steam bellows: a vessel is filled with water, the hole at the top is plugged but one at the side is left open, it is placed near the fire where the water is heated, producing a jet of steam (more air than water vapor) that issues from the side hole to blow back on the fire and keep it going. The vessels were generally made in the form of a human, particularly like the Aeolian heads, so that the steam emerges from the mouths from which the winds issue.[51] This *sufflator*, as it was called, reminds us of the abundance of *souffle* and hot air that Rabelais not only attacks in others but also puts to excellent use himself. We also think of the *souffleur*, the prompter, who makes his appearance in medieval theater at this time, although it is incorrect to say he makes his appearance, as this is, like *acteur*, a position for a "no one," but one nonetheless necessary to propel things, keep things going as they shift from one "someone," one constated agent, to another. Might we not see here, in the rediscovery of this instrument *sufflator*, the portent of a new kind of agency that keeps propelling utterances by supposedly drawing only on their effects and properties and by supposedly saying, adding, or originating nothing?

Certain signifying practices attempt to internally establish agency, identity, and stability. Historiography will find itself unable to do so and will, like traditional signifying practice, be powerfully drawn to an external deictic position. And yet, at the time of the emergence of prose, it will begin to see its world, and historical truth, as residing to a great extent *within* the movement of historical events. Therefore it is in the field of history that, at this time, emerging prose will take its greatest bound forward.

Chapter 7
Prose History

The phenomena constitutive of, and attendant upon, the emergence of prose are indicative of profound and far-reaching changes that affect the social, epistemological, ethical, and political dimensions of life. We live today in a world of change; it could even be said that change is the one constant element on our horizon of expectations. It is therefore difficult for us to grasp how a traditional society, largely inured from change, reacts to its irruptions. To be sure, change occurs in such societies, but it is not perceived or acknowledged as such. The new is taken to be a version of the old, of the known. It is the function of myths in such societies to provide explanatory regresses that "absorb" the novel and show it to have been provided for beforehand so that its advent is seen as, let us say, the fulfillment of a pre-diction. One only need recall here the reception given to the Spanish conquistadors upon their arrival in Aztec Mexico: their otherness was resorbed in the Quetzalcoatl set of prophecies. This was far from an isolated occurrence: Claude Lévi-Strauss observes that as late as the 1930s Deep Amazon Indians still dealt in this manner with the arrival of non-Indians in their territory.[1]

Traditional societies accept change readily as long as it fits into preexisting molds. We do too, of course, although we have a rather broader array of such molds available to us and a conception of them that is quite distinct: not all our molds are handed down, some are vested under our very own eyes in ways that we do not always fully understand but which ensure that the new is absorbed—perhaps the proper term would be "processed"—in conformity with established, or at least available, procedures. This extended capacity to handle the new, and thus to accommodate ourselves to change, is undoubtedly a definitive characteristic of modernity. Indeed the very idea of modernity rests on an understanding of change, a mode of understanding that is associated with history, or more precisely with historicism: phenomena, events, living conditions of social life, mental structures, all are to be understood both in terms of the interaction occasioned by their co-occurence and in terms of their relation to the ground from which they spring, in terms of their presentness and their pastness. Prose is deeply implicated in the constitution of historicism and may well have been its privileged vehicle. In this chapter we will examine prose in relation to change, more specifically, to history as a discursive mode, and to historicism.

A caveat at the outset: any attempt to make sense of the passage from the relatively ahistorical outlook of the early Middle Ages to the more fully historical later one will be undermined by the fact that the learned Latin tradition is in a time warp with respect to the developments on the vernacular side. Yet, given the fact that our understanding of these phenomena is mediated by texts, all of which were produced by individuals trained in the learned tradition (scholars were the only ones who could write), we cannot keep a neat distinction between the two at all times. In some respects this is distressing, for it introduces indeterminacies and uncertainties while we strive for precision and certitude, but, as we have seen in chapter 6 and shall continue to see, indeterminacy and uncertainty are important epistemological dimensions of what we are attempting to describe. Furthermore, such dating of documents as we have is in general approximate and speculative. As a result, we cannot offer a clear chronological narrative, only a description of some articulatory clusters or configurations in the relation of prose and history.

The myths and tales told in traditional societies are at once immanent and transcendental: they are located in a spatiotemporal dimension *sui generis*, somewhat like that of the Christian God. They are transcendental because they do not function according to the rules of our world: on the contrary they hold the key to these rules; they determine them, yet escape from their applicability. They are immanent, for the workings of the world are but their instantiation.[2] One does not ask oneself questions of *imminence* with respect to them. One knows that they are about the world as it is. From our modern perspective, we tend to think of these myths as cosmic, atemporal, eternal, but these are all notions that belong to us rather than to the world of such myths and tales. In such a world, the myths and tales are taken to be true but in a sense of "true" that again is not ours. They are true because they are unchanging. The model of their truth is the Old Testament rock, which does not change through the ages.

Memory is put in the service of this unalterability. Such tales lack spatio-temporal specification: we are not told precisely when a given event has occurred, or if we are, it is with more stress on the day and the month than on the year so that its eventfulness would be cyclic and it would serve as a day of celebration. The same is true of places: they are identified only for purposes of avoidance or, on the contrary, for special invitation. What is being recounted is ultimately independent of these spatiotemporal coordinates. Myths have often claimed a legitimacy having its source outside the culture, but all myth and tale analysts have seen that it is the inner logic of these texts that is important: how the events or actions they recount relate to one another. Their signification is established in this way. In the cultures of performance in which these myths or tales flourish, the performed telling is a reminder of their immanence and of their transcendence. It brings the assurance of available certitude to such perplexities of everyday life as may arise.

We do not know whether or to what extent such a civilizational state obtained in the early Western Middle Ages. The presence of the church, the remnants of Latin learning, the awareness of such flourishing cultures as the Byzantine, the Judaic, or the Islamic, all point to a far more complex situation; furthermore, conditions must have varied widely between, let us say, the Rhine Valley, Ireland, southern France, and Scandinavia. The structural multilayeredness of medieval society and its concomitant potentialities ought not to hide from view, however, the generally prevalent earthboundedness of life for most people. As late as the ninth and tenth centuries, much of the territory of what is now northern France was exploited by agricultural stations that were the descendants of the Gallo-Roman villa. The lord or baron (freeman) lived there with his family and often participated in toiling the land. The bulk of the work was done by slaves who were considered members of the master's household. Such "cultural" events as took place, no doubt songs and epics, were addressed to this undifferentiated audience. It is not that social hierarchies were not recognized—far from it—but that the values articulated and promulgated in the songs and epics had everyone's allegiance. Just as everyone was a Christian even though only the church really knew and sought the implementation of Christian values, so everyone believed in epic values even though it was only the nobility that was meant to incarnate and implement them.

When, as a result of complex and still little understood processes,[3] the old order gave way to the new feudal one, the more "organic" audience of the older order collapsed. Lords freed their slaves, the cost of which they could no longer bear, and turned them into serfs, thus, in one swoop, freeing themselves (that is, the lords: such is the meaning of the emancipation of the slaves) from the burden of feeding and housing slaves and, in return, obtaining the right to tax them in kind—labor—and, more importantly, in money.[4] We will not concern ourselves with the rise of this money economy. For our purposes, it will suffice to note that the collectivity of the older agricultural stations was broken up: the lords still lived in their villas, now dubbed castles, the serfs lived in fields and newly cleared lands. Owing to their military obligations, the lords retained a strong interest in the epics, but it ought to be expected that wonder tales about forest creatures and treasures (gnomes, dwarves, elves, etc.) proved more appealing to the servile populations, laying the ground for what the eighteenth century will call folklore. This differentiation, purely speculative on our part, does not result in any conflicts, but it indicates greater cultural specification and audience specialization.

The changes brought about by the instauration of the feudal order precipitated some changes in the texts of the culture as well, although it is difficult to say with what degree of consciousness. To take two examples from the epic: it is quite clear that both the *Chanson de Roland* and the *Chanson de Guillaume* deal with traditional knightly values. At the same time, however, both raise matters that are more contemporary: in the *Roland*, it is the question of preeminence between loyalty to the king or to blood ties, resolved in favor of the former by means of the judicial trial won by Thierry. In the *Guillaume*, it is the vexing problem of what to do with the surplus population of young knights for whom land could not be found, thus effectively barring them from the privileges of their estate: the solution was to conquer more land from the Saracens. The dual thrust of these epics (and this is quite true of others) points to the fact that this form was functional: it both transmitted traditional values and addressed contemporary problems. Change was acknowledged but it was contained. The epic form—performed verse—had proven itself equal to the challenge.

It is interesting to observe that the oldest epics that have come down to us have this dual thrust. It cannot be presupposed that this was the feature of all epics. The rather extensive research done in the origins of the *Roland*, although highly speculative, has shown that the older parts of the text were free of this concern.[5] This suggests the conclusion that the epics were *written down* only insofar as they included this double concern of how to conjoin the traditional with the contemporary, the known with the unknown. The inclusion of the contemporary problematics, which clearly are of a different "ontological" order than traditional values, probably precipitated this act of writing down: they were too evanescent and certainly not transcendental enough to be preserved in standing memory, yet preserved they had to be, for they articulated an important form of knowledge. They were not true as a rock, let us say, but they deserved the permanence of a document provided by writing. This marks the beginning of a historical consciousness. And, at the outset, this consciousness will adopt as its vehicle the performance of epic and the verse that is its verbal component.

The double structure of the Old French epic is a well-known fact of medieval literary history,[6] although the reasons for its existence are controversial. It is clear that literary scholars sense that the epics we have are not homogeneous, yet they cannot locate the causes of the doubleness in the commingling of two different stages of culture. The medieval audience must have sensed it as well, but they were even less prepared to understand it. Contemporary events could always be spoken of but only if they evidenced the immanence of larger regresses.[7] Such was not the case with the contemporary problems dealt with in the epics. These were new and unanticipated problems, attendant to the establishment and continuance of the feudal order and to the hegemonic pretensions of the monarchy. In relation to the events themselves, whose meaning must have been perceived but dimly, their inclusion in the epics must have allowed them a measure of transcendence, although not the transcendence enjoyed by the traditional matter of the epic.

The act of writing this verse down implies some unease with the signifying practice of performance. When change becomes severe, it needs to be accounted for, immediately and in its difference from traditional culture. At a certain moment, events were seen as contemporary in the sense of having a certain uniqueness, which exceeded the capability of the mechanisms of traditional culture for their storage, interpretation, and ascription of significance. Traditional practice can make no room for distinctively current events. Questions are raised about the formal mechanisms of traditional culture, and in this way a historical consciousness is born. Perhaps one day, when the significance of contemporary problematics becomes clear, they will qualify to be dealt with in a practice seen as traditional; until then, the writing-down is a sort of memorandum, aide-mémoire, a document for future memory when the right kind of transcendence can be exercised. On the other hand (and this line of thinking may prove to be more fruitful), this writing-down represents a search for a purport more adequate than performance for the treatment of these matters.

What is not problematized here but soon will be is a distinction that we take entirely for granted: the distinction between form and content. The myths and tales of traditional society, we have seen, are based on the notion of truth as unchangeability. There cannot arise with respect to them any sense of distinction between form and content. Again, in his chapter on the Nambikwara in Tristes tropiques, Lévi-Strauss expresses his wonderment at the fact that he could understand the layout of a village, the workings of kinship relations, and the form of women's face-painting as a peculiar form of asymmetry to be found in Nambikwara myths as well. To us this is indeed surprising, but if one conceives of truth as the unchangeable, the immanent, and the transcendental, it must pervade everything, including what we call form and what we call content, such that a distinction between them is not pertinent. As change is excluded *a priori*, form and content are permanently wedded to each other and occur in perfect synchronicity. There is an integration here similar in effect to that which occurs when the history of a culture is repeated, in identical oral form: how can there be a history other than in that particular form? Consciousness of the noncoincidence of form and content is closely connected to historical consciousness.

When truth changes, there is a lack of synchronicity between the signifying practice and its message: a lag is sensed between what is then seen as a new content versus an old form. Attention is called to a form-content distinction, which was irrelevant up to that point. The decision to write down contemporary events in the verse form of the epic, the form of authorized collective truth, will discombobulate the traditional synchronicity and precipitate a crisis of verse.

The representation of current events in written verse initially takes place under the aegis of the epic and thus draws for its own acceptability upon the latter's standing as credible form. But as soon as written historical verse begins to operate independently of the epic, it calls forth a number of questions having to do with its mode of authority. The epic was vouched for within the signifying practice of performance, into which authority is built in. The inclusion of new historical material within epic structure was also initially covered by association. But as soon as it presented itself as historical verse per se, the question of its standing had to be raised.

In the case of Yolande's request for a prose translation of the pseudo-Turpin, we pointed out in our introduction that verse is rejected on the ground that it lies. We reiterate here the relevant portion of the prologue to the translation. "Many people have heard it told and sung, but it is nothing but lies that they tell and sing, these singers and jongleurs. No rhymed tale is true; everything they say is a lie for they know nothing of it except through hearsay." What is evidenced by this accusation is a critique of verse and a discrediting of the jongleur and of the signifying practice articulated around him, insofar as that practice has a means of transmission found to be faulty: "oïr dire," hearsay.

Historical verse escapes the strictures of a Baudouin and a Senlis when it no longer depends on its traditional mode of transmission, that is, when it is written about current events. However, in a world of writing and with prose now as its incipient competition, verse finds itself the target of another critique. For example, the author of *La Mort Aymerie de Narbonne* (1180) writes:

Nus hom ne puet chançon de jeste dire
que il ne mente la ou li verse define,
as mos drecier et a tailler la rime[8]

No one can recite a *chanson de geste*
without lying where the verse ends
by raising words and pruning rhymes.

Our introduction showed that even attacks on the veracity of verse could
take place in verse, particularly when the attack is in a prologue to a prose
work, for one is still uncomfortable with prose as a beginning or ending boundary. *La Mort Aymerie de Narbonne* has these lines in the middle of what is
a totally verse work, and we see as we continue to read that it is more than
an attack on verse; it is specifically an attack *ad hominem*, against the class
of versifiers among which it counts its author as an exception. The text continues:

Ce est bien voirs, gramaire le devise,
uns hom la fist de l'anciene vie,
Hues ot non, si la mist en un livre
Et seela el mostier Saint Denise.
La ou les jestes de France sont escrites.

This is quite true, grammar (the written) asserts it,
A man from olden times did it,
Hues by name, he put it in a book,
And deposited it in the monastery of Saint Denis.
There where the *gestae* of France are written.

This is rhyme that overcomes the limitations of rhyme because of a particular,
individual rhymer, whose authority is guaranteed by documentarians.[9] The
move here is toward the conception of the origins of documents as being
individual authors, who are more or less "gifted" in language. As exceptional
status has to be claimed for such individuals, it is clear that versifiers in general are not now trusted because of demands seen to be imposed on them
by the formal workings of verse. This kind of attack echoes the term of controversy among Latin historians who were also taking verse to task but from
an established written tradition. We will briefly examine what was happening
on the Latin side.

The distinction between Latin verse and Latin prose was less powerful
than might be expected because of traditions seeing writing as subordinate
to and bespeaking speech and even checked against memory.[10] For example,
contemporary rhetorical training regularly involved paraphrasing from verse
to prose and back. Curtius recalls to us that

antiquity did not conceive of poetry and prose as two forms of expression differing in essence and origin. On the contrary, both fell within the inclusive concept "discourse." . . . Turning poetry into prose is introduced into the schools of rhetoric as an exercise about the first century of our era. Quintilian recommends it to orators (X, 5, 4). Augustine had to paraphrase passages from the *Aeneid* in school. In late Greek and Roman Antiquity, as in the Byzantine Middle Ages, paraphrase became an end in itself. Statius boasts that his father not only explained the most difficult poets but also bore "the same yoke as Homer," turning his verses into prose "without falling a step behind."

It has heretofore remained almost unnoticed that a large part of early Christian poetry is a continuation of the antique rhetorical practice of paraphrase. We first find books of the Bible recast in hexameters. . . . The *vita* of St. Martin by the Aquitanian Sulpicius Severus (*ca.* 400) was versified in the second half of the Fifth Century by Paulinus of Périgueux who calls his work a "translatio" or "transcripta oratio." . . . But it was possible to go still further, and turn a versified version into prose afresh. . . . This practice of double versions had many disciples among the Anglo- Saxons . . . About 1050 Onulf of Speyer composes his *Rhetorici colores* in prose and adds a versified version with the words: "idem idem eidem de eodem." This is the last example of the stylistic transposition which the Middle Ages took over as a heritage from the antique schools of rhetoric. The practice shows us that metrical and non-metrical discourse were felt to be interchangeable arts.[11]

That prose and verse were in some sense interchangeable also shows that prose generally adopted the same subject matter as verse. Ogle states that

even though Quintillian . . . emphasizes the need of the study of geometry, music and astronomy, he does so only because these subjects were considered necessary for the appreciation of poetry, and poetry, in fact, was the chief matter of study . . . Since . . . poetry was to such a large extent the subject of study, the language not only of school exercises but of prose generally tended more and more to become poetic; ordinary language was tabooed, and its place was taken by a prose which was adorned with all the artifices of poetry. And not only was the style of prose made poetic, but the matter, which in the best period had belonged to the province of poetry, found treatment in prose, especially descriptions—descriptions of objects of nature, objects of art, . . . and panegyrics of great men and praises of their deeds."[12]

Poetry was studied rhetorically, and rhetorics included oration, so that, as two branches of rhetoric, prose and verse could be seen as demonstrating the same skill. When Cicero talks of prose rhythm, he uses terms of versification. The commonality between the two extends to the Middle Ages: Brunetto

Latini (1220-95) says, "Le grans partison de toux parleors est en .ij. manieres, une qui est en prose, et une autre qui est en rime; mais li enseignement de retorique sont commun andui" (The major division of all speech is in two kinds, one which is in prose, and another which is in rhyme; but the rhetorical doctrine is common to both).[13]

We do not of course propose that within the medieval Latin sphere verse and prose were completely interchangeable, but clearly the relation was not such that the authority of one could be substantially overthrown in the face of the other. The character and development of Latin nonverse must first be understood in its own terms (and especially in its special relation to the rhetorics of formal, magisterial speech, *oratio*). Prose must be studied *in situ* because of the striking differences between the linguistic and historical circumstances that accompany its emergence and flourishing.

Most noteworthy is that Latin writing was *taught* and dwas the object of an increasingly elaborate scholastic discipline. Grammars, like those of Donatus and Priscian, were written to teach how to do it correctly. But the grammarians believed they could deal with all writing because of the techniques that all writing shared, such as *amplificatio*. Consequently, oral language, oratory, came under their province, as did poetry, which, from Ovid on, was submitted to grammatico-rhetorical exegeses.[14] There were distinctions to be made, to be sure, but ultimately grammars could deal with it all, and much of the confusion we experience trying to disentangle, in inventories of rhetoric, the different sets of often overlapping and duplicate rhetorical devices stems from the fact that different and overlapping kinds of discourses are involved.

Whether one sees it as the extension of the field of "rhetorization," as Curtius does, or of grammar, as Murphy does, there is a move to cover all kinds of language, what Murphy calls a *reductio ad completam*.[15] Clearly the phenomenon here is: once everything is seen to be treatable as language and thus can be dealt with linguistically, whether logically, grammatically, or rhetorically (*i.e.*, the trivium), the tendency is to make *internal* to one's field whatever distinctions there are rather than to view these distinctions as limitations upon one's field; seen in this light, the whole *reductio* is not unlike how we find prose to approach *its* field. John of Garland, in his *De arte prosayca, metrica et rithmica*,[16] included, within the category of prose, *ars dictaminis*, the written communications necessary to the efficient functioning of chanceries and royal courts and thus assumed authority over the whole epistolary art. What about letter-writing as prose?[17]

In the ancient world, messages over distances were transmitted orally or, even if written, read aloud. Common practice was to dictate a letter (*dictare*) for a scribe to copy. Used for a relatively limited set of official functions, the language of letters could be reused, to which the letters of Cassiodorus, published as *Variae* (sixth century), owe their immense popularity in the Middle Ages for they covered a multitude of cases. From the seventh to the ninth century, when even the literacy of kings was not ensured, extensive use was made of handed-down formulas (which still dominate legal discourse today): standardized statements capable of being duplicated under various circumstances, in which spaces of names, dates, et cetera, are left blank. Because they were already written down, they could also serve as the written record of the official act once they were filled in. There was virtually no distinction drawn between the form of a letter and an oral communication.

Letter-writing was found to have forms specific to its particular type of communication with the Benedictine Alberic of Monte Cassino circa 1087. In his *Dictaminum radii*, he refers to the addresser of a letter as *scriptor* rather than speaker and the addressees as *lectorem* rather than *auditores*. As for structure, the letter was seen as having five parts, virtually cloned from the six-part Ciceronian oration. Alberic's most significant modification was to split the functions of the *exordium* into a *salutatio,* to capture attention, followed by what would come to be called a *captatio benevolentiae.* Subsequent *ars dictaminis* spent a preponderant amount of time on these introductory parts, many amounting to nothing more than examples of salutations. "[T]he whole subsequent history of the *ars dictaminis* indicates that these first two parts of a letter were the most important in the eyes of dictaminal theorists."[18] Each combination of social standing between sender and receiver, each type of occasion demands its particularly appropriate salutation. We know from what we have seen of the chantefable and John of Garland's notion of *ydioma* that here is a question of *sermocinatio,* determining the appropriate level of discourse (*sermo*) and address at a time when communications had to arbitrate between different social levels. In general, when the letter is perceived as being different from a speech by someone who is absent, it becomes immediately necessary to deal with its frame. As only written, where does it come from, how does it begin, what is its deixis? Who is meant to be uttering it, and to whom, and how can this be revealed in the communication? It is significant that attention is paid to those points at which the language meets boundaries, introductions and conclusions. As far as conclusions are concerned, it is here that the cursus (the rules for marking an accentual end to a period) finds its greatest trust. *Rithmus,* rhythmical prose, was important for church speech and had been used for oration, particularly at its end, the peroration, which for Cicero should be rich in rhythm, weighty and resounding terms ("numeris, verba gravia et sonantia"). But the cursus particularly caught on in letter-writing: John of Gaeta, a student of Alberic, went on to become Pope, at which point he introduced it "firsthand," we might say, into curial style, and from this it took the role of a letter's most visible stylistic demand or accoutrement. If letter-writing is a precursor of prose, *ars dictaminis* spends most of its effort on situating the writing between individuals, with its salutations and protocols, and on the problem of closure.

Because official letters were highly formulary before Alberic and because he and his successors began an "art" of letter-writing (short-lived: there was not much more to say after 1200), one would anticipate the entrance of a certain writerly freedom into the field. For the most part, however, "models are posited instead of theories."[19] *Dictaminis* did not go very far before it became filled with formulas, samples, and models for every occasion, increasingly automatic (e.g., Lawrence of Aquilegia), and increasingly close to the parallel development of an *ars notaria* (not surprising because *ars dictaminis* was concerned with legal or quasi-legal public and official communication).[20]

To return now to the question of verse, prose, and paraphrase, let us recall that paraphrase is part of a larger rhetorical strategy of variation. A text was varied or renewed by changing its words (*permutatio, transsumptio*), often by just changing a letter, changing verbs into nouns, or adjectives into verbs, and by exploring all paths of circumlocution. With written *auctoritates* firmly in hand, teaching and preaching (*artes praedicandi*) encouraged variation for effective pedagogy and dissemination of the message. To put forward change in repetition, to show it to be desirable or necessary, is possible only in a culture that has already conferred the permanence of writing on its most precious texts. In an oral culture, variation is kept within strict parameters to avoid confusion and drift. In a written culture, one can bother, if one likes, to traffic in form and variation, in a kind of oratory that is now seen as not carrying the burdens of the whole cultural patrimony, and so is free, even by means of writing that offers permanence, to be *occasional*. The way is opened, at the same time, to questions of individual *style*.

Medieval Latin history was firmly in a *written* tradition at the time, not in an active oral one, and it was meant for readers. Occasional paraphrases aside, history in Latin had been in prose until the year 1000. And much writing about history during those years proclaimed that the appropriate style for the writing of history was a simple one, a *sermo simplex*. Three purposes were claimed for such a style: (1) It was considered as a quicker and more convenient way of writing,[21] (2) It was put forward as a form of discourse that could convey the truth in a less adorned and more accurate way (Otto of Friesing saw "sermo simplex" as "amica veritatis"),[22] and (3) it was a way to attract a wider and less literate audience, an aim of preaching, which legitimated the vernacular for such purposes in the ninth century, and thereafter began to view elaborate rhetorical figures as confusing and inappropriate for sermons (e.g., Wycliffe).

In fact, however, this direction was contrary to the rhetorical styles loaded with oratorical models and formulas, which were found in the *ars dictaminis*, taught in the schools, and practiced by the chanceries. Even though a wider lay audience was desirable, the fact was that writing was done by the learned for the learned, and all appreciated elaborate style. Historians could use an extensive stylistic repertoire to distinguish themselves from mere chroniclers. Furthermore, as we mentioned earlier with reference to Geoffroi de Vinsauf, style was implicated in differences in social level and importance: to great deeds only an elaborate style could do justice. Levels of style were particularly problematic in Christian writings, to which we have already alluded: when the humble is the divine, does it too demand high style?

> Not only had many of the early Fathers—and these the most influential—been educated in Greek or Latin rhetorical schools, but many of them had themselves been teachers of rhetoric. And although in theory they might have accepted Tertullian's view that, so long as they believed, nothing else mattered, or agreed with Gregory the Great that it was an unworthy thing to subject the word of God to the rules of Donatus, their practice shows that they were well versed in the use of the tools they affected to despise. Some, however, were bold enough to declare, on the one hand, that the Holy Scriptures conformed to the highest laws of rhetorical art and, on the other, that only by the training obtained from the traditional methods of grammar and rhetoric could the Christian teacher and preacher gain the eloquence necessary to overcome the claims of the heathen."[23]

As a result, prose grew more ornate and complex, with attention paid increasingly to matters of style by way of Latin rhetoric, and the claim of simplicity was often little more than a topos. The search for a style appropriate to historical narrative led the writers to experiment in the area of form also, for it is around the year 1000 that rhythmic and cadenced prose (of which the cursus was particularly attached to curial and epistolary writings) and versiprosa texts made their appearance in history. The former was relatively unknown in antiquity and in the early Middle Ages, except as rhythmic oratory, but became widespread in the eleventh and twelfth centuries under the influence of liturgical scansion, whereas the latter, although of rare occurrence among the ancients, enjoyed a certain vogue from the sixth century onward, in the works by Boethius and Martianus Capella in the forefront, although not in historical works. It was Dudon de St. Quentin who was the first to insert verse in a work of Latin historical prose, in the eleventh century.

The proliferation of verse within Latin historical prose gave fresh impetus to those Latin historians who objected to the verse on grounds of form. According to Lacroix,[24] verse was to be avoided because it was not dignified enough for some of the subjects with which history dealt. And Guibert de Nogent is said to have rejected the idea that "these things ought to be said in *sonorous* language or that recourse ought to be made to the *sonorousness* [*sonorité*] of versification."[25]

Returning now to the vernacular side, we initially find a difference in attitudes toward verse. For Nicolas de Senlis and other *prosateurs*, verse is disqualified because of the inadequacy of the signifying practice of performance. Verse *as written* should have put that difficulty to rest, but it also has the effect of foregrounding verse as form. This leaves it open to attack in the vernacular as *referentially* inadequate: forming the rhyme distorts the truth, says the author of *La Mort Aymerie de Narbonne*.[26] The attack on verse has changed, from one that is basically aimed at the functioning of oral tradition to one aimed at form as such: verse is rejected inasmuch as it impedes access to facts. This critique coalesces with the backlash against verse by the contemporary Latin historians, who have come to it from writing alone. According to Lacroix, Guibert de Nogent thought, "Prose makes the narrative clearer; versification runs the risk of getting it tangled up."

Until the twelfth century, surviving written history remains by and large Latin history, Latin having such a strong hold on writing. At that point, the courts of noblemen developed into enough of a counterweight to begin to give respect to a vernacular culture. There was, as Auerbach says, a new, vernacular, literary public. Furthermore, as we saw at the end of the Senlis prologue to the *Pseudo-Turpin* translation, there is developing, earlier than one might have expected, a social class that is literate but not with respect to Latin. Corollary to the spread of vernacular literature from the twelfth to the fourteenth century, the elaborateness of Latin disappeared, in favor of a simpler style, and almost no historical work in Latin contained verse after the fourteenth century. This is just the time when prose is emerging and spreading rapidly in French writing.[27] The very success of prose from the twelfth century onward determines the mode of language in which historical knowledge will henceforth be transmitted.

Questions of signifying practice come sharply into view as traditional content—myths and heroic tales—is encroached upon by the written records of contemporary events. Jean Le Bel (d., 1370) started writing history, he claims, to correct the mistakes of a minstrel whose account did not conform to the events that Jean Le Bel himself had witnessed. His *Chronique* begins:

> Qui veult lire et ouir la vraye hystoire du proeu et gentil roy Edowart, qui au temps present regne en Engleterre, si lise ce petit livre que j'ay commencé à faire, et laisse ung grand livre rimé que j'ay veu et leu, lequel aucun controuveur a mis en rime par grandes faintes et bourdes controuvées, duquel le commencement est tout faulx et plain de menchongnes. . . . Et de là en avant peut avoir assez de substance de verité et assez de bourdes, et sy y a grand plenté de parolles controuvées et de redictes pour embelir la rime, et grand foison de si grand proesses racontées sur aucuns chevaliers et aucunes personnes qu'elles

debveroient sembler mal creables et ainsi comme impossibles; par quoy telle hystoire ainsy rimée par telz controuveurs pourroit sembler mal plaisant et mal aggreable à gens de raison et d'entendement. Car on pourroit bien attribuer, par telles parolles si demesurées, sur aucuns chevaliers ou escuiers proesses si oultrageuses que leur vaillance en pourroit estre abessée, car leur vrais fais en seroient mains creus, de quoy ce seroit dommage pour eulx, pourquoy on doibt parler le plus à point que on poeut et au plus prez de la verité[28]

Whoever wants to read and hear the true story of the brave and gentle king Edward who presently reigns in England, let him read this little book that I have begun to put together, and let him leave aside a big rhymed book that I have seen and read, which some poetaster has rhymed in great feigned rhymes and poetastric fabrication, the beginning of which is entirely false and full of lies. . . . And from that point on there is both true matter and fabrication, as well as many poetastric words and repetitions to adorn the rhyme, and a proliferation of so many feats told about some knights and persons that they should appear hard to believe and even impossible, and because of this a story rhymed thus by such poetasters could appear unpleasant and disagreeable to people of reason and sense. For one could well attribute, by such exaggerated words, such outrageous feats to some knights and squires that their bravery could be lowered, for their true accomplishments would be less believed, which would cause them harm. That is why one must be as much to the point as one can and as very close to the truth.

And he ends his prologue with the following programmatic statement:

Et pourtant que en ces hystoires rimées treuve on grand plenté de bourdes, je veul mectre paine et entente, quand je pourray avoir loisir, d'escrire par prose ce que je ay veu et ouy recorder par ceux qui ont esté là où je n'a pas esté, au plus prez de la verité que je pourray, selonc la memoire que Dieu m'a presté, et au plus bref que je pourray, sans nulluy placquier.

And because in these rhymed stories one finds a great plenty fabrications, I want to apply my labor and mind, when I have the leisure, to write in prose what I have seen and heard recalled by those who were there where I have not been, as very close to the truth as I shall be able to, with the memory that God has granted me, and as briefly as I shall be able to without overadorning anyone.

We have seen that, despite paying lip service to the ideal of a "sermo simplex," there was a great deal of style embellishment in Latin history in the name of appropriateness to the deeds recounted. Le Bel states at the beginning of his work that embellishment of the form, even for great deeds, entails an unacceptable distortion of fact ("leur vrais fais") and destroys credibility:

"high" style for "high" actions can be inappropriate and even counterproductive. It is but a short step to see form itself as such embellishment, and to condemn it in favor of being "au plus prez de la verité que je pourray."

"Closeness" to the truth is associated both with the physical and temporal proximity of the utterer to the referent ("ceux qui ont estée là," "au plus bref," "sans nulluy placquier") and with the utterer's nonverse writing ("le plus a point que on peut," "escrire par prose"). This notion is identical to that of the use of *sermo simplex* for those for whom time is scarce. The closer one gets to the referent, the more verse as form is seen as distance and distance is seen as distortion.

"Au plus prez de la verité" holds out as its unreachable goal a location at no distance from the event itself. The closer one gets to the historical event, personally or by reliable substitution, the more referentially valid one's discourse will be. (One cannot, apparently, be totally at one with the event, totally immanent, but that is what one strives for.) Such a validity, founded in immediacy to the referent, was not a goal of the performance: if proximity and immediacy were underlined in the performance, they were between the addresser and the addressees, not between the addresser and the referent. Between the addresser and the referent there was a "respectful" and well-ripened distance.[29] When performance falls and verse is left with only the distance (formerly a traditional distance, now an empirical one, experienced as a physical distance from an outside, remediable by coming close), a critique of verse, as linguistic form, can and will be formulated. Verse is too far away and too late: it does not inhabit the referent the way the jongleur inhabited the communicative act.

Note that although the denunciation of Le Bel resembles that of Nicolas de Senlis, Le Bel is speaking not of a *chanson de geste* or a *conte rimé* but of a *grand livre rimé*. With prose opposed not to the jongleur but to a *livre rimé*, the vernacular debate fully enters the culture of the written (where the Latin debate has been). Again we see delineated the two distinct battles of prose against verse, both in the name of truth: the first rejecting verse as a relic of performance, in the name of documentary, not handed-down truth; and the second, within the established culture of the written, considering verse to be "form" and rejecting "form" as at a distance and a delay from "content," to which it is claimed that prose is referentially truer and is thus the appropriate medium of history. It is only a short step from here for scholars to characterize this distancing demanded by form as an *artisanal* distance, and this might very well be the point in time when a breach is effected, a communication pragmatics is ignored, and a poetics receives attention (following the tradition of *poesis*, making, craftsmanship) while a prosaics, lacking a tradition, fails to constitute itself.

For Le Bel, the antidote to *livres rimés* is personal knowledge (what he has seen and heard, and sometimes read) not included in the immemorial past of the collectivity. A new conception of truth is at work here, one that is articulated under the aegis of writing and along with the spread of prose. The question of the referent did not arise in the world of the *Roland* because the meaning of the performed text functioned as something that resided not in an outside but in the relations of the intratextual events. For a historiographic text, however, the external relation is crucial because its task is to represent the real that is conceived as external to language and to the text. This is precisely a relation constructed by prose.[30] (Verse is still reliable in lyric because lyric deals with exteriority only secondarily.)

A study of Froissart strongly suggests that this very famous French chronicler began to write history in verse, in 1353, but his next writings (1369) were in prose and he did not return to verse.[31] In the interim, he had been requested by his sponsor, Robert de Namur, to write in prose, but more importantly he had discovered the work of Le Bel, which he subsequently used wholesale in his own writings. His second prose version includes this statement:

> Plusieur gongleour et enchanteour en place ont chanté et rimet lez guerres de Bretagne et corromput par leurs chançons et rimes controuvées, le juste et vraie histoire, dont trop en deplaist à monseigneur Jehan le Biel, qus le coummencha à mettre en prose et en cronique et à moy sir Jehan Froissart, qui loyaument et justement l'ay poursuiwi à mon pooir, car *leurs rimmes et leurs canchons controuvées n'ataindent en riens le vraie matiere.*[32]

> Several jongleurs and public square singers have sung and rhymed the British wars and they have corrupted by their songs and their poetastric rhymes the rightful and true history, a fact which greatly displeased Milord Jean LeBel, who began to put it into prose and into chronicle, and it displeased me, Sir Jean Froissart, as well, and I have continued his work with loyalty and rightfulness to the best of my ability, *for their poetastric rhymes and songs in no way attain the true matter.*

As a measure of the success of prose over verse versions of history, it is worth noting that the *grand livre rimé* attacked by Le Bel has never been found (although it was noted among the books in a royal library at the time), and Froissart's early verse histories have not survived.

The attack on verse was (sometimes more, sometimes less consciously) an attack on form as such. Prose is presented as remedy, as successor to verse as form, but no claims are made *for* prose *as* form. Prose is considered less false only because of the marks it lacks, because it is *un*marked. It is not claimed that nonverse tells the truth, just that verse lies. Simply because we can locate lies does not mean we can locate truth. The attack on verse leaves prose with hegemony obtained by default. But just to go from verse to nonverse is not enough—that is why prose will take a long time to mature. "Form" was not really the problem, or the only problem, and by dropping verse one does not drop the cognitive models based on performance, which presented, among other things, situations of cognitive plenitude in which certain individuals or "offices" (e.g., jongleurs) could be in a position to know fully and speak their knowledge. For one thing, dropping verse does not necessarily bring the desired immediacy.

We will now look at the way in which prose fulfills this task of historical representation, and what happens to history in the process, by examining the prose *Chronique de Louis XII* by Jehan d'Auton (1466-1527), in particular the lengthy passages in volume 4 in which he describes the king's campaign against the rebellious city of Genoa.[33] D'Auton's chronicle immediately displays some of the features advocated in Le Bel's programmatic statement. The goal he assigns to himself and of which he repeatedly reminds the reader is as exact a representation of the referent as he is capable of achieving. He thus comes to privilege what we have called, discussing Molinet, the witness discourse, wherein the narrative instance presents its discourse as the result of visual and auditory ascertainment. In this respect, it is easy to see that d'Auton takes Le Bel's manifesto quite seriously, as he carefully establishes the actual conditions of his witnessing. Thus, in the very first pages of the account of the campaign, just as he is about to relate the Genovese motivations for the war, d'Auton states that he has culled the information he is about to impart *in loco,* but unfortunately after the fact ("comme je l'ay sceu estant sur le lieu . . . " [as I learned from being at the site . . .], p. 38), drawing attention to the conditions of his testimony.

The cognitive reliability of this text is always put forward in direct relation to the reader's ability to determine *d'Auton's relation and position vis-à-vis the events that he recounts:* whenever he recounts a set of occurrences that he knows only secondhand, he inserts in the account an indication that he was subsequently present in the very site where the events had occurred and therefore could personally testify to the traces that they had left there. Let us examine three examples.

1. Par quoy, n'espargnoyent icelle eglize, mais tiroyent au travers, de tous costez; et tant que, tantost *apres ce, je estant dedans ladite eglize,* viz partye du coeur et piliers d'icelle par terre, et les voultes perce en plusieurs lieux, etc. . . . Somme, la baterye estoit merveilleuse de tous costez.

2. Les nouvelles de ceste entreprise furent tost semees . . . et tellement que plusieurs villes mutines . . . pencent que Gennes deust tout

confondre y envoyerent soubdartz a grant nombre: desquels me vouluz enquerir, estant a *Gennes apres la prise d'icelle.*

3. Somme, de tous ceulx n'en eschappa que ung tout seul . . . ils [the Genovese] le musserent et deguiserent, puys luy baillerent de l'argent, et tellement firent qu'il se sauve et se retira au chateau de Gennes, *où depuys me trouvay* et parlay aluy.

1. [Concerning an attack on Genoa] Wherefore they did not spare this church but bombarded it from all sides, so much so that *some time later when I was in the aforementionned church,* I saw part of the nave and its pillars knocked down and the vault shot through in several places. . . . In sum, the artillery was horrific on all sides.

2. [When the Genovese initiate their rebellion] The news of this undertaking spread quickly . . . so much so that several rebellious cities . . . came to believe that Genoa could fuse them all, and they sent soldiers there in large numbers, which I wanted to inquire into *when I was in Genoa after it was taken.*

3. [Recounting the aftermath of the massacre of the French] In sum only one escaped from the lot . . . and the Genovese hid him and disguised him and then gave him some money and did so much that he escaped and retired to the castle of Genoa, *where I have since found myself* and spoken to him.

And in the last instance, d'Auton goes so far as to ask this eyewitness of the massacre to put his testimony in writing, and he indicates that he has relied on this document as well as on other accounts in his relation of the events.

Even though historiographic practice incorporates much of this technique, particularly in the form of the pilgrimage (as in *Le Saint Voyage de Jherusalem* of Ogier d'Anglure at the end of the fourteenth century),[34] we might ask what credit the chronicler deserves for having visited the site of an event when he was not present at that site at the moment of the occurrence of the event: he was not *there then.* We could speculate broadly as to what motivates this attachment of the utterance to a presence, however delayed and deferred, but it may suffice for our purposes here just to ask ourselves whether such attachment to presence is inherent to the writing of history in prose. We will in fact find that it interferes with that very writing.

By itself, such notations of presence and proximity may well be negligible, but their very occurrence constitutes a break with the habits of previous vernacular historiography, which always positioned the enunciative instance in a locus of cognitive certainty at a far remove from the events that were to be related. D'Auton, on the contrary, writes from a new awareness of the cognitive fragility of what he relates. Here history is to be plunged into, although the question seems to be the extent to which one is *there then.* D'Auton's account is surely as cognitively reliable as he can manage it to be under the circumstances, but the circumstances are as much *his* circumstances as they are history's. His making explicit of his relation to the historical object makes his reliability depend upon where he happens to be. History remains larger than him and to a great extent *passée;* he gets to see only its traces. Having scuttled the formal distance that builds in a transcendental view of the proceedings, he necessarily exposes to view all the physical limitations incumbent upon actual, even documented, personal presence: he simply cannot be in two places at once. His account thereby has a certain measure of reliability but also labors under a good deal of obstruction. It is *he* who is too present. Can one really *not* be in two places at once?

Although his goal is to make the historical event immediate, he confirms its absence by the implicit distance betweens the event and his own presence, on which he continually insists. His account is always "after the fact," meaning both "too late" and *à la chasse de.* As absence, the event is a trace, an emptiness that calls for a discursive filling-out. The historian finds this place of absence and begins to inject some presence in it, notably his or her own, or more accurately, some *language* that will now take place here and reconstruct the referent known to us only through the trace that it has left. The trace is what the discourse of the historian will *anchor* itself in, hence the stress laid upon the actual visit to the site, which at the time is clearly the nature of the deictic functioning of historical discourse. This historian proceeds to collect all remaining traces, including such discourses as may have survived, to achieve as much presence, as much of the matter, as possible. However, as we have seen, language is inherently incapable of presence: it offers only effects of presence or at best simulacra of presence. A structural predicament of history lies here. It can have language take place only on the premise that a referent was once there. In addition, the representation provided by the historian is forever caught in its own shortcoming: it never achieves plenitude, it never totalizes. The historian's own presence at the site of the event is mystifying: it draws attention only to this incompleteness and to this absence. I just missed it. It is too late. D'Auton, bound to presence and reconstruction, is historian as collector and curator. He is not able, as Commynes will be, to give us history while it happens.

Le Bel attacks the *grand livre rimé* because of his concern that praise for the prowess shown by the king's men would not be properly allotted and appreciated. "Car l'istoire est si noble, ce m'est advis, et de si gentile proesse, qu'elle est bien digne et merite d'estre mise en escript pour le en memoire retenir au plus prez de la verité" (For the history is so noble and of such exquisite prowess, in my view, that it is indeed worthy and deserving of being put into writing to preserve it in memory as very close to the truth as possible). He goes on to state that all individuals who were valorous should be mentioned. Praise is also the primary professed motive for Froissart and d'Auton. D'Auton cites and uncritically accepts speeches and testimonies that draw praise to his subject. For example, some student had written his own Latin verse inscriptions in praise of the king and had left them at various turning points in the road all the way from Genoa to Milan, and d'Auton found it pertinent to cite and translate each one. Although written, one cannot help thinking that this is history as praise for the praiseworthy, and praise for such heroics is very much a part of the oral sphere of communication. Great deeds call for an act of praise, and that act, even if it is an act of a historian, is one of testimony to greatness. Thus it should be only a little surprising for us to discover, at the end of d'Auton's account of Louis's march to Milan, a short passage in verse. Perhaps d'Auton uses it in an attempt to restore some sense of plenitude to his enterprise. He introduces it as follows:

> Apres que les dictes choses furent mises a fin, la ville de Gennes fut de tous pointz accoisee, les pays circunvoisins espouventez, les Francoys tus rejouye et le Roy tout a souhet. Dont je, qui lors estoye audit lieu, voyant la grace de Dieu si largement estandue sur l'affaire des Francoys, la gloire du Roy prosperer et son honneur accroistre, pour commaincer a luy vouloir donner louange de son bienfaict et lui divercifier passe temps, luy presentay ce peu d'escript comme s'ensuyt.

> After these things were brought to an end, the city of Genoa was pacified in all respects; the surrounding lands, terrified; the French, very happy; and the king, as good as one could wish. Wherefore I, who found myself there then, seeing the grace of God so generously pervade French interests, the king's fame prosper and his honor increase, presented him with the little written piece that follows in order to begin to praise him for his good deeds and to divert him.

There follows a short poem lauding the victory of Louis, "Master of land and sea," and comparing him to the great conquerors of the past. And then the chronicle returns to the narrative of the further Italian campaigns, beginning with the king's departure for Milan.

So d'Auton is also a poet on occasion.[35] The poem he has written does not narrate: prose has narrated for over two hundred pages. The poem seeks to immortalize the agent of victory, to give him his due place in history; it monumentalizes, whereas prose runs the risk of only locating him in the flow of history.[36]

So, the goal is history. But the goal of history here is to a great extent commemoration. To commit to memory is to commit to repetition. Commemoration is already part of a structure of rememoration, repetition, rehearsal, and all that goes with it. History-writing as unqualified praise entails history-making as clear-cut deed, the res gestae to which one testifies. This is the past as performance values it, and the mere dropping of verse will not leave the signifying practice of performance totally behind if such values persist.

It will also be noted that d'Auton's poem is not continuous with the prose text: it appears here by way of citation, with a clear indication that it existed in writing before being presented to Louis. The same goes for the Latin inscriptions laid out along the journey. This is not a disruption or interruption of the prose, as it would be were this a true versiprosa text. D'Auton's poem can be seen as an early instance of postprose verse, in that verse is now a precious object within prose.

Where is this insistence on presence coming from? It appears to be a last remnant of speech and performance, but it was not a problem for the jongleur, who was a stand-in for universal presence. D'Auton's presence is part of his gathering of fragmentary evidence in the construction of a referent. And he credits such presence and proximity with whatever immanence he gains with respect to the historical material. The more immanence he has, the more transcendence he will get from it. The aim is for the audience to gain the impression that it is the recipient of an immediate, rather than mediated, semiotic matter, to which it is compelled to give its assent.[37] However, d'Auton runs the risk of blocking transcendence because of the opacity of his presence. We will now look at a historian who knows how to write from within the historical event. He also knows how to establish his credit by discounting his personal involvement. He knows how to duck, how to get himself out of the way. He knows when and how to use this immanence for the kind of transcendence he takes as appropriate to an understanding of the course of history.

Philippe de Commynes (1447?-1511) played a major role in the struggles between the king of France and Charles Duke of Burgundy. He started on the Burgundian side as a result of feudal obligations, and eventually wound up counselor to the king. Having thus seen and participated in the events on both sides, he was asked by Angelo Cato, the archbishop of Vienne, to write his memoirs, which stand as a striking achievement in the history of historical prose.

Commynes's own role in the events was extremely controversial and indeed resulted at one time in his imprisonment. (Such are the risks of having your presence overly opaque.) It could thus be expected that he would avail himself of the occasion of his *Mémoires* to exonerate himself from all accusations and to provide a credible (not to say laudable) rationale for all his actions. But his *Mémoires* are no *apologia pro vita sua*. (This is not to say that the *Mémoires* are not self-serving: they are very self-serving but not in the rhetoric of apology.) Commynes endeavors to put us in the very midst of history rather than at a judgmental distance from it. As we have seen in d'Auton, the biggest obstacle to success in such a project is the historian's "self."

That Commynes has been able in great measure to overcome this obstacle is no doubt owing, at least in part, to his experience as a diplomat, not only between King and Duke but also between neighboring states. Having carried out numerous missions at a time of intense bargaining and routine double-crossing,[38] his activities as a whole reveal only a shadowy figure. Many of his missions are not referred to in any of his writings, and the extent to which we are aware of some of them has depended on other fragmentary and suggestive sources. While in diplomatic service, his ability to efface himself is particularly striking in his purposefully unsigned dispatches and reports; his signed messages are accompanied by his request that they be destroyed immediately after reading. He knows the special value of untraceable information.

His duties as a writer of memoirs are carried out in similar self-effacement. He speaks of events that he has clearly witnessed, but his presence as a witness is rarely openly thematized. He is in the retinue of the duke or of the king. There is, for example, a Council of War taking place, and he is clearly part of it, but his role is given as minimal. Then a secret conversation has been arranged, yet we do not know who has arranged it, even though we may well surmise, on the basis of the details that are given to us, that the suggestion may have emanated from him and that he served as the go-between.

The reluctance on Commynes's part to indicate his role in a historical action is not just a gesture of modesty; it is more part and parcel of his view of history and of the mode of its proper representation. His approach is not to focus on actions that somehow constitute epiphanies of history or on the agents of such actions. Rather, we get an endless and prosaic process of receiving information, evaluating it, obtaining advice from advisers and other parties of political weight, and drifting toward decisions of uncertain outcome. Prowess and other heroics are occasionally demonstrated, and there are the requisite formulas of praise from time to time, but there are no unalloyed heroes here, no one capable of seizing the bit of history and bringing it to a halt or launching it in the direction of his or her choice. Commynes's understanding of the limitations placed on individuals at that time and place is underscored by the emphasis (new at the time) that he gives to the more impersonal factors in war: geography, topography, and the increasing use of artillery.

There are hardly any agents, for no one is capable of conceiving of a complete action that can be successfully carried out from beginning to end. There are too many variables, too many imponderables. The very events and the forces that constitute them are shrouded in indeterminacy. The two courts, including their putative leaders, operate in the realm of uncertainty. Their followers are often in a state of confusion about the broader stakes and directions and thus frequently pursue personal and more immediate goals that wreak havoc with any attempt to constitute more global policies. The text reads as the crisp apprehension of details, but all must be weighed, nothing taken at face value. And yet, in the midst of all this, things do happen, history is made, although no one can reasonably take credit for it. History, agency, is not localized in any one individual or group: it is not substantial.

Why is history so seemingly complex now? There were always conflicts, always ruses, always negotiations. Up to this time, they were local conflicts, upon which one can focus one at a time. But the move by the king to establish a state over which he would exercise a new kind of sovereignty now calls for consideration of the *totality of local conflicts*. In other words, there is someone who wants to be in control of the whole process but who operates by means of local conflicts (e.g., playing one baron against another). Although the king's attacks seem to be against one local sovereign or another, they are more broadly and profoundly attacks against the notion of a sovereignty that can be decided only locally, between and among localities.

One has a situation in which there is too much information, the effects and pertinence of which remain to a great extent undetermined. Commynes brings to this situation an outlook that seeks not to master history but to make sense of it, that is, to see the instability and flux of events, to understand the direction of their flow, and to formulate the mode of one's participation in them, thereby exercising a different kind of agency based on such understanding. (One primary mode is a particularly fluid one: among these historical figures, Commynes is a wielder and an adjudicator of *influence,* in a world governed to a great extent by influence.)[39] The complexity of the historical process as flux is frequently thematized at this time as magnitude so overgrown and proliferation so unchecked that no distance is possible. Consequently, the shape of what is is indeterminate. Prose is clearly associated with these phenomena, as we will illustrate with a brief look at another versiprosa text by Molinet.

"Overgrowth" and "proliferation" are not our terms, not critical *trouvailles:* they are used, by the Grands Rhétoriqueurs and those around them, as one concept in a journey to self-understanding. Images such as the overgrown tree are prevalent at the time, in the works of Alain Chartier, Christine de Pisan, and Charles d'Orléans. This tree is likely to bring on its own demise through, for example, the weight of its fruit, or the sheer number of its leaves and branches. The Grands Rhétoriqueurs have brought this proliferation to the surface in their own style, which has usually been condemned in botanical terms, as "overgrown," "luxuriant," "in need of pruning," and has been the principal reason for the marginalization of their work in current canons. The text, like the tree, cannot be "contained," is out of "control."

In chapter 4, we mentioned that these writers were experimenting with forms, so excess itself is to be anticipated. Their "excess" in verse is easy to characterize, with its richness of rhymes, anagrams, wordplay, and so forth. That is, excess in form is still form: one has only to refine the taxonomy of one's poetics and critics will be mollified. Excess in prose is less easily recuperated.

Molinet's "L'Arbre de Bourgonne Sus La Mort du Duc Charles" (1486) is a versiprosa text, alternating four prose and four verse sections. We will look at the first two sections.

Il n'a pas dix ans que au tres fructueux et opulent vignoble de Bourgonne flourissoit ung gros arbre de admirable altitude, fort aorné de precieuses vertus, par lesquelles non seulement le jardin, mais la maison, le court et tout l'heritaige en furent grandement famés; sa haulteur attaindoit les nues, sa parfondeur perchoit les terres, sa rondeur obumbroit les champs, son odeur tresperchoit les mers et de faict estendoit ses palmes et raincheaux sy avant sus les limites de ses voisins que ceux ne le pooient tiller; souvent se mirent en paine de l'esbrancher, mais tousjours multiplyoient nouveaux jettons, pourquoy les dictz voysins, doubtans en fin d'avoir leurs possessions occupees par succession de temps, jetterent leur regard vers les corps celestiaux, prians aux dieux par vive affection de coeur qu'i les vaulsissent delivrer de ce fort puissant et gros arbre, car s'il perseveroit en grandeur, il auroit preeminence sus les plus haultz de ce monde et pour ce qu'il donnoit refection aux famileux, recreance aux coeurs desolés, protection aux envaÿs et asseurance aux espantés, plusseurs gentilz pastoureaux et nobles bergeronnettes s'estoient logiés soubz ses ramyers, lesquelz, comme luy, croissoient, flourissoient et fructifioient en honneur, loenge et vertus. Les dieux, assés records et bien memoratifz comment anchïennement les fors geans avoient accumulé montaignes les unes sus les aultres, pour les voloir expuser de leurs trosnes, legierement se consentirent aux requestes des supplians et donnerent la commission du faict a Mars, le grand dieu des batailles, et a Vulcanus, le dieu du feu, marissal de l'ost de Juppiter, lesquelz tellement exploicterent par une longue nuyt d'hiver que, par force de feu, de flaïaux, de ferailles, de fulminations, de fouldres et de grandes tempestes, ce hault arbre fut abbatu, brisiet et reversé par terre, ensemble plusseurs pastoureaux assommés de crueux tonnoirres, dont la perte fut lamentable et dommageuse et angoisseuse aux nobles coeurs. Se ce tres hault et puissant arbre s'eust vollut ou daigniet fleschir, ainsi que font plusseurs jongz et roseaux qui ploient a tous vens, espoir qu'i eust evité ce terrificque et mortel oraige, mais il avoit le coeur sy vif, le troncq sy dur et l'escorche si ferme que luy ne ses branches fort roides ne se voloient jamés ploier, car tant plus avoit grande attainte, tant plus estoit percus des vens. Aucuns bons pellerins, voiant ceste pitoiable destruction, considerans la sublimité de tel fort sumptueux chief d'oeuvre tant soudainement tresbuchié, ne polrent contenir leurs larmes, qui, vaincus de compassion, amerement le regretoient, le regrettant souspiroient, le souspirant plouroient, et en plourant proferoient ce qui s'ensuit:

> Cy gist la fleur de roial parentaige,
> L'arbre d'honneur, de vertus le plantaige,
> L'ardant raincheau, espris de hault pretendre,
> Qui, non content de son propre heritaige,
> Gaigna la mort par soy trop loing estendre.

> C'est le flaïau qui fut par ses explois
> Terreur des Frans, refuge des Anglois,
> Extermineur des Liegois rebellans,
> Dont on cremoit plus enfraindre les lois
> Que d'aborder entre dragons vollans.

> Cy gist l'escut de Bourgonne anoyeuse,
> Son grand posteau, sa lance vertueuse,
> Son chier tresor, le salut du païs,
> Qui de sa perte est trop plus angoisseuse
> Que aultre cent mille ayant coeurs esbahis.

> Ce sont les yeux qui bien peu sommeilloient,
> Mains, bouche, voix qui sauldars resveilloient,
> Poings, jambes, pieds, qui d'armes se parerent,
> Coeur, vaines, sang, qui fort se traveilloient,
> Pour gloire avoir et a cop trebucherent.

> Cy gist le picq qui roches trespercha,
> L'air esclarcy, les fleuves estancha,
> Pierres fendyt, le terre fist crouller,
> Puis au meilleu d'autruy champ tresbucha,
> Par trop voloir haultain bruit accoller.

> C'est le bourdon agu de toutes tailles,
> Ducteur des ostz, assembleur des batailles,
> L'effroy d'Europe, armigere puissant,
> Qui ne admiroit feu, ne fer, ne fustailles,
> Ne riens qui fust trop chault ne trop pesant.

> Cy gist l'estocq de noblesse et l'afficque,
> Poing de justice et maillet terrificque,
> Rainceau de foy, tres devot christïen,

Qui tint estat et court plus magnificque,
Que nul vivant, tant fust grand terrïen.

C'est le batton de proesse esprouvé,
Second Hector, Hannibal retrouvé,
Vray Alexandre et Scipion d'Aufricque,
De qui le nom vif doit estre eslevé
Entre les preux de ce mondain fabricque.

Cy gist sans peur le gentil conquerant,
Le champion, grands triumphes querant,
Qui de regner avoit tel appetit
Que, s'il euist vescut en prosperant,
Le monde grand luy estoit trop petit.

Cy gist le corps pour qui dix mille testes,
Autant de bras et de gens et de bestes,
Sont desrompus en portant son grand fais;
Dieu, qui cognoist des haulx princes les gestes,
Le mette en gloire et pardoint ses meffais.[40]

Not ten years ago in the very fruitful and rich vineyard of Burgundy, there flourished a large tree of remarkable height, adorned with precious virtues, and which brought great reputation not only upon the garden but upon the house, the court, and indeed upon the entire line as well; its height reached the clouds; its depth pierced the earth; its roundness shaded the fields; its perfume crossed the seas; in fact it extended its limbs and boughs so far over the boundaries of its neighbors that they could not bear it, and they often attempted to prune it, but new shoots multiplied nonetheless. Therefore the neighbors, fearing that their possessions would ultimately be overtaken, turned their eyes to the heavens and prayed the gods from the bottom of their hearts to deliver them from this powerful and large tree, for if it went on growing it would reduce the preeminence of those on high in this world, and also because it gave nourishment to the famished, restored the faith of the broken-hearted, protected the assaulted and reassured the frightened, some gentle shepherds and noble shepherdesses took up residence under its branches, and like it, grew, flourished and multiplied in honor, praise, and virtue. The gods, still mindful of how once mighty giants had piled up mountains one upon the other in order to evict them from their thrones, readily acceded to the request of the supplicants and commissioned Mars, the great god of battles, and Vulcan, the god of fire and marshall of Jupiter's army, to carry out this task. The latter performed such deeds one winter night that, by the powers of the gods, and by means of flails, shot, lightning, thunderbolts, and big storms, this high tree was felled, broken, and knocked to the ground, together with several shepherds stunned by cruel thunder, whose loss was deplorable, damaging, and anxiety-provoking to noble hearts. Had this high and mighty tree wanted, or deigned, to bend as do various rushes and reeds that twist in the wind, it would hopefully have avoided this terrible and deadly storm, but it had such a quick heart, such a hard trunk, such a solid bark that it never wanted to bend its very straight branches, and the greater its reach, the more it was battered by the winds. Some good pilgrims, seeing this pitiable destruction, and considering the sublimeness of such a magnificent masterpiece being brought down so suddenly, could not hold back their tears and, overcome with compassion, bitterly regretted it, regretfully sighed, sighfully shed tears, and tearfully proffered what follows:

Here lies the flower of royal lineage,
The tree of honor, the stalk of virtues,
The ardent stem, given to high claims,
That, not satisfied with its own inheritance,
Received death for overextending itself.

It was the source that, through its deeds,
Was the terror of the French, the refuge of the English,
The exterminator of the rebellious people of Lièges,
Whose laws one feared to contravene more
Than land among flying dragons.

Here lies the shield of troublesome Burgundy,
Its great staff, its virtuous lance,
Its dear treasure, the salvation of the land,
And Burgundy is more anguished by its loss
Than by that of a hundred thousand gaping hearts.

These are eyes that slept but little;
Hand, mouth, and voice that woke up soldiers;
Fists, legs, and feet that dressed in armor;
Heart, veins, and blood that labored mightily
To gain glory, and suddenly they fell.

Here lies the pickax that broke through rock;
That cleared the air and dammed the rivers;
That split stones and moved the earth;
And then, in the middle of someone else's field, it fell,
For having wanted to reach too high a fame.

It is the sharp-pitched great bell,
Leader of armies, master of battlefields,
The alarm of Europe, mighty war-maker,
Who feared neither fire, nor lead, nor ordnance,
Nor anything however hot or heavy.

Here lies the sword and mattock of nobility,
The ironfist and terrible hammer of justice,
The stalk of faith, a very devout Christian,
Who ruled over a state and held a court more magnificent
Than anyone alive, so great a lord of the land was he.

It is the proven staff of courage,
A second Hector, a Hannibal born anew,
The true Alexander and Scipio Africanus in one,
Whose living name must be raised high
Among the valiant of this worldly contrivance.

Here lies fearless the gentle conqueror,
The champion questing for great triumphs,
Who had such an appetite for reigning
That had he lived and prospered,
The great wide world would have been too small for him.

Here lies the body for which ten thousand heads,
And as many arms and people and animals
Were broken in carrying his great weight.
May God who knows the deeds of high princes
Grant him his glory and forgive him his misdeeds.

The question we will discuss is simple: why does the text move from prose to verse? The prose describes the tree as undergoing a continual metamorphosis, as constantly growing, as everywhere. How can this tree be described when it is difficult to establish a distance with respect to it? The difficulty is one of encompassing it: from where do you perceive it? Are you under it, over it, beyond its edges? If you describe it from the circumference, do you risk losing its heart? And this spatial problem is completely at one with the temporal problem: it is growing all the time and must be described in its growth. So it must be described from disparate perspectives. It is itself unstable.

Prose can handle this immanence, this flux. The tree threatens those who have staked out ground (the neighbors, the gods); no place is safe from encroachment, it is just about everywhere. (Prose does not stake out ground and stand apart, so it can live with the tree.) The gods see themselves threatened as if by the Titans, but it could just as easily have been the threat of Babel: how to hold in check reproductive powers and the discourses they increasingly produce? The tree must be cut down to size.

The tree is destroyed. Thereafter, it is but a ruin, it grows no more. It is reduced not only in its glory but also in its visual problematics: it can be taken in in one glance, it can be encompassed. It can now be understood in its transcendental dimension, it can be given a final utterance, it can be spoken of and named. Molinet will not have prose do so. He will use prose to bring us to the moment for naming (it will literally "clear the ground") and then have prose cede to verse: the bulwark against any unchecked growth, the procrustean bed. A clear retreat in the development of historiography as we have unfolded it.

So Molinet will call in utterers, brought in just for the occasion: pilgrims. To the pilgrims will be the naming. To the verse will be the naming. For here is an utterance as staged, here is a consecration, a dedication. Having passed from the flux of its historical situation, from the prose, the tree is fit to be known. In the flux, you lose the possibility of transcendence. Molinet cannot sustain the prose when transcendence is called for. Verse operates here because the move is from immanence to transcendence, and it dubs the tree a monument, transcending its place and time, immanent now only as monument, that is, offering its transcendent dimension unequivocally, univocally, knowable finally as "Burgundy."

But this is history as postmortem. The pilgrims arrive too late. The tree cannot be revived materially, it can only be revived formally, through a generation of metaphors. (The later parts of text will recount attempts at regrafting.) Or *is* it too late?

Verse does not see it as too late. The longer the distance, the more fit for commemoration, the more monumental the verse. For verse, the lateness permits the erection of a transcendent stance vis-à-vis the object, enhances the formulatability of the description, *perfects* the naming. D'Auton also comes to the ruin, as did the pilgrims. But his is a lateness he does not desire, and cannot overcome, in spite of having dropped the verse. Although not a versifier, he is nonetheless a pilgrim, come to commemorate in praise and to praise through commemoration. To this extent, Molinet's use of prose to describe the tree might be considered as merely preparatory to the historical move seen in the verse naming. Historical interest is going to change, however, and it will manage to stay in prose, focused upon the tree: inchoate, ever-changing, and imperfect. These aspects cannot be recounted from a dominant position only: they demand a position *subject to* the tree, where the tree quite simply extends beyond the grasp. From the epic consciousness seeing history in a distant past, history becomes a dimension of people's lives now.

But then, what dimension does it have? Traditional modes of transmission are put under strain because their kinds of distance, dominance, transcendence, form, verse, appear inappropriate now. When history is seen as treating objects that extend beyond the grasp, objects that one must operate within, objects that find a good deal of their *raison* in perplexity, objects whose effective *mesure* is unavoidable *démesure,* thus objects over which the consistent establishment of a dominant position, a position of pronouncement and commemoration would be impossible, meaningless, or just too late—when the historical object (here, the tree, a *matière* in the process of formation and formulation) is seen in this way, history will remain with prose. Prose will be able to incorporate such change.[41]

A transcendental position from which to view and judge this proliferation and flux, which Molinet seeks and for which he appeals to verse, appears to Commynes as untenable and undesirable inasmuch as it withdraws one from history while it happens. *Nous sommes tous embarqués,* we are all in the same boat. No one, even Archimedes, can stand outside history, whether close or far (Le Bel, d'Auton), and therefore it behooves us to understand *where* we stand *in* the historical process, where it makes room for us or how we secure a niche for ourselves, where it is going, and how it can be made to work for us.[42] This restricted form of transcendence which remains bounded by human finiteness, is what Molinet does not want to, or cannot, find for himself in the tree, yet it is what Commynes attempts to establish in history.

Molinet's predicament is that the unchecked proliferation and growth of the tree prevents any sort of naming from tasking place. Words ares designed to designate entities, as far as Molinet is concerned, and before they are applied one must be certain that the boundaries of the entities are set. Once the boundaries are set—*the encounter can be staged between the knowing subject and the object to be cognized*—the object can be simply seen and said. For that, verse is fully adequate. The deep-seated critique of verse by the early Prosateurs is at least as epistemological as it is formal or strictly referential, to the extent that verse has characterized (within performance) the language in which such knowing encounters have been recounted.

Commynes will indicate the limits of this practice: in his history, the task is not to construct cognitive situations, wherein the flux is arrested so that an object can be constituted for a knowing subject (turning d'Auton's trace into fullness), but to efface the subject, so that the flux underlying the objects can come to the fore, thereby allowing access to the objects. One makes sense of historical flux by managing referential indeterminacies and cognitive uncertainties, so that they are oriented in the direction of the flow. What you're reading is differences, not substances. "Au fort, il me semble que Dieu n'a créé en ce monde ny homme ny beste à qui il n'ayt fait quelque chose son contraire pour le tenir en humilité et en craincte" (All things considered, it seems to me that God has created neither man nor beast in this world without establishing some counterpart to oppose him, in order to keep him in humility and fear).[43] Different things complement each other. One must go beyond the parts to the relations between counterparts. Substances are negotiated on their own margins.

As events unfold, the king or the duke (take your choice: they are really variables, that is why in Commynes's line of work you can easily play the game from either side) is called upon to make decisions. He has a need to know what is going on because competing rumors circulate. Advisers are summoned and asked to provide their evaluation of the unfolding situation, which takes the form of competing naming claims. The partiality, fragmentariness, and competitiveness of these claims effectively denies them the status of a transcendence. To the actual flux of events there corresponds a flux of discourses. The historical referent is thus doubly indeterminate, in its very nature and in its representation. But to Commynes this situation does not call for resolution, a final pronouncement that would have to be his own and, thus, in which he would be forced to stage *himself* as the knowing subject who takes the floor and *speaks* or who writes as if speaking: to do so would be to stage everything and lose "prosaic" history. (Therefore, as Jean Dufournet, a reader of Commynes, says when referring to decisions made at court, "Commynes ne se prononce pas" [Commynes makes no pronouncement, Commynes does not commit himself].)[44] Nor does this indeterminate situation constitute an aporetic one in which one ought to throw up one's hands and surrender to the nonsensicality of the world. On the contrary: it provides cognitive as well as political opportunity. Information needs to be managed, but it should be weighed and balanced in doses of certainty and uncertainty, with every shade in between.

Commynes will leave opposing opinions standing, often without even indicating their accuracy in retrospect; he will leave questions unresolved, although we sense that he personally would have considerable light to shed on them. (Maybe he means us to sense that.) He will draw in other discourses, other subjects, *porte-paroles,* so that the commitment is not his. Even with the words of other subjects, *Commynes will rarely couch them in represented speech* (this in dramatic contrast with his contemporaries) because of all that such speech implies in terms of a final knowing and pronouncement.[45]

For example, in the *Mémoires* the suggestion is made that the king was profligate in his donations to the church. Dufournet points out that Commynes does not himself suggest it. The *Mémoires* go as follows:

De grandes offrandes faisoit et trop, à l'advis de l'arcevesque de Tours, homme de saincte et bonne vie, cordelier et cardinal, lequel, avec plusieurs au[l]tres choses, luy escripvit qu'il luy vouldroit myeulx hoster l'argent aux chanoynes des eglises, où il faisoit ses grans dons, et le departir aux povres laboureurs et aultres qui paient ces grans tailles, que de lever sur ceulx-là pour le donner aux riches eglises et aux riches chanoynes ou il le donnoit.[46]

He made great gifts—too many for the archbishop of Tours, a man of good and holy life, a Franciscan and a cardinal, who, among other things, wrote him that it would be better to take money from the canons of the churches to which he was making these large gifts, and to distribute it to poor farmers and others charged with heavy taxes, rather than levying these taxes upon them in order to give the money to the rich churches and the rich canons to whom he was giving it.

Then, in a dispositive move, shifting discourse again, to one of "fact," Commynes will follow this "opinion" with a long enumeration of the gifts given, as if proving the archibishop's (not Commynes's) point.[47] Clearly, Commynes's way of writing history does not eliminate the possibility of his serving his own interests: in reality, it offers particularly underhanded possibilities. It is just that it allows him to be self-serving without serving up himself.

Frequently, God is invoked. This usually occurs at the point where a rendering of a situation comes to its term, and one feels that Commynes has dissected the situation and showed the limits inherent in all those involved. God is said to be the mover of last resort, that which truly determines the course of history, but if He has *influence* it is not in evidence: for the mortals, it is too late. God is a means of termination: as such, and like the verse that *Acteur* must speak at the end of the *Ressource* and which the pilgrims speak in the *Arbre,* his invocation is antiprosaic. At the end of book 1, for example, Commynes will say:

> Mais, tout bien regardé, nostre seulle esperance doit estre en Dieu, car en cestuy-là gist toute nostre fermeté et toute bonté, qui en nulle chose de ce monde ne se pourroit trouver; mais chascun de nous le congnoist tard, et après ce que en avons eu besoing. Toutesfois vault encores myeulx tard que jamais.

> But, all things being considered, our sole hope should be in God, for in Him lies our security and good fortune which cannot be found in any worldly thing. But each one of us recognizes this too late and after we have had need from Him. Yet it is better late than never![48]

Is it? This we will have to take on Commynes's *word.* As far as his actions are concerned, however, as far as the kind of history that Commynes has chosen to record for us, God *is* too late.[49]

A text that invokes Him escapes at that point the mechanisms of immanence and transcendence because God's transcendence operates in a totally different realm. Commynes is always saying "toutesfois je ne sçay pas de vray" (however, I do not know the truth of it) about one thing or another, but when he approaches the end of a given treatment, as the text seems to call for a kind of transcendence that his prosaic managing cannot achieve, because this kind of transcendence is not what he is aiming for, he truly "does not know"—he truly has nothing more to write. Like the *Arbre*, prose presumably has staged, brought us to, a knowing situation. Rather than pilgrims who enter to see, it is God who comes in, because only God sees, only God knows. Unlike the pilgrims, however, God does not *say*, and the transcendence he can offer functions not as a culmination to but rather in a relationship of exclusion from his historian's work.

God marks a threshold, which can only be invoked, not crossed. God stands for the capacity of cognitive reach to achieve fulfillment, but invocations of Him, occurring when they do, show this threshold as one beyond which it is only God who plies His trade, not the historian. He is invoked to hold out to us the promise of a fulfilled cognition, but that is the same moment when our success at fulfillment is revealed to be but partial. His invocation functions as a limit to the kind of understanding we can hope to achieve: He is here a closural device; a closural device of the kind prose needs, paradigmatic of what prose must do to close.

Because prose appears to leave situations undominated, unfinalized, and unknown, it immediately has a problem with closure. Having no form as such, prose can only approach closure but cannot, as prose, put it forward. It might be said that prose does not close but must delegate the task, by investing in one discourse at its end, and it is that discourse which closes, which marks the margin, for example, the discourse of invocation (here with Commynes), of prayer and return of an agent (at the end of the *Ressource*), of epitaph (with the *Arbre de Bourgonne*). As we have seen, verse is the richest source to which prose turns, when faced with the need to close.

Without edges or margins, what does prose look like? As its stance is to extend beyond what it contains, what is *its* shape? A piece of prose is like a *swatch* of fabric. By examining it one can see its particular fashion of fitting things together or juxtaposing them, such as how one color or pattern serves as a background for another. But its edges are ragged and unfinished; it is to be understood as extending beyond them. Although in fact not infinite, a swatch has no border. A border must be imposed upon it by something other than itself.

This is why prose cannot really be cited, at least in small segments: it comes out as just discourse. Walter Benjamin has suggested that the modern novel marks its close in a partial, oblique way, we would say in a typically prose way, with a penetrating comment by some character about something heretofore unnoticed in the text, not happening there at the close but having already happened, an insight that makes us look back and maybe read again.[50] Not a final gesture but a little touch, a backward glance at what was already seen and said, a simple backstitch.

A resort to such indirect devices is what we would expect from a signifying practice that leaves situations unfinalized. As we turn away from this digression on closure in prose and back to Commynes, let us remember that history is now also unfinalized, never closed to another backward glance. Once history has come to include us, once we have entered into it, we cannot mark its ending. To do so is to remove ourselves from within it. And we have seen that prose allows no such final outside position.

That "Commynes ne se prononce pas" is all the more astounding because his real role at the time, which he is recounting, was precisely that of an adjudicator of advisers, that of an *opinion giver,* a councillor with the same status as the prose Conseil in the *Ressource.* Commynes is "silent" in the very arena in which his competence was exercised, and exercised so successfully that he was stolen by the competition. Let us more closely examine his change of sides.

Commynes starts out as the duke's man. The position of his fiefdom, his family history, the system of alliances in which he has entered, all compel him in that direction. He achieves a high position in the retinue of the duke, and then occurs what is perceived to be a baffling development on the part of an individual who has apparently shown little desire for personal gain or opportunism in a world in which such ambitions are more the rule than the exception: he unexpectedly becomes the king's man. Of course, he *says* almost nothing about this. (We can see, however, how it enhances what he says as a historian: to be a valued adviser to either man, he had to constantly shift perspective to that of the other side, anyway. So the switch was probably not difficult at all.)[51]

This shift of allegiance must be understood in the context of Commynes's own conception of history, based on flux and on the inevitability of certain directions, irrespective of figure or tradition. To remain on the duke's side must have appeared to him as a sterile attempt to arrest history. The king, he ascertained, represented the future of history. Commynes provides here a vision of the transcendental that can inform judgment, decision, and action insofar as action has become *knowing how to be positioned.* His abilities allow him to reject the eddies and ride the currents, while he looks beyond figures to history itself, "Mais j'ay peu veü de gens en ma vie qui sachent fouyr à temps, ne cy ni ailleurs"[52] (I have seen few people in my life, either here or elsewhere, who knew how to flee at the right time). He is not, of course, referring to himself.

Commynes is always evoking past historical experience in recounting the actions of those before him. He has the gift of seeing history in the making. As a result, he can give us history as an understanding of the past that is *constantly present* (thus not invisible) *but not constant.* A historian, Commynes would say, not only can but must be in at least two places at once. D'Auton *is* too late.

Latin prose was becoming increasingly elaborate at this time, but, as we previously mentioned, there were countervailing forces at work. In the seventh century, Gregory Bishop of Tours developed a *simplex* but worthy style.[53] In response to those who would criticize his "uncouth" style, he says in the preface to his hagiographic work:

> Opus vestrum facio et per meam rusticitatem vestram prudentiam exercebo. Nam, ut opinor, unum beneficiem vobis haec scripta praebebunt, scilicet ut, quod nos inculte et breviter stilo nigrante describimus, vos lucide ac splendide stante versu in paginis prolixioribus dilatetis.

> I do the same work as you, and by my very roughness will provide matter for your skill. For, as I think, these writings will bring you one benefit, namely, that what we describe rudely and abruptly in our turgid style you may enlarge in verse standing clearly and sumptuously in more ample pages.[54]

And at the end of the *History of the Franks,* he says to those who have such skills: "[I]f in all this you are practiced so that my style will seem rude, even so I beg of you do not efface what I have written. But if anything in these books pleases you I do not forbid your writing it in verse providing my work is left safe."[55] Gregory invites a versifying of his writing, in line with the practice of parapharse to which we alluded earlier in this chapter, but he also clearly holds to the standing of his prose as such. It is his writing that provides for versification and, even if reworked, should be kept safe. So that whereas this is an early example of apologizing for a prose that is not verse, it is an apology with a second edge: do with my rude writing what you will, he says, but do not eliminate anything: it has value even in its rudeness. If something pleases *you,* he suggests to his readers, *you* can put it in verse. *You* construct the knowing situation. This kind of writing can be reused. It stands outside your verse.

In his prologue to *Mémoires,* Commynes states that what he has written is only that which has sprung quickly to his mind, and that his reader, the archbishop, may want to put it in Latin. (Commynes was apparently not proficient in Latin).[56]

> Toutesfois ne pretendz e.n riens ,. .en le louant en cet endroit, diminuer l'honneur ne bonne renommée des aultres, mais vous envoye ce dont promptement m'est souvenu, esperant que vous le demandez pour le mectre en quelque oeuvre que vous avez l'intention de faire en langue latine dont vous estes bien usité; par laquelle oeuvre se pourra congnois-

tre la grandeur du prince duquel vous parleray, et aussi de vostre entendement.

Nevertheless, I do not claim in praising him [King Louis] here to detract
at all from the honour or good name of others, but send you a record
of that which sprang promptly to my mind, hoping you asked for this
in order to put it into a work which you have planned to write in Latin,
which you do so proficiently. This work will demonstrate the greatness
of this prince of whom I tell you, and also your own learning.

It was actually translated into Latin in 1545.

Commynes finds himself in the following position: the request from the
archbishop provides him with the opportunity to write something that is unfinished, open-ended, and subject to revision, reconstrual, and rewriting. Commynes's writing, therefore, need not concern itself with form because, as form
can be imposed on it at a later stage, it is positioned at an earlier stage. Commynes couches his work as raw material in its relation to finished form. In
fact, in relation to that "form," it will be "matter." And the form that is to
come may be the Latin of Commynes's archbishop, but it could just as easily
be the verse of Gregory's readers or, indeed, any other form of *hoche Sprache*
or *Kunstprosa*.

Montaigne follows the same strategy in stating that if he thought his prose
Essais were worth saving, he would have written them in Latin. We recognize
this as a topos of affected modesty, but, at a time of shift in signifying practice,
it is much more than that. It is the negotiation of the niche that the new signifying practice of prose will inhabit among other vernacular and learned signifying practices. It is specifically a *distinguo:* "I write of things other than that
of which High Latin writes." Of what does he write? In his prologue, *Au
Lecteur*, he states that *he* is the simple matter of his book and sends the reader
elsewhere if he or she is looking for something more elaborate:

> Si c'eust esté pour rechercher la faveur du monde, je me fusse mieux
> paré et me presenterois en une marche estudiée. Je veus qu'on m'y
> voie en ma façon simple, naturelle et ordinaire, sans contantion et arti-
> fice: car c'est moy que je peins. . . . Que si j'eusse esté entre ces na-
> tions qu'on dict vivre encore sous la douce liberté des premieres loix
> de nature, je t'asseure que je m'y fusse très-volontiers peint tout entier,
> et tout nud. Ainsi, lecteur, je suis moy-mesmes la matière de mon livre:
> ce n'est pas raison que tu employes ton loisir en un subject si frivole
> et si vain. A Dieu donq.

> Were it to have been to seek the favor of the world, I would have made
> myself up better, and presented myself with a studied gait. I want to
> be seen in my simple, natural and ordinary fashion, with neither strug-
> gle nor artifice: for it is I that I paint. . . . Had I been among those

nations said to live still in the sweet freedom of the first laws of nature,
I assure you that I would have quite willingly depicted myself completely, and completely naked. Thus, reader, I am myself the matter
of my book: no reason then for you to use your leisure on such a frivo-
lous and vain subject. Farewell then.

The *matière* of this book, Montaigne tells us, is "tout nu." Exterior adornment
and studied gait ("marche estudiée") entertain a relationship to his simple
vernacular prose (*prorsa*, "going straightforwardly") analogous to that of "ar
tifice" to rude *matière*.

"I will play matter to your form"—this will be the position that prose will
come to occupy with respect to other signifying practices. Here, in response
to the accusation that it is amorphous, prose will find a ready reply: "I am
not yet form." This may seem to be a subordinate position, an invitation that
form be imposed upon it, but in fact it is a very powerful one. As we read
Commynes's vernacular prose, that of Montaigne, and on and on, we understand that this reply functions more precisely to locate the position in which
prose can stand *alone* and from which prose can claim a certain priority
by virtue of a lack of secondary elaboration, rendering itself immune to the
critiques addressed to both the jongleur and the written verse as inadequate
modes of representation.

Since the critiques addressed to it in the twelfth century, written verse
has been construed as a form in problematic relationship to its content. No
longer grounded in the organic environment of the signifying practice of performance and limited to being seen as empty form, as "versification," verse
is in need of something that will stand under it, that will *underwrite* it. Verse
will take the signifying practice of prose, which now asserts its hegemony,
as a substitute for performance, but it, and ultimately all of us, will not take
prose as a signifying practice in its own right. That is prose's subterfuge: not
to be recognized for what it is but for the way things are. Verse will take
prose as matter to its form. And in such a world, if history is not to be construed
as imposing a form, then it must be an attempt to give us the world in its
prosaic state. The request of Yolande, with which this book started, was specifically one for a prose *history*. With Commynes and beyond, the relationship between prose and history is cemented.

Not only verse and history but also other signifying practices and the culture as a whole will take prose as matter to any form, matter irrespective of
form, matter prior to all form. What this means is that the signifying practice
of prose is now achieving both its autonomy and its genuine hegemony by
invading all forms and making them dependent upon itself. All these forms
can no longer conceive of an existence without prose. They are in a world
now understood and accepted as prosaic.

Chapter 8
Prose Fiction

In the winter of 1984, one of us witnessed an oral performance in a small village, some 60 kilometers north of Dakar, the capital of Senegal. The performance was in Wolof, the vernacular language of the vast majority of Senegal's population, even though the Wolof, as an ethnic group, are but a significant minority among the officially recognized ethnicities. The village itself was a Sereer village, the second largest ethnic group, but the griot gave his performance in Wolof, which is the vernacular *lingua franca*. Our interpreter, a member of the Hassounke group (one of the smaller ethnic groups, which inhabits northern Senegal, southern Mauritania, and eastern Mali) grew quite agitated during the performance, an agitation he later characterized as outrage at what the griot was doing: apparently the griot had introduced a Hassounke hero into a Wolof tale without indicating that he was doing anything of the sort, indeed, treating it as a matter of course. Later on in the tale, the griot went further, attributing to a Wolof hero feats that were characteristic of, and proper to, the Hassounke hero. The interpreter was quite shocked at such a procedure, which he described in terms of cultural appropriation and Hassounke genocide. The Sereer audience had no such qualms and apparently raised no objection when the griot included some of their ethnic material in his talk.

Folklorists and anthropologists have studied these types of performance, of course, and have proposed such terms as "acculturation" and "syncretism" for its apprehension. Literary scholars have been less attentive to them, and it may be worthwhile to dwell a little upon them, especially to better understand the divergent reactions of the Sereer inhabitants of the village and that of the Hassounke interpreter. To the latter the Wolof griot was clearly the cultural representative of an ethnic group that, by dint of number, of a privileged linguistic position, and of the geographical distribution of its population, had managed to impose a certain cultural hegemony over a country that is the result, in any case, of colonial carving-up of territory. As a member of a group that until recently led a nomadic existence straddling three countries and thus does not readily accept the sovereignty of any, the Hassounke was very sensitive to the cultural encroachment and felt proprietary about the contents of his culture: his heroes and their feats were not to be shared; at most they were to be appreciated in the wholeness of the culture that gave birth to them. By contrast, the Sereer people, who had invited the Wolof-speaking griot to join them, viewed him as part of a contemporary vernacular culture in the making, one whose official language is Wolof (as opposed to French, which is the administrative language and is used by about 17 percent of the population). As such they did not feel threatened or proprietary about elements of their culture that were making their way into this new communal culture, the vehicle of which is Wolof.

This situation was not without problems for the griot himself, however. When questioned about it, he readily acknowledged his *bricolage* and saw it both as a burden and as a realm of opportunity: the attribution of feats to a different hero is an act that must have consequences; discrepancies are created that must be resolved; gaps in the whole of genealogical narratives must be attended to. He spoke wistfully of the movement whereby all the tales of all the groups he knew could be harmonized and ordered in a coherent and cohesive whole. He certainly did not view this as a Wolof project but as a Senegalese one.

What are the chances of such a project being realized? The authority and self-confidence of the griot, like that of the jongleur we have been discussing, is rooted in his being the expositor as well as the repository of a collective memory. In his oral world, there is one collective memory of the Hassounke, and another one for the Sereer, and yet others for the Wolof, Bassari, Dioula, Lebu, Manjak, et cetera, but there is no collective memory for Senegal because the Senegalese culture that the griot was constructing is a project of the present into the future and not the transmission into the present of the past. The notion of a vast compilation in which the collective memories of the various groups would be gathered into one large whole is in fact a curious and ultimately untenable project. Were we to grant that such a compilation were possible, and even that all problems of discrepancy and conflict among the various traditions were resolved (bearing in mind that many of these originate from people who until recently saw one another as hereditary enemies), we would still have to ask ourselves the question the griot did not ask: whose collective memory is this now? We may want to answer: "That of the Senegalese," and, indeed, that is the answer provided in Senegal, as well as in many other countries of Africa, by the research teams of universities or ministries of culture, which fan out into the countryside to capture on audio or videotape the performances of oral culture. The answer is disingenuous, however worthy its political and historical cause: this is no one's collective memory; it does not represent the slow accretion of materials in people who transmit them to one another across time. It is something other than collective memory. Indeed, it is a project that abandons the terrain of collective memory to move to another, that of state culture, with its centralizing institutions that ultimately depend on writing. The griot already saw himself as a sort of state functionary, and the interpreter would have been correct in perceiving what was happening as the end of all traditional culture, not merely his own.

The griot is out of his element. He attempts to resolve within the signifying practice of performance a prosaic problem and thus introduces yet another transitional or hybrid form.

Let us speak of this so-called syncretism. The various myths of a given culture were hierarchized in order of their importance and received their justification in one myth that played a central role in relation to all others. By virtue of this process, there was set in motion a centripetal force that would draw toward this myth all the most telling elements of the others. The central myth would then become progressively enriched in its injunctive force and appropriateness as model for more and more heterogeneous present experience (because, as we know, the guardians of the cultural patrimony, written or unwritten, must always respond to demands for more information), leading to a comprehensiveness that makes present-day descriptions of its "encyclopedic" role (Homeric epics, for example, have been so described) only mildly anachronistic. The myth begins to function as a sacred text, which, through interpretation if necessary, reveals all that needs to be known.

Once the culture turns to literacy, this process is accelerated. For one thing, writing will try to flex its muscles and show it can contain as much as possible. Consequently we get written texts of a magnitude that exceeds any practical possibility of single performance. For another thing, because writing is not only permanent but also mobile, it can move from the locale where its "matter" was indigenous and in circulation, into other regions with different homegrown heroes and myths. This possibility was enhanced (in modern Senegal and in medieval France) by the tremendous increase in means of physical communication in general: roads, commerce, and the expansion of the administrative tools of a centralized state. When our wistful modern griot attempts this sort of encyclopedic compilation, his personal belonging to one ethnic group stands in the way of his project, for he is perceived as acting in a far from disinterested way.[1] Writing has no such burden; it is indeed neutral in relation to traditional forces. It gives them all the same standing and thus can hold them together. But what it actually holds together is the heterogeneity of a differentiated society.

Something of this sort seems to be occurring in the thirteenth century as well, in relation to the vast storehouses of traditional material. Some writers, like Jean Bodel, could draw clear boundaries between the subject matters of Rome, France, and Brittany, (the Arthurian *matière de Bretagne*),[2] while in the works of others, including those as careful as Chrétien (cf. the *Cligès*, with its admixture of Byzantine and Breton materials), such boundaries no longer obtain.

The integration of material of such diverse provenance is difficult to effect, and new forms must be sought. What will be called upon is the same mechanism by means of which clan and family boundaries are renegotiated, namely a procedure of extension—the system of marriage and affiliation alliances. Thus are the great medieval narrative cycles born, one epic extending into another, massive works of a multiplicity of wandering knights. The eponymous heroes of these cycles turn out to be members of a vast kinship structure, one that can even be invoked to account for the undercurrents of tension that may exist among them as a result of their prior inscription in myths and tales of hostile people. Is it not conceivable that the enmity between Ganelon and Roland in *La Chanson de Roland* may stem from the fact that Ganelon is a Breton hero whereas Roland belongs to the matter of France?

The reterritorialization under centralized imperial rule, as in the case of Charlemagne or under subsequent royal rule, has the effect of placing local heroes from differing traditions in the same time and place, the same chronotope.[3] The difficult passage from local preeminence to a hierarchized order must be negotiated. In *La Chanson de Roland*, the top order of the knights is referred to as the *Peers*. In the *matière de Bretagne*, the *Round Table* may well be the very material embodiment of the effort to conciliate conflicting claims of preeminence. To so reconcile is, for the prose cycles, to attempt to impose a hegemonic view upon the culture. In the Grail cycle, that is certainly what happens as clerical interests assert themselves and begin to favor knights such as Perceval and, even more so, Galahad, to the detriment of Gawain, Lancelot, and their cohorts. Once the various tales are given the same standing, by being linked in extended cycles, they can be drawn into the service of competing ideologies that are far more interested in the present and future direction of the society than in the preservation of past glories. Indeed, the ideologies may be ready to sacrifice the preexisting texts altogether to create a space for their own dominion.

The cycles, built up from the linkage, continuation, and extension of epic and courtly adventures, are in prose. Many are even distinctively named as such: the *Lancelot en prose*, the *Tristan en prose*. Nevertheless, there are entanglements reminiscent of verse, like those we saw in the verse *Bérinus* relative to Orchas's rescue of Aigres. These are related to the signifying practice of performance, which in the early verse *Bérinus* leads to the recounting of all sorts of actions and perceptions of Orchas in the rescue of Aigres, as opposed to the subsequent derhymed version, which calls on Orchas ("out of nowhere," we might suggest) only at the necessary moment in Aigres's consciousness. We see here the particular inability of performance to effect what we in a cinema culture now know as "cutting" or "montage."[4] As a result, although the basic device used to construct such cycles is just simple linkage of affiliated adventures, any reader experiences such linkage as far from simple. Each hero had existed in his own space and time (not unlike the jongleur, who carries his own space and time with him), facing his own obstacles, challenges, and destiny. How can they all share the same space and time? The minimal necessities of an integrated work demand intersections, a bringing-together, encounters that themselves become challenges and obstacles.

A modern reader's most immediate impression of these works is of a total lack of cohesion. The prose cycles have been attacked by scholars through the ages as not only entangling but unwieldy in the extreme, an incohesive grabbag of differing tales indiscriminately thrown together. A typical case is the Grail cycle, full of individual knights going on their separate quests, encountering distractions, meeting with strangers or with each other in ways that often entail the slaying of one by the other, separating and coming together. The attention of the story drops one knight to pick up another, then returns to the first, in a narrative of detour and *retour*. For example, here is one sequence of transitions in *La Mort Artu:*

> But now the story stops telling about them and returns to King Arthur.
> Now the story stops telling of him and returns to Sir Lancelot.
> But now the story stops telling about them all and returns to King Arthur.
> But now the story stops telling of him and returns to Sir Gawain's three brothers *at the moment when* Lancelot escaped from them after they had found him in the queen's room.[5]

Because of the very magnitude of these works, the reader struggles to keep all these intersecting strands in some kind of order, but it is difficult. A knight we are reading about reveals his name, and we may or may not realize that he is in fact some "nameless knight" introduced 300 pages earlier and not referred to in the interim. Strands of narrative extend as if organically, wander in particular directions, and give birth to their own offshoots and "ramifications," in an amorphousness and lack of control for which the "Arbre de Bourgonne," as rendered in Molinet's prose, is a fitting model.

The accusation of lack of cohesion was countered in 1918 by Ferdinand Lot, who showed that rather than being a potpourri of actions, everything in the prose Lancelot is carefully connected and timed.

> Aucune aventure ne forme un tout se suffisant à lui-même. D'une part des épisodes antérieurs, laissés provisoirement de côté, y prolongent des ramifications, d'autre part des épisodes subséquents, proches ou lointains, y sont amorcés. C'est un enchevêtrement systématique. De ce procédé de l'entrelacement, les exemples se pressent sous la plume.[6]

> No adventure forms a self-sufficient whole. On the one hand, previous episodes, left aside temporarily, extend themselves in ramifications, on the other hand, subsequent episodes, coming sooner or coming later, are initiated. It is a systematic interlacing. Of this interlacing procedure, examples abound.

The Micha edition of the prose Lancelot raises questions about the perfection of the "enchevêtrement" that Lot sees, and there are other cycles about which such a claim of well-craftedness could not credibly be made, but the strategy adopted to handle these various strands, "entrelacement" or "interlace" (as it was coined by Lot in the above citation), has justifiably obtained common acceptance.[7]

The problem of how various specialized interests mesh into a cohesive whole has been approached by the philologically minded scholar at the formal level. However, our Hassounke interpreter and others who must live through a period of cultural remapping are much more attentive to ideological issues expressed as the advocacy of *specialized interest*. And at the level of lines of interest, confusion prevails, a confusion that can extend even to the bearers of that interest. For instance, is Perceval an advocate of clerical or knightly interest? Even he may not know for sure, and in fact the text stages that confusion as an opposition between his father's legacy and his mother's instructions. So he appears as a character divided, seeking a resolution, one which comes with considerable difficulty, not only for Chrétien's characters but for those of the other cyclic material. The courtly code itself is brought into serious question, as presumably courtly characters, even the royal king Marc in the *Tristan en prose*, subvert it, break the rules. And the results of this state of affairs are certainly graver and more bloody than mere psychological confusion or rule-breaking may suggest. Encounters become openly confrontational, resulting in victory for one and crushing death for the others. We see one knight of the Round Table aligned against another, brother against brother, father against son. Aggression is directed less toward outside enemies or magical forces (one major appeal of *La Mort Artu* for modern readers is its lack of magic and fantasy, its more human scale) than it is toward each other. The confrontations are like present-day "elimination matches" or "sudden death."

Ultimately it is not one against the other but a kind of implosion, a generalized and uncontrolled carnage. It is as if written culture were to be the field on which oral culture plays itself out, until there is nothing more to sing about. In the Grail texts, the phrase that begins to occur with regularity and becomes the leitmotiv of *La Queste du Graal* is "la fin des enchantements de Bretagne" (the end of the enchantments of Britain). In *La Mort Artu*, before the final battle, it is clear to all what is coming: "Thus the battle began on Salisbury Plain; it was to lead to the destruction of the Kingdom of Logres and also of many others because afterwards there were fewer noble men than there had been before. Moreover, after their deaths, lands remained devastated and waste, through lack of good lords, because they were all killed in great pain and slaughter."[8] Where Galahad and Perceval have passed, the land is left without mysteries and no longer holds any potential for adventure. There is no possible continuation, it is the end of the line. Referring to the battle between King Arthur and his illegitimate son, Mordred, we are simply and sadly told: "The Father killed the son, and the son gave the Father a mortal wound."[9]

Facing a differentiated audience, in an interest that is no longer transcendent but one with which the state will identify, our jongleur-writer or syncretist griot must bring competing forces under control. How? We have seen two strategies evolve. One is the defeat of one party by another, with the winner taking the spoils. That is, the imposition of one set of cultural values over the whole of the newly constituted society. The defeated culture loses all right to express itself and so must go underground. The other strategy, as shown in Arthur's death, is simple mutual annihilation, in which contending forces, unable to prevail, fall to some third party whose presence is not suspected, as in the Grail material, where all the various strands of oral culture are brought into a final conflict on the altar of the newly victorious written culture which clears the ground for itself. These rather extreme solutions foreground a cultural discontinuity, which, if allowed to generalize itself, would be found intolerable by any culture. Another solution emerges, which we shall examine presently.

In a differentiated society, the overall cultural orientation of the society becomes an object of contention. Although all groups may have paid lip service to the hegemonic ideology, which in the Middle Ages was Christianity, there existed nonetheless considerable space for contention, as evidenced by the endless theological controversies, accusations of heresies, and mutual excommunications. And such conflicts were not limited to the theological sphere: there were all the conflicts between written and Roman law on the one hand and oral and customary law on the other.

This level of contention was contained for a while by being limited to themes and their specialized populations or to localities. As national boundaries were expanded to those approximating modern European nations, problems grew qualitatively as well as quantitatively. A new national identity had to be forged out of particularities (which is the situation in present-day Senegal). The forging of such a national identity required the meshing of the various groups that had considered themselves culturally autonomous before then, and it forced at least a partial renunciation of their foundational myths and tales. We may well imagine how difficult this renunciation was and can cite as an example the Maya, whom the Spaniards converted to Christianity relatively easily but who were nothing short of aghast when they were brutally brought to the realization that their adoption of the Christian God had apparently demanded of them a total renunciation of their own deities. All these traditions could not be simultaneously true, and yet a forced distancing must not be total. A mechanism had to be found to prevent one's beliefs in the truthfulness of one's own set of myths from leading to absolute social intransigence in the face of similar claims from others. The only avenue open was to void the claim to truthfulness, while preserving and indeed showing solicitude toward the texts that previously were the objects of such claims. The texts become fictional. And the preexisting opposition between what is *our* territory (the inside, the true) and what is not (the foreign, the untrue) is remapped to allow what is ours to be either historical or fictional. Truth and lack of truth become, respectively, the historical and the fictional, both ours and both precious. These differing myths can be ours, can coexist on the inside without being mutually exclusive of each other, as long as the ground for which they compete has changed. (We can understand why in these transitional cyclical texts, outright fantasy must be purged: one must make way for a new fiction.) Fictional texts are valued as remnants of tradition, indeed, constitute tradition itself (as we see in the American use of the fictional works of Norman Rockwell and Mark Twain), but they do not have the injunctive power possessed by explanatory myths endowed with truthfulness.[10] They may admit of casual as well as serious use and can be at the disposition of, and invocable by, anyone. They may even be seen now as in themselves *beautiful*. They are prized, but they are no longer worth fighting for. They are consolatory. The myths have been neutralized (no longer *uter*, of either the one group or the other). Their fictionalization is the price to be paid for peaceful coexistence in a larger, differentiated society.

No absolute claim about the origin of fiction in medieval France is being made here. In fact, a theory and a history of fiction remains to be written.[11] Rather, we are seeking to identify a mechanism by means of which a differentiated society, for its own purposes, will come to invest heavily in the fictional to the point of establishing institutions such as literature for its safeguard and perpetuation. Such a move completes a certain type of cultural development: a sociological institution will be put in place to manage the adjustment of territorial distinctions (ours, theirs) to ontological ones (truth, falsehood) now seen as no longer congruent.

As a consequence, the heroes do not disappear. By means of the interlace structure, a certain kind of effectivity of a model class of heroes is wiped out, but, that having been accomplished, they remain, and on this new ground they can be, rather remarkably, freestanding again. They no longer need complex intraplotting but can now be part of "stories." Guarded by an institution of literature that ensures that such texts are classified and visibly remain fictional, they can be taken back as story, if not history. Here is the point at which the philologist's romance also becomes the literary romance. The shift is most apparent in the way in which Sir Thomas Malory adapted the cyclic material. We quote Eugène Vinaver in his introduction to the critical edition of Malory:

> The French Arthurian prose cycle with its various ramifications was not an 'assemblage of stories,' but a singularly perfect example of thirteenth-century narrative art, subordinate to a well-defined principle of composition and maintaining in all its branches a remarkable sense of cohesion. It was an elaborate fabric woven out of a number of themes which alternated with one another like the threads of a tapestry: a fabric whose growth and development had been achieved not by a process of indiscriminate expansion, but by means of a consistent lengthening of each thread. Malory's adaptation, on the other hand, was far from possessing or even attempting the unity which is claimed for it by the critics. He never tried to reduce his French romances to 'one story'; the method he used was both more subtle and more drastic. With great consistency, though with varying degrees of success, he endeavored to break up the complex structure of his sources and replace their slowly unfolding canvas of recurrent themes by a series of self-contained stories. It was a delicate and difficult process of unravelling, of collecting the various stretches of any given thread and letting it unwind itself with as few interruptions as possible. Sometimes, as in certain parts of the romance of Arthur and Merlin *(The Tale of King Arthur)* and in the long and monotonous *Book of Sir Tristram,* Malory found himself defeated by the ingenuity of the French writers. But his successes were more impressive than his failures. If his *Noble Tale of Sir Launcelot* is, by modern standards, eminently readable, it is because it consists of three judiciously chosen short episodes which in the French *Lancelot* were hundreds of pages apart. Dismissing all the intervening matter, Malory makes these episodes into one 'tale': the tale of Lancelot and Lionel, which is con-

cluded by a reunion at Arthur's court of all Lancelot's victims who have survived his great strokes. Still more significant is the handling of the story of Balin, the unhappy knight whose Dolorous Stroke lays waste two kingdoms. In the French romance the story is an expansion of the theme of the Blighted Land which belongs to the *Queste del Saint Graal*. In Malory's version the Dolorous Stroke comes as a sequel to an event which occurs within the Balin episode itself; and because it can thus be understood without reference to any other work the whole perspective of the tale is altered: instead of a chain of events stretching far beyond any single romance there is a sequence which is complete in itself, a 'circle of destiny' drawn tightly and firmly around the protagonist's life.

    . . . The central theme [of the story of Arthur's death and of the destruction of the Round Table] is disengaged [by Malory] from all concomitant elements and freed from links with the other branches of the cycle. The events leading to the downfall of Arthur's kingdom are no longer interwoven with others, and the tragic destiny of Arthurian knighthood is divorced from the earlier account of how the 'worldly' knights failed in the quest for the Grail. The final catastrophe becomes a human drama conditioned from first to last by a clash of loyalties and explicable within its own limits. It is Lancelot's loyalty to Guinevere that causes him, in his anxiety to protect her, to destroy unwittingly the man he loves most—Gareth, Gawain's brother; and it is grief that turns Lancelot's truest friend, Gawain, into his sworn enemy and causes the mortal strife. Mordred's rebellion and the battle of Salisbury Plain are no longer treated as repercussions of extraneous events; they are links in the chain of human actions and feelings developed as the story progresses: fateful shadows arising from the depths of man's own noblest passions.[12]

The learned editor of Malory's text extends Malory's enterprise to our own day: what had been competing class interests (knightly vs. clerical) are now turned into human passions, transformed from particular and specialized interest to the universal. In this way, the institution of literature fosters the belief in a universal ground on which culture can be established. The critic lends his hand to the author in that enterprise.[13]

Boccaccio takes the story of Troilus and Criseyde, which in the *Roman de Troie* was only an intermittent interruption to the series of battles, and makes it into *Filostrato*, a story of unrequited love, which he uses to console himself in his own plight.[14] And in the hands of Chaucer, the same story also participates in the fourteenth- and fifteenth-century extraordinary interest in Troy—a culture that "died" but led to a multiplicity of cultures. This was a move from a religious, and particularly apocalyptic, consciousness to a historical one: what exactly does it mean for a culture to die, or is it reconstituted in new nation-states? How do cultures pass on one to the other?

We are less able to resolve the question of whether Troy is fact or myth, history or fiction, than we are to note the interest in that kind of status at that time, when people were living through, and seeing with their own eyes, the fabrication of their own culture.[15]

There is more here than the geopolitical aspect. Until this time, interactions between individuals were more genuinely between collectivities: for example, in a traditional society those who meet exchange genealogies to establish their degree of kinship. Now, rather than mere tokens of collectivities, the individuals interact by means of their difference (as a more differentiated society is constituted), yet bear the marks of the culture they come from or of the experience they have acquired within a newly differentiated society. Those marks, the way individuals situate themselves, are stories. In the *Canterbury Tales* and the *Decameron,* it is stories that function as the tokens of exchange, stories possessed by individuals rather than by collectivities.

Such a possession already implies a consumption of tales that is individual and a reading that is private. The distinction between historical and fictional is mapped upon—and refashions—the distinction between the sphere of the public and the sphere of the private. The latter becomes "subjective," no longer possibly encyclopedic because its reality is seen as problematic. And the aesthetic becomes a private and subjective matter, which will eventually call for Kant's Third Critique.

Chapters 7 and 8 show a *history* and a *story* that come from verse and establish themselves in prose. While they differentiate themselves before our very eyes, we see little that actually does differentiate them. The distinction seems to be more a social one, on the order of the development of a new institution, rather than one residing in some formal property of the texts themselves.

For prose, fiction is an open door, the beginning of a glorious future.

The Prosaic World

We have explored the emergence of prose by specifying and analyzing the conditions under which it arose and the kinds of changes in signifying practices and in the conceptions of meaning that were first necessary for, and then attendant upon its emergence. Prose eventually achieves a considerable degree of hegemony in the entire field of signifying practices. In this concluding chapter, we wish to place the moment of emergence in a broader historical sweep and thus see what role prose has played in the establishment of our modernity.

In the introduction, we stated reasons for privileging France in the Middle Ages as the locus of our investigation into the emergence of prose. We recognized then that prose had existed before, and in different places, but we also saw that an inquiry into prose would be more productive if focused on France. We need to recognize that in antiquity, prose did not stand for the same signifying practice within the same configuration of signifying practices that it did in the Middle Ages and beyond.

In antiquity, poetry held the place of honor, but public speech that was not versed aspired to that same position. First Gorgias with his extreme elaborateness and then his student Isocrates showed oratory to be the equal of poetry by putting forward an oratorical prose that could attain artistic form. In the words of Isocrates,

> For there are men who, albeit they are not strangers to the branches which I have mentioned, have chosen rather to write discourses, not for private disputes, but which deal with the world of Hellas, with affairs

of state, and are appropriate to be delivered at the Pan-Hellenic assemblies—discourses which, as everyone will agree, are more akin to works composed in rhythm and set to music than to the speeches which are made in court. For they set forth facts in a style more imaginative and more ornate; they employ thoughts which are more lofty and more original, and, besides, they use throughout figures of speech in greater number and of more striking character. . . . All men take as much pleasure in listening to this kind of prose as in listening to poetry.[1]

For Isocrates, however, such prose has to have some metrical character: "Prose must not be merely prose, or else it will be dry; it must not be metrical for then artifice is manifest; it must rather be compounded of all sorts of rhythms, of which the ones most commonly used should be the iambic and the trochaic."[2] This is of course the modern conundrum that we saw in Frye: prose is to be recognized only in its impure state.[3] It more fundamentally poses the question of what one means by prose at the time of the Sophists: what is pure prose?

To the extent that prose is oratory, the metrical and rhythmic marks that it inevitably has can be foregrounded. This is clear from the Sophists on but is expressed particularly well by Cicero: "The poets have given rise to the inquiry as to the difference between them and the orators. It once seemed to be a matter of rhythm and verse, but now rhythm has become common in oratory. For everything which can be measured by the ear, even if it does not make a complete verse—that certainly is a fault in prose—is called rhythm."[4] Once the Sophists succeed in showing that its lack of rhyme did not disqualify prose from being "artistic," that is, "poetic," the orator can get up on the poet's podium and beat verse at its own game. By the time of the Romans, oratory attempts to assume this primary position, and most orators interest themselves in poetry only to the extent that it can enhance their own speeches. Public speaking becomes a powerful signifying practice and means to temporal power in Greek and Roman democracy. As oratory competes more and more successfully with verse, the differentiae between prose and verse become fewer. Discussions of their differences begin to show prose and verse more as partners than as competitors, sharing the same devices (skillful word order, rhythmic feet) and learning from each other.[5] Cicero will even claim oratory as a higher form than poetry, seeing the poet as struggling within his constraints (but also benefiting from more license) to attain what oratory can achieve. This is a shift whose dynamics are not dissimilar from the move of prose to encompass its predecessor, verse, in the Middle Ages.

There is clearly a limit to what can be formally learned from all this, but for our purposes it is enough to see that prose, or at least "poetic prose," and verse are in a more and more relative relationship, one to the other. Verse has now become just a sign, and not even a criterion, of the poetry, that is, of the higher forms to which speaking and writing in general, and *oratio* in particular, can aspire. Thus, to return to the writing of history, we end up with remarks like Quintilian's, which are about as far from any of Commynes's as can be: "History has a certain affinity for poetry and may be regarded as a kind of prose poem [*carmen solutum*]."[6] To talk of a *carmen solutum* is to unfetter the whole distinction between prose and poetry and to show how difficult it is to keep prose distinct from other signifying practices in antiquity because one is really talking about the signifying practice of oratory, even if much of it is written (whether prior to the act of speaking, after it or instead of it). This should not surprise us, however, when we realize that nonverse not only aspires to but basically exists within (does not definitively step out of) an authoritative signifying practice that has been characterized by verse, which dominated cultural life and education, an education which for the early Greeks consisted of the improvisation and memorization of poetry, and, as Havelock has said, "the oral delivery of a prose rhetoric based on verse principles."[7] We pointed out in chapter 6 that these principles were quite forceful throughout the Latin Middle Ages.

The ancient "situation" of nonverse, examined from the standpoint of the medieval emergence of vernacular prose, can be quite puzzling. An indication of the direction prose will eventually take can be found in Aristotle and his successors the Peripatetics and Stoics. Although Aristotle admired Isocrates for his prose style, he saw prose as existing along a stylistic continuum from the very elaborate to the very bare. And he singled out certain subject matter (real issues before the assembly and the court) as those whose style should be kept at a conscious and unequivocal distance from any elaborateness that could draw it close to verse. Such matters should be couched only in clear and appropriate language: any more elaborateness would involve distortions introduced to sway what must be a debased audience.

Theophrastus follows by making Aristotle's preference an absolute opposition between style-types. As Ammonius says:

> Language is divided into two types, according to the philosopher Theophrastus, the one having reference to the hearers, the other to the matter concerning which the speaker aims to convince his audience. To the [first] division with reference to the hearers belong poetry and rhetoric. Therefore its function is to choose the more stately words, and not those which are common or vulgar, and to interweave them with each other harmoniously, to the end that, by means of them and the effects which result from the employment of them, such as vividness, sweetness and other qualities of style, together with studied expansion and contraction, all employed at the suitable moment, the listener shall be charmed and moved and, with respect to intellectual persuasion, overmastered.

The [second] division looking to the matter will be the especial concern of the philosopher, refuting the false and setting forth the true.[8]

But neither in Aristotle nor in Theophrastus is there a description of this second division, except that (like Isocrates) it cannot be absolutely plain, which would make it "mean" (i.e., base): it must also be appropriate. The back-and-forth movements and qualifications involved in pronouncements on this subject can be dizzying. From Aristotle's *Rhetoric*:

> For justice should consist in fighting the case with the facts alone, so that everything else that is beside demonstration is superfluous; nevertheless, as we have just said, it is of great importance owing to the corruption of the hearer. However, in every system of instruction there is some slight necessity to pay attention to style; for it does make a difference, for the purpose of making a thing clear, to speak in this or that manner; still, the difference is not so very great, but all these things are mere outward show for pleasing the hearer; wherefore no one teaches geometry that way.[9]

Furthermore, it is not always clear, when a description of this unelaborate prose is attempted, whether one is talking about a prose that stands alone or that is only one part of a larger oration, other parts of which can or even should contain grander style (e.g., prose is appropriate to proof, but proof is not a whole speech). This is emblematic of the treatment of prose in antiquity: when it is not a question of prose competing directly with verse, and thus basically occupying the same position, it is a question of making divisions between subject matter, for which certain kinds of language use are analogously distinct, without our knowing what the status of these divisions is, that is, how deeply they cut. There are always mitigating factors: for example, it must be plain but not too plain; or it is really a mix of one style and another; or it must bear the style particular to the valued individuality of the given speaker.

The Stoics took this rhetoric of proof, stripped of its emotional factors, and widened its application to more everyday and pragmatic situations. They looked to a more conversational idiom—what we would see as a *sermo* rather than *oratio*. *Oratio* is firmly rooted in external deixis (e.g., where one stands, the podium). *Sermo* is more indifferent to a deictic dimension—it is more offhand—and in this way is similar to poetics, which is blind to deixis as well. (In fact, *sermo* has been looked at only poetologically, as an artifact.) But the Stoics feared a true conversational idiom as too loose and unregulated, and they balanced their move away from elaborate speech and toward some sort of freedom with a preponderant Atticist concern not only for brevity but also for *proprietas verborum*, the necessity to find the very word that correctly applies to the thing. We now know that prose is not headed in that direction; it is rather elaborating a process by which, given the *verba*, a temporary, unfounding position can be constructed from which that *verba* can then be seen as *propria, apta, idonea,* a position from which a reading is then available.

All this remains, however, within the broad and continuing Attic-Asiatic controversy, where Attic criticisms of overdone and artificial style are countered by attacks on plain style as bloodless and arid. And here grand style will win: it is what gave oratory its legitimacy in the first place. If one sticks with language, with speech, with style, then grand style is where the power is. It can tangle with public poetry not only in ceremony but also in oratory, where success is measured by results. It can also overpower plain proof. Theophrastus said it—"overmastery"—and that holds true for classic Rome (and beyond), which recognized that intellectual persuasion can be overwhelmed by that which plays on the emotions. Aristotle is disturbed about precisely this danger and attempts to defend against it with his distinctions and distancing, but such a danger cannot be overcome if one remains within the situation of an individual manipulating speech for immediate effect. We have seen that if one stays within the conception of *styles* along a continuum, one finds that they compete but are also adjacent, they vary but are also complementary (e.g., in the same oration, the grander style is fitting for the *exordium,* the plainer for the *narratio*), they are mutually exclusive but are also inseparable (e.g., the simpler as the "bones" and "muscle," the grander as the "flesh," the exterior appearance). The individual speaker becomes very important as a way of holding the mix and of finally having a *style* that is just *his.* Such an outcome is in perfect accordance with notions of ethos at the time: Aristotle talks of a "virtue of style," which is aligned with moral virtue as he sees it: an avoidance of extremes. This is picked up again and again throughout the ages, as in the notion of the "honnête homme" of the seventeenth century, who is both morally reasonable and moderate, and speaks in a reasonable and moderate way. Hendrickson says in a note that the attempt to reach a plain prose is to draw out a *res* of philosophy that is not the *verba* of rhetoric. But in the ancient world, that *verba* cannot be completely disengaged.

And, in any case, is this really a move toward prose? Were the Peripatetics and Atticists to somehow draw out this *res,* were they to succeed in constituting and legitimizing a freestanding and consistent "bare" style, would that be prose? Is prose plain? Only to those like Le Bel, who takes as his goal to write "à point."[10] Prose is not a style, it is not a *sermo,* it is not an *ydioma.* Prose contains styles, much like oratory does, but it cannot be seen through style. Prose is a different signifying practice. It is to that depth of *distinctio* that the ancients will not venture. Once having realized their limitation, however, we can recognize and acknowledge that there are certain stakes raised in antiquity that are identical to those adduced in the fifteenth and sixteenth centuries. The terms of Plutarch in the following passage connect neatly to Montaigne:

> For the use of language is like the currency of coinage in trade: the coinage which is familiar and well-known is also acceptable, although it takes on a different value at different times. There was, then, a time when men used as the coinage of speech verses and tunes and songs, and reduced to poetic and musical form all history and philosophy and, in a word, every experience and action that required a more impressive utterance. . . . But, as life took on a change along with the change in men's fortunes and their natures, when usage banished the unusual and did away with the golden topknots and dressing in soft robes, and, on occasion, cut off the stately long hair and caused the buskin to be no longer worn, men accustomed themselves (nor was it a bad thing) to oppose expensive outlay by adorning themselves with economy, and to rate as decorative the plain and the simple rather than the ornate and elaborate. So, as language also underwent a change and put off its finery, history descended from its vehicle of versification, and went on foot in prose, whereby the truth was mostly sifted from the fabulous.[11]

What does *prose* mean here? All terms must be historicized but particularly prose because, if we are to follow its common meaning as all that is not verse, its meaning depends on whatever else there happens to be there then. There is no single word in Greek that corresponds simply to our common understanding of prose. The Greek word set most often *in opposition to verse* in the above passages, and thus translated as prose, is *logos,* the word that combines in its meaning both speech and reason, the word by which a thought is expressed, and the inward thought or reason itself (thought, calculation, relation). *Logos* means word, saying, conversation, mention, fable, chronicle, and, particularly in Athens, it was used as the term for formal speech, like the Latin *oratio.*[12] We see it quite clearly in Isidore of Seville's *Etymologiae,* a seventh-century extraction from and compilation of earlier encyclopedists and classicists. His entry on prose, for which he uses the word *prosa,* is as follows: "Prosa est producta oratio et a lege metri soluta" (Prose is extended speech that is free from the law of meter).[13] In some cases, what modern translators give us as prose, because the Greek opposes it to verse, is not *logos* but *ton koine,* vernacular, speech, "what is poured forth promiscuously: in flowing, unfettered language" (Liddell and Scott). There is a distinction between koine and logos, that which is actually spoken in an unreflective manner and that which is the product of a work of elaboration. This distinction was available to Greeks quite early. That was the kind of understanding that the pre-Socratics achieved.[14]

Our word goes back to the Latin word for prose, built from the Greek preposition *pros,* meaning "near," "toward," "to," and *pro,* "before," "ahead." Thus it should not be so surprising that prose is commonly understood as having priority, as "coming before." Although Greek terms for prose do not seem to be based on *pro,* we should mention the use in Greek theater of a *prosopon protaticon,* a character who opened the play by revealing the situation for the audience, a technique to solve problems of early exposition in theater. *Prosopon* is "character," "face," same usage as *prosopopoeia,* "to make a face," "impersonate"; and *protaticon* is from *protasis,* "beginning," from *proteinen,* "to stretch out before," "put forward." Although prose is clearly neither of these things, we see it as a language use that attempts to "stretch out before." Doesn't this *prosopon protaticon* seem an ancestor to *l'Acteur?* One puts prose forward, and what is put forward, the theater requires to have a face on. Must writing require that? Here we meet again the impossibilities of establishing a position both *prior* and *faceless,* an aporia that prose will come to solve. Were we to continue this speculative etymology of prose, we might continue to προλογος, *pro-logos,* Aristotle's term in the *Poetics* for that part of a tragedy or comedy that precedes the first song of the chorus. Perhaps prose as we have come to understand it looks back to the *pro* or *pro-logos,* understood not as "the *logos* before" but as "that which is meant to precede and underlie *logos,*" or to the *pro* of *proteron,* "antecedent."

Etymologies of the modern term begin with the Latin *prosa,* from *prorsus,* "straightforward," "direct," making *prorsa oratio* or *prosa oratio* or *prosa,* which means "a straightforward speaking without diversion or interruption, right through to the end of the period." Dictionaries oppose *prorsus* to *versus,* but etymologies derive the *prorsus* from *prouorsus (proversus),* through the elimination of the *u* and the assimilation of the *r* to the *s.* The meaning of the Greek *pros* when used with the accusative is, in Liddell and Scott, "of Place, *towards, to,* Lat. *versus.*" Verse and prose clearly have instability built into them. It has been suggested that the first stable term for prose is not *prosa* or its related terms but Cicero's *oratio soluta,* unfettered, free speech, which we see now as discourse in solution, suspended speech.

Prose is an extremely general term, which, if extended to any utterance that is not verse, tells us about as much as it told M. Jourdain. To use this term is either to apply it in this minimal, general, and really quite uninformative way, or to actually, and often unconsciously, apply a specific, modern notion of prose. The principal tendency is to do the latter; but to use modern conceptions as categories for whatever is not versed, anywhere, at any time, can be fatally distorting.[15] The use of the term by philologists to describe nonverse in ancient Greece is such a move. It is put to similar use by anthropologists who categorize as prose any nonverse oral narratives they find. This was pointed out in as early as 1925 by Franz Boas: "The form of modern prose is largely determined by the fact that it is read, not spoken, while primitive prose is based on the art of oral delivery and is, therefore, more closely related to modern oratory than to the printed literary style."[16]

The oldest unrhymed texts in French are called prose texts by their editors Brian Woledge and H. P. Clive in *Répertoire des plus anciens textes en prose française depuis 842 jusqu'aux premières années du XIIIe siècle.*[17] They start in 842 because that is the date of the Strasbourg oaths, which occur in a Latin history of the conflict between Louis the German and Charles the Bald over division of Charlemagne's empire: at one point a settlement is reached (recounted in Latin), speeches are given to the crowd (also recounted in Latin), but the oath of peace is stated by the French brother in German (so that the German soldiers present can understand it) and likewise by the German brother in French. For those oaths, and the oaths of response by the troops, the chronicler Nithard switches to the vernacular. He then resumes in Latin.[18] We value these *Sermons* not as prose but as the first transcribed vernacular speech (speech, moreover, cited within, deictically situated within Latin). They are a landmark, to be sure, but just that of the vernacular as written. They are called prose by Woledge and Clive because of the subsequent extended authority of writing, in spite of the fact that the use of the *oath* as obligation predates writing and, certainly at this point, is not dependent for its meaning and authority on its own transcription.

But things do not change so much. Eight hundred years later, M. Jourdain arrives at his "revelation" about speaking prose not because he is enquiring into speech but because he is initiating a writing project.

To move from the prose of classic Greece to the prose of the Middle Ages involves an earthshaking shift in the locus of power from that of the public arena to that of writing, and the growing legitimacy of a vernacular.

The situation that prevails, then, is as follows: On the one hand, we have the learned culture, based on Latin, which is used both orally and in writing, but where the writing clearly holds all of the privileged positions since it is the guarantor of the purity of the Latin, at the very least. Within this learned culture, verse and oratory share a ground determined by their belonging to the remnants of Roman culture such as it has been preserved in writing. On the other hand, there exists an oral culture, of vernacular languages, in which verse holds all the prestige in opposition to everyday speech. As the vernaculars come to be written, thus evidencing an abandonment of the communicative situation of the oral in favor of the prestige of writing, a reconfiguration occurs that now sees a distinction within the vernacular culture between written and oral aspects, in which the oral is still divided between verse and speech but no longer has the prestige that it used to have, and in which the written consists of prose as well as verse. There is also a new and distinct vernacular literacy. In this configuration, some verse may well be written, but it is burdened by its former life in the now devalued oral culture. Newly emerged prose, however, untainted by any previous oral life, stands to reap the fruits of this shift, as the very embodiment of writing and eventually of language prior to the imposition of any form.

Whereas ancient nonverse competed with verse on verse's own ground, medieval nonverse in the vernacular found itself in a situation in which the prestige of the podium was dwarfed by that of the written. Although the aspiration, traditional of vernaculars, to attain the position of Latin persisted,[19] the vernacular—*verna*, home-born slave, native, indigenous—was given the opportunity to emancipate itself from the dominance of Latin by establishing a form of writing unachievable by a language weighed down by its own history and social regulation and imprisoned by a clerical class jealously guarding its prerogatives. The vernacular grew enough in respectability to be itself written (no small accomplishment: it took centuries) but did not become so respectable as to be immediately burdened by already-formulated cultural messages and as to be codified and monopolized by an identifiable power structure. It avoided bespeaking its sources too much; it retained its diversity of *ydioma*. Not sharing the Attic concern for preciseness, tightness, and appropriateness, the vernacular could overcome a single *oratio* with its plural *sermo*, a shift basic to the birth of modern prose.[20] It could occasionally reach the status of not being for attribution, just at the time when that quality was also associated with truth in language, and was an effect of writing. As vernacular, "homegrown," and of the moment, it was both changeable and rooted. It was an under-language and could serve as an underpinning. The vernacular was out there, it was dispersed and around, it was available, *disponible,* and every instance of it was not held to be the product of an agent, a do-er and a maker. Unlike Latin, it was not owned, and thus it could be an instrument of change.

To restate: at the beginning of the Middle Ages, France finds itself between a high culture that is in Latin and monopolizes writing and (because of invasions from the outside, the outside position) a vernacular culture that is oral and in verse. This is the language of the people, but, in contrast to the ancient citizens' democracies, the people are now disenfranchised and cannot use their speech for power because any power available through the exercise of language involves becoming learned, through the church, a process that purposefully strips away the indigenous language. Even when power is exercised by the illiterate kings, it must exercise itself and circulate beyond the immediate reach of the king through the written word, for in the wake of the Roman Empire,[21] and particularly with the steady expansion of written law, written juridic procedures and bureaucratic administration, authority without documentary evidence as its backing has no credibility. For a while the separation between oral and written, Latin and vernacular holds, and interaction is limited. It is not an interaction that the church would see as necessary, for it considers its language to be universal, standing at the opposite pole of the particular.[22] Speech remains the particular. Vernacular culture defines an intermediate space between the universal and the particular, namely the diverse, that is, the sum of the particulars, which are not immediately subsumed under a universal that can discount their differences. There is a problem of management between and around the particulars, and that will be the task of prose.

The question then becomes: can the vernacular be written? Which means not whether it can be transcribed, as it was in as far back as 842, but whether it can draw unto itself the authority of writing. Up to that point, there was no evidence that authority as such inhered in writing: writing was totally at one with externally established learned authority, which spoke and wrote only Latin. It is in the thirteenth and fourteenth centuries that one began to believe that a translation could be written from the learned language to the unlearned language that would retain authority, by virtue of what is now seen as an authority in writing . . . *but* it is now a particular kind of writing: one that must be free not only of the marks of performance but also, like *acteur*, of the marks of any public utterance *or act;* a writing that must be free, in some ideal sense, of any marks, a writing whose only marks, whose only "styles," are to be of those discourses it contains and frames.[23] Such writing is seen as authoritative insofar as it is a means of getting "close to," or "within" what is an evolving sense of truth or fact as "raw," understood as perhaps extralinguistic, perhaps ephemeral, in any case gradually but fundamentally inimical to speech, inimical to statements made by one to another *in presencia,* inimical to an *oratio* that now seems to be too much *with* us, too monumental, already in a mode of secondary elaboration. The stakes then are very different from the stakes of the ancients, which had to do with demonstrations of individual skills in a world of personal advancement. The ground of the conflict between verse and prose (and thus the meaning of verse and prose) has shifted, away from one that (even in a literate culture) compares modes of elaboration within the realm of speech (where it is particularly difficult to eliminate "sonorousness," personal style, *rythmus,* which is why in the realm of speech, as well as in a discipline of "literature," which focuses on "style," one keeps drawing prose back to form) and toward one that pretends to stigmatize elaboration in favor of the exploitation of the *absencia* unique to the *tekhne* of writing, which does not seek to be understood as speech, and in which a subject need not be stable or even localizable.

Within the Western tradition, there are at least two ascertainable traditions of prose, the antique and the one that emerges in the Middle Ages. Let us examine the extent of the latter's effect on us.

One thing still with us is the way prose withholds itself from view. In chapter 7 we discussed how it becomes identified with the linguistic substratum so that whereas one recognizes that it emerges relatively late, it presents itself as prior to verse or any specific discourse. It thus can claim a foundational role and functions as the ground of reference, a sort of degree-zero of language for all further formal elaboration. We stated at the beginning that verse is seen as developmentally second. But we know it to be developmentally first. Well then, if verse is first *and* verse is second, where is prose? That there has been virtually no answer to this question, that is, that prose is considered omnipresent, is an indication of the success of prose. Prose is meant to have no place; prose does not happen. Prose is what assigns place.

In relation to verse or indeed any other form, prose assumes the position of matter. Let us recognize what is significant about such a move. Matter is the unavoidable, the indestructible, *l'incontournable*, "that around which you cannot get." It is there from the beginning, as the *hyle* of the world, and it is what will remain after the destruction of whatever forms may have been imposed on it. Unlike ancient *hyle*, however, prose is not inert: it does not wait for the inspirational breath to set it in motion, it animates and motivates, disposes, arranges, assembles, and orders by itself. This is a position that prose has staked out for itself, or, if you will, that culture has demanded. It is a position of considerable power, for in a world of change, a world that acknowledges and demands change, prose, unsubstantial though it may be, *holds*.

The question may well arise: where does this change originate? What causes it? This is a question to which prose provides no answer, for it does not acknowledge its legitimacy. Answers come more in the form of how other factors in the culture answer the challenge of prose. Change is a given, and if anything, poetological thought must be seen as an attempt to arrest change and to contain it within specifiable forms, for which agents can be assigned or identified. Prose is much more heraclitean, it begins with change and seeks only to find ways of managing it. We have seen that in the social sphere it is the function of the state to be the manager of change, the holder of conflicts, the definer of limits. Against these functions there stands an older form of thought, a throwback to the world of performance, which resists what it sees as nothing but an accommodation to change that is left out of control. In this view, the world is static, agents come along and in a heroic feat animate it and transform it by imposing their will and their vision on it. In such a view, the position claimed for prose is an illegitimate one, usurped from its rightful owner, speech. Unable to maintain the primacy of verse over prose but unwilling to "fall" for prose's claim that it underlies verse, holders of this view derive both verse and prose from speech as the underlying practice. Speech, as an act or deed of an individual, spontaneous, unregulated, is the means by which the individual expresses himself or herself. Both verse and prose then represent secondary elaboration upon this foundational act. Historians such as Jean Marot (sixteenth century) provide an example of this kind of resistance when they systematically exploit voice and speech to pinpoint the origins of their ideology. From this perspective, then, it is important to show (but at a length and in a detail that would far exceed this book) that the agnosticism of modern prose with respect to its own origins is but an ideological stance designed to occult the interests that would be revealed were prose's sender identified.

Speech, then, will be located preverse and will inspire myths similar to prose. But speech is not the end of the regress: speech is body-generated language; under and around speech, as in performance, is the individual *soma*. To resist prose and cling to speech is to look for the bodily presence underlying the words, to seek the certainty that is the individual. And both verse and some nonverse will continue to do this. In other words, the implicit argument is still one of deixis. We saw in D'Auton, and can see even more in Jean Marot and others, whose writings stage the speeches of mastering historical figures, how historians have the option of sticking to the kind of deixis and presence that obtains in speech. (Historians like Commynes invest very little in speech, recognizing the speech of historical agents as a place of obfuscation. His practice should be compared with that of Herodotus and Thucydides, who give us something that is clearly no longer sung epic but is still a world comprised mostly of speeches.) For a long time, the competition, the skirmishes, will be between speech and prose as the underwriter. But it is an unfair battle: in most cases prose will win hands down because it can contain speech, whereas speech does not contain prose. As it reaches into the foundations of language as "taking place," prose can make allowance for speech within it. Put differently: once having worked out the basic problem and mechanisms of deixis (how language connects itself with what is under it), prose can pretend to be both language and what is under it. This is what a body cannot do: a body relies upon deixis, uses it, but does not constitute it. Prose can *hold* speech. Speech cannot hold prose.

Prose can situate itself in a foundational position with respect to all language. It will under-stand and under-write speech and verse. But it will not display such understanding, which would only bring it out of the background that is its ground.[24] Prose has no dimension of display because, without margins, it cannot be isolated. The dimension of prose is extension. Only single discourses of it, or single signifying practices within it, can be highlighted, cited, and put on display, but they are not prose.

It is precisely because of this that prose requires a specific form of literacy, which is generally not the one that is taught. Whereas most literacies concern themselves with the mastery, both encoding and decoding, of single discourses, whether individually or *seriatim,* prose requires a literacy that would be attentive to this managerial function of the discourses and thus beyond them to the play of deixis within it. Such a literacy, as we have just seen in relation to history and change, and as was exemplified by Commynes, is not restricted to textual operations but is a mode of living and acting in a world that is now prosaic. In other words, if there is such a thing as a prosaic hermeneutics, it is not restricted to the world of linguistic artifacts but constitutes the dimension of understanding in modernity. With respect to what goes on around us, as readers we must be aware of the position we occupy in relation to the processes we seek to interpret, and such acts of interpretation are not of the contemplative type but represent forms of intervention, requiring that the positionality that is inevitably ours be invested with aforethought and adjusted to the needs and desires we may have. This is in marked contrast to the fixed position of the cocelebrants of ritual and the audience of performance. Unlike them, the prose readers, the inhabitants of the prosaic world, can and indeed must take initiatives. They are the observers-participants who can block, accelerate, redirect, invert, or even abort processes. Thus they do have at their disposal a form of agency commensurate with their powers; they do not transform the world through heroic deeds, but they see potential directions and can channel change that will occur anyway.

Under these circumstances, it is clear that it will be very difficult for two readers, let alone several, to share the same sort of reading. Besides the inevitability of change, there is also the structural impossibility of occupying exactly the same position in relation to ongoing processes. A latent anarchy threatens here. It can be banished only by a significant investment in institutions that will specify and socially sanction privileged positions, something that can be achieved only by mounting a considerable pedagogical apparatus. (Thus, either education will be handled by the state or it will turn its back on prose and be assigned to religious groups, which read prose according to nonprose literacies.)

The shift between verse and prose in which a secondary form emerges as the primary one may at first seem improbable. Yet it is part of a number of shifts of a similar nature occurring at this time. For instance, in the High Middle Ages, the church stands as heir to the prestige and thus to the legitimating power of the Roman Empire. The pope, by virtue of his position in the church, that is, as the vicar of Christ on the earth, as well as by virtue of the fact that his see is in Rome, grants legitimacy upon the princes of this world. And as we know from the conflicts with Frederick Barbarossa, this is a considerable power; the failure by a pope to legitimize an emperor is interpreted by the latter as an incitation to rebellion on the part of his subjects. The secular world is thus contained within the domain of the universal church. This state of affairs shifts, and not without conflict, with the notable Avignon Captivity. Here, the kings of France (as it happens), in the fourteenth century (as it happens) sought to reverse the relationship of dependency between secular and sacred power: it is they who would be the guarantors of the church rather than the other way around. The church would retain all its powers, without any hindrance in their exercise; indeed it would find a state eager to assist it in the exercise of such power. All the church need do is accept the state's protectorate over it. The church is not altered, but it is now contained. In the larger economy of the state, it becomes one contender among many. It is privileged by the state, to be sure, but it is a privilege that can be withdrawn because it no longer derives from a grounding of the church other than that of the state. The privilege accorded to the church by the state stems from the position that the state assigns to the church within itself, and such power as the church possesses within the state is a function of the relation of that position to other positions within the state, assigned by or perhaps merely permitted by the latter within a polis in contention. The church is no longer a domain but a force among others. This is precisely what prose will have done to verse. The process, occurring both at the level of signifying practice (prose) and at the sociopolitical level with the state, gives rise to a new space, which we will name the culture of the state.

Such a culture takes on some specific forms. Traditionally, agents were understood either as enacting the will or destiny of the collectivity or as putting forth the claims of a subgroup within the collectivity to which they were linked by ties of blood or honor. In the culture of the state, the first type of activity will be reserved to the state itself, which alone acts on behalf of the collectivity. Such action is carried out at the instigation of state apparatuses, that is, faceless mechanisms of intervention without any heroic dimension. The second kind of activity falls within the adjudicating power of the state. The agents here are seen as claimants for special interests, and, to act justly, the state must take a position of disinterest in relation to such claims. As a first step, this requires that all claimants be considered as formally equal to each other, and thus must be stripped of what may constitute their unique advantages. In practical terms, this means that their claims must be handled through the mediation of writing ("reduced to writing" as administrators say these days), thus eliminating from view what may be formidable or pathetic about their presence, that is, all their differential marks. They become faceless and are handled by an equally faceless bureaucracy with their fate being determined not in terms of their own interests but rather depending on the congruence of their concerns with the larger aims of the state. Bureaucracy presents itself not as an instrument of will but as merely processive. Bureaucracy is like prose but the language it uses is not prose, for it needs to elaborate a discourse that is going to be specific to it and into which other discourses have to be translated (e.g., filling out a form), and it is not interested in the articulation of discourses to each other but rather the articulation of interests, once put on as equal a discursive footing as possible. It is in this sense, then, that the bureaucracy participates in the culture of the state, modeled on the operations of prose, whereas its discourse is but one discourse among others, however privileged or monotone it may be.

Insofar as state action is concerned, the matter of agency presents itself in a rather different way. Conceptually it is not until a Hegelian notion of the state that one finds the state carrying out actions directly. Prior to that, the state will seek to identify instruments for the carrying out of its decisions. This requires that the state possess the ability not only to formulate goals, policies and decisions for itself but also to identify potential agents for their realization. In other words, the state must have rather precise knowledge of its inner resources at its disposal. This is where experts like Conseil, from our versiprosa text, come in, for they must be able to see beyond the narrow thrust of a particular interest and toward the potential of this interest, narrow as it may be, to serve as the instrument for the realization of the transcendental interest of the state. Such an expert is not an agent himself, for he does not carry out an action, whether on his own behalf, that of an interest group, or even of the state. However, he makes action possible by specifying the felicity conditions under which it can be undertaken, by whom, and to what end. He himself is a faceless functionary in the management of the deixis. Again, the discourse of an expert such as Conseil is not prose, yet he too functions in a proselike manner, which is why Molinet will not put even his *speech* into verse.

The sort of knowledge that an expert has is of considerable importance within the culture of the state. What sort of knowledge is it, and what does it say about knowledge within that culture? It is first and foremost disinterested knowledge, that is, the expert is not an advocate; on the contrary, he must stand at a distance from both his object and his own inscription within the social sphere. In other words, in the exercise of his expert function, he must detach himself from all appurtenances. That this was a strategy for the efficient functioning of the state is shown by the means France had to adopt to effect the rapid bureaucratization that was occurring at the time: great pains had to be taken to eliminate any ties between the petty official and that which he processes, because such ties would encourage the private appropriation of power. French district officials *(baillis)* were outside the fealty relationship, frequently transferred (thus positioned from above, not rooted from below), and "were forbidden to acquire land where they performed their official duties or to have their children marry property owners in that locality."[25] Juridical procedure provides a useful model of what goes on here: blood vengeance is replaced by state prosecution, with the specification that the functionary representing the state, the general prosecutor or public attorney, may in no way be related by blood or by any other ties to the other parties involved. His only stake in this process should be that of seeing justice done. He must construct a unique type of relationship, which we will come to know as the subject-object model of cognition, in which he will be the knowing subject of an object, as the latter is *assigned* to him. This may seem rather abstract, but it is saying only that from that point on, knowledge is to be mediated through institutions and disciplines.

Knowledge does not come from being rooted in a place, having grown in it; rather it comes from being able to distance oneself from that which one is to know. In order to know (as we saw in the *dérimage*), one has to occupy fleetingly a fragile position for the purposes of the knowing.[26] Such positions and purposes are precisely what disciplines specify. By contrast, he who simply "inhabits" is now but a native informant. His perspectives are not positionally constructed for purposes of knowledge, and thus they demand interpretation, demand to be themselves juxtaposed, overlaid, *put* in perspective.

We have found the functioning of the state very suggestive with respect to processes occurring within prose, just as prose's handling of discourses has turned out to be very illuminating with respect to the state's handling of agency. We are not suggesting that prose and the state are isomorphic; rather, we see in thirteenth-century France a culture delimited and empowered by operations characteristic of both prose and the state.[27] We certainly cannot at this stage do more than merely note such a similarity.

If we look at the fate of earlier signifying practices, we see that little is totally discarded. Many are framed and recycled within prose: a limited place is found for them. Many others prevent prose from invading their domain. For a signifying practice to resist prose means to a great extent to keep the writing that may exist within that practice subordinated to that practice's other particular literacies (e.g., the Koran means "recitation," and recitation it has remained). And many of the lasting signifying practices evolve in other directions. For example, theater clearly appears to be carrying on much of what performance did not yield to written verse and prose but kept as presence, presentation, and representation. The single jongleur, however, did not stay; each actor represents an agency limited *within* the production, and there is an agency (a playwright or director) who is not locatable among the presences on stage. Reciprocally, the audience begins to occupy a unique set of perspectival possibilities, not necessarily shared by anyone on stage or even, in a subsequent step, identified with an individual, biographical "vision."

Verse, as the displaced predecessor, poses particular problems, and it is instructive to follow its fate to see how a signifying practice negotiates its boundary with another major signifying practice. In its emergent state, prose does not invariable confront verse directly but rather grants it a privileged position, one that nonetheless restricts the scope of verse by surrounding it. Verse seems intact, even highlighted or fetishized (as in D'Auton, for example), even though it has lost its deixis, which has now been transferred to prose. Thus verse is literally at the mercy of prose. This is a state of affairs against which verse will rebel and resist.

One means of doing so is to elaborate the entire poetological tradition, which asserts that utterances can be freestanding and have to be considered autonomously from one another. In this instance, the safeguard from prose is institutional. Thus Renaissance poetics could be seen as part of a broad-based resistance to prose, which we will discuss later.

Another means is by privileging the lyric (Petrarch), which allows verse to attempt to recapture the ground of its own deixis, anchoring it in the *subject* who produces the verse and for whom there is no other discourse. The way the subject manifests itself in the verse is as unique voice, singular, whole, specifiable as to time and space, univocal. In performance, voice was but one element among many others; its transcription is taken to be the inscription of a deixis and thus a trace of presence. In other words, in writing, all that is left of presence is "voice." But voice raises the problem of the subjectivity of the subject, that is, the ability of the subject to experience his or her own presence to himself or herself. Thus the lyric covers a segment staked out by the terms trace and presence and oscillates in a dilemma so delimited. Verse can function within this segment and successfully resist the encroachment of prose, for it will either ground its deixis in presence or thematize its inability to do so. In any case, it does not ground its deixis in prose.

The integrity of voice soon comes under attack and from two different quarters. First, a romantic inquiry into the origins of verse comes up with the idea that such an origin is always a plural collective, a *Volk*voice, as Herder and Grimm put it, that is unspecifiable in space and time. All the great themes of poetry, all the archetypes, many of the forms, emanate spontaneously from this *Volk*, yet all the power of nineteenth-century historical science proves unable to go beyond more than mythic specification of such origin. Voice-based verse is deprived of its deixis, and a mythic origin has no standing in a world defined by historical science.

At the same time that univocity dissolves into a collective emanation, the integrity of the individual subject also comes under attack. Far from being a whole, the individual subject is a place of division, cleavage, uncertainty, territorialized by multiple social, psychological, cultural forces, each of which manifests itself in a different discourse. In effect, the subject is dialogic and not monologic. Here, too, verse loses its deictic underpinning, and it must now define itself differently in relation to prose.

Verse will either seek to revive and reauthorize myth, as in much of romantic verse, or accept its place in the world of the written and explore ways of outflanking prose by determining what makes for the power of language on paper. At this point, what occurs is no longer a competition with the considerable deictic manipulatory power of prose but an exploitation, by verse, of what has been learned about prose literacy. What results is Baudelaire's exploration of the prose poem, and Mallarmé's reflections on prose and experimentation with layout.[28] Symbolist and postsymbolist poetry are a result of this reflection.

What they discover by looking to prose is an articulation within it, an articulation similar to that of verse. Prose and verse are not really at loggerheads, for they do share some underlying entity that would be the ground of articulation, prior to both prose and verse. They locate that ground in language. The focus on language is misguided, however. Prose does not invest in language as a foundational category. It knows language to be a construct of philosophers, philologists, and *poètes en manque* (poets suffering withdrawal pains). Language is an abstract system, unlike prose, which is an operativity or an efficacy. Thus, to discover it is to discover a dead end, as is clearly demonstrated by the inability of forty years of German scholarship to make anything out of Valéry. Perhaps it is here that Rimbaud sensed the lack of future.

To be sure, the poets frequently lived these changes in a tragic mode and thus favored a rhetoric of crisis ("Crise de vers") to describe them. There was concomitantly the keen discovery that prose is not an element among others, that it does not bear looking at. It evades you or ignores you, dedicates no single position for you, leaves you no where. Flaubert commits himself to working *on* it, and surely has the keenest sense *of* it to date, but finds himself unable to get a grip: "J'en arrive à la conviction qu'il est *impossible d'écrire*" (I am coming to be convinced that it is *impossible to write*).

Mallarmé was suspicious of the turn to language, for it did not in any way deal with the problem of the power of prose. And thus he came to be much more concerned with the problem of limiting the extension of prose, as well as of verse, by formulating the project of the Book. Mallarmé's deconstruction of prose was carried out at the level of syntax and lexicon, however; categories of language and not of prose, which deals in discourses. It will be only the surrealists, and writers such as Boris Vian and Raymond Queneau in the French tradition, or Broch or Musil or Proust or Calvino, who will recognize the discursive basis of prose. In Bakhtinian terms, Proust would be someone who acknowledges the novel as dialogic, but channels it through an author who bears the responsibility for the dialogical quality of the novel. He thus usurps traditional conceptions of prose and reconstitutes the category of the author, making it important again. He is an example of an author totally at home with prose, able to dramatize the experience of living in a prosaic world, that is, a world supremely indifferent to categories of wholeness and autonomy. He knows its mechanisms intimately and identifies himself within it. Prose usually hides behind all its discourses, and to think of it as an "author's words" is a distortion. Prose can stand behind the authorship of Proust, however, and conserve all its operations intact.

After this very cursory sketch of where verse is going, we can now ask, what is the promise of prose? We have attached ourselves to the description of its emergence and thus to the specification of the conditions that would permit it. We have seen prose become progressively stronger and less beholden to previous signifying practices, as it begins to provide one of the underpinnings of the culture of Western modernity. It would be a mistake, however, to think that once it has emerged, prose will no longer encounter any obstacles on the path of its further development. On the contrary, it will find in its way residues of older cultures and signifying practices and new constructs that seek either to block it or to espouse its movement without understanding it. In other words, its path will be a tortuous one. We must bear in mind that unlike the Hegelian concept, prose is not itself an agent, containing within itself a program that it needs to realize. It works more by occupying the interstices between existing entities, which it then redefines and realigns within its own domain. Every obstacle is thus a new challenge, which sends prose into a new direction or reconfigures it. It does not have a linear history. Beyond its emergence, its course is far from certain or clear: some of the features attendant to its emergence appear to regress only to reappear more recently. There is no ultimate shape that prose needs to achieve.

To begin with, we must stress that what we have been calling prose poses considerable problems of apprehension. Over and over again, we have seen that in all the processes it ordains and regulates, prose does not highlight or feature itself, for there is no "self" to feature. It is not a substance, in the sense that the taxonomically oriented poetician would like it to be, hence his external disappointment with prose: as soon as the poetician thinks that he or she has found it, he or she discovers that it is something else, be it the essay, the novel, a piece of rhetoric, or perhaps just one discourse. The frustration of the poetician, however, is slight when compared with the puzzlement that those who lived contemporaneously to the emergence of prose must have felt. They were bred and raised in a world of substance in a way that is almost entirely beyond our present powers of comprehension. Today, we know of abstract workings and forces, whether in the structure of the atom, the nature of light, the black box of information theory, the operations of black holes, or psychological phenomena. We also have a sense, no doubt pivotal to the very conception of this book, of both the active power and the nonetheless concurrent immateriality of *media*. Our predecessors, however, came from a world of substance in which it was important to identify the materiality one dealt with. We have seen that one of the ways in which prose will indeed be apprehended is as the *materia* that stands ready to be informed.

We have also seen, however, that, as material as prose might be, an apprehension of it as thereby inert and inactive is blind to prose's fundamental operativity. This operativity, however, is difficult to disengage, as our efforts in this direction make abundantly clear. Historically, though, it will not be without *effects*, and it is through these effects that the operations and historical development of prose can be apprehended. No more than a few landmarks can be indicated here, in a book that after all has been devoted to the emergence, and not the entire course of prose.

We have seen that one of the most radical features of prose is its ability to articulate discourses one to the other so that local deixis is produced at will and to permit a relative autonomy to discourses that otherwise would necessitate elaborate specification of anchoring. The result is one of seamless flux, of constant displacement, and it must have proven quite disturbing to those raised in an environment dedicated to the values of stability, localization, and presence. The effect that prose will produce here is the problematization of the subject whereby the latter now needs to develop an introspective dimension, what we call a subjectivity, which will be taken to be the locus and the container of this flux. The shifts, overlays, and uncertainties that we have seen prose effect are barely tolerable as features of the world, for they literally disorient the subjects living in the world, but they can be ascribed to something that will eventually be called the mental life of the subject. *It* can be in flux, the immemorial evidence of dreams suggests. (If the Renaissance spent so much time on dreams, it is not by chance.) The subject can try to keep track of this flux and in the process see itself not as an entity but as the flux itself. Such is certainly the project of Montaigne's *Essais*.

It has been often remarked that Montaigne lived at a time of considerable sociopolitical turmoil: the Italian wars, the wars of religion, the imposition of strong central rule over areas only recently brought under the direct control of the Crown, and yet how little of this turmoil transpires in his essays. Some have made the rather facile suggestion that Montaigne internalizes these external forms of turmoil, but it would be more accurate to say that unlike many of his contemporaries, who found in literacies derived from other signifying practices the deictic anchoring from which to gain a view however partial of the turmoil, Montaigne seeks to apply a different literacy, one that is clearly based on his remarkable skills as a reader—as is made clear by his citational approach to the problem and by the site of his musings (his library). Here he discovers that he is neither the source nor the location of deixis. He cannot construct stable distinctions between object and subject, and thus he achieves a kind of cognition that he is used to. He can produce only a record of the shifts, uncertainties, and displacement, that is, he attempts to track this prosaic process that he wishes not to internalize but to extirpate from the interiority in which he conceives himself to be and to objectify in an artifact cognitively attested: what we call a "book." For if his subjectivity can be apprehended in book form, it may be presumed that it will be amenable to the readerly skills that literate individuals possess. But Montaigne is sufficiently literate in prose skills to know that this will not produce either a stable or a final reading: it will only give the processes of subjectivity an objective existence.

Montaigne's manner of dealing with the problems of flux and redefinable deixis was bearable inasmuch as it was limited to subjectivity and contained by it. In the broader sphere of interpersonal relations, let alone in the king's court and the sociopolitical sphere at large, these proselike processes threaten anarchy. The structural impossibility of fixing determinate, permanent, and external deixis unmoors values, individuals, and groups. Danger lurks in such circumstances but so do opportunities. Rhetoric regains favor, although its function is now quite different from the one it played in antiquity. Then the boundary of the *polis* was clearly known, and the mobility of citizens was based on the premise of their formal equivalence in the eyes of the law. Now the society of feudally determined position begins to move to a state form of organization. Rhetoric is one of the means by which this reassignment of place is accomplished: it can loosen existing attachments and be used to define distances between speaker and hearer, thus contributing to the remapping of the social sphere. At the hands of master rhetoricians, it becomes the practice of power, either for the establishment of a new social order or for the more readerlike exploitation of opportunities for the acquisition and control of power. Machiavelli will be quick to understand this opportunity and see that the very threat of disorientation, breakdown of relations, and general nonsensicalness, are now powerful weapons to be harnessed in the exercise of power.

Shifting deixis leads, on the one hand, to various attempts to limit its mobility. The nascent modern state may be a beneficiary of this feature, to the extent that it can, like prose, establish a breadth of field of its own, within which these moves can be contained, observed, and juxtaposed. But the state is also in a position to appreciate or to recognize its disruptive potential to itself as it seeks to impose a new order. One of the tasks of bureaucracy is to establish parameters for such shifts: the dating, recording, and archiving of documents conceived of as "deeds" testifies to this desire to master deixis from the outside. On the other hand, the gap that shifting deixis constantly opens between what seems to be and what is comes to be thematized as the problem of being and appearance and leads to a vast problem of social semiotization: one seeks to take on the guise of what one feels oneself to be or wishes oneself to be. In the sixteenth and seventeenth centuries, the theater flourishes under such circumstances, which permit of both tragic and comic modulations. And of course theater can have recourse to speech and presence that allow the illusion, at least, of deixis under control, although playwrights such as Shakespeare, Molière, and Racine are quick to see that such deixis as theater offers participates in the play of being and appearance regulated by a deeper deixis, which we see as a working of prose.

The uncertainty of the external world, the inability to immediately determine whether one is dealing with reality or appearance, leads to an epistemological crisis. Nowhere is prose's effect more deeply felt than in this area. For its very processes represent the abandonment of the Parmenidean belief in the equation of language and being. With this equation problematized, the search for epistemological certainty will have to switch from the real to the subject but a subject that now must be cleansed of all the flux, which is then ascribed to the sensory apparatus, to function as the source of all reliable cognition. In our terms, then, the Cartesian *cogito* is an attempt to ground deixis in a thinking self. Method is used to establish internal order and to arm the subject with a carapace that will make him or her immune, or at least resistant, to the surrounding flux. Covered by such a carapace, the individual subject is then ready to confront the external world, a world from which he or she is currently cut off, a place of danger and opportunities. It is a world to be conquered by imposing on it the instrumentality of reason.

Structurally, prose offers another possibility that will also be realized. The world of discourses must have some boundary, it suggests, and whereas combinations of these discourses are indeed infinite, the basic elements cannot be. Thus, from the medieval compilation to the eighteenth-century encyclopedia, there persists a dream of totalization, of containing all that is relevant within one space, and thus of finally being able to orient oneself both within and in relation to it. Such a space will require the fourth dimension of time, of course, and it is precisely what Hegel will use to impose an organization on it.

Hegel conceives of his own project as the bringing to consciousness through the temporal dimension of something that was secretly at work and producing its own effect. The development of the spirit, thus, would be the progressive investment of the world by the spirit. It would be tempting to read the course of prose according to this model. But we have seen that it is not prose that achieves self-consciousness in the nineteenth century—rather, it is verse. It is the Mallarméan project to identify verse with such self-consciousness, so that verse ultimately must, in his light, conquer prose as consciousness conquers all that is unconscious. Mallarmé is thus able to announce the end of prose as being in sight: he said, "Il n'y a pas de prose."

The Hegelian model appears powerful because it threatens prose where prose seems most vulnerable. We have seen that prose indeed does not offer itself to view and plays what could be described as a game of self-concealment. Therefore, to bring it into the light would be to affix it and thus dominate it. It would be the end of prose. We may well wonder, then, whether this book is not one step in that direction. Indeed, as we turn to the world around us and hear the cries about growing illiteracy, observe the apparent receding of language in front of media that exploit other parts of the sensorium and those that delve into the immaterial itself, such as forms of electronic communication, we may begin to think that our ability to conceive of this project and to carry it out as far as we have may stem from prose's losing its wind, as it were, and offering itself to our inquisitive gaze, and to our mercies, like some behemoth risen from the deep and pathetically beached on our shores.

But if there is anything we have learned in this inquiry, it is that prose is not a substance that can be apprehended in such organic terms. Its fundamental power derives from the fact that it understood a basic mechanism of language, namely its ability to refer to its own enactment and thus to construct deixis. As opposed to previous signifying practices, which had to rely on elements that they did not control for the establishment of their own deictic inscription (hooking up to something that is outside themselves, having to colonize and bring in a piece of the world), prose is deictically autonomous. Prose, able to carry its deixis from within itself, can give us the world.

The deictic mechanism we have taken to be the exclusive property of language turns out to be proper to all semiosis, not just to its verbal fraction. It is from here that media derive their efficacy. A progressively prosaic world is not only one that is now inscribed more and more within prose but also one in which the deictic play characteristic of prose pervades the nonwritten and indeed the nonverbal as well. New media, then, do not contain prose, nor do they establish their own reach at its expense, they extend the scope of that deictic discovery. As a result, as it becomes less visible, prose may appear to recede. But then again, that is what prose is wont to do.

APPENDIX

La Ressource du Petit Peuple
Jean Molinet

1. —Pour ce que naguaires vent failli aux volans de mon molinet, qui multitude de nouvelles histoires debvoit tourner entre ses meules, pour en tirer fleur et farine, pensant oublier merancolie, je me tiray aux champs et, ainsi que, par admiration, je reguardoye les plaisanz flouritures dont les preaulx herbus estoient ricement parez, soubdainement s'ouvri la terre, se vis ung tres parfond abisme, duquel, aveuc feu, flame et fumee qui premiere en sailli, sourdi sur piez une tres laide, espoentable satrape, fille de perdicion, fiere de regard, horrible de face, difforme de corpz, perverse de coeur, robuste de bras et ravissant des mains : elle avoit le chief cornu, les oreilles pendans, les yeux ardans, la bouche moult tortue, les dens agus, la langue serpentine, les poings de fer, la pance boursouflee, le dos velu, la queue venimeuse et estoit puissamment montee sur ung estrange monstre a maniere de leuserve fort et corageux a merveilles, jettant feu par la geule, chaulx et soufre par les narines, chargie a tous letz d'espees, couteaulx, dolequins, rasoirs, soyes, faulx, dagues, planchons, paffus, picques, pinces, pouchons, forches, fourches, ars, dars, hars, licolz, chaines, cordes et cagnons, ensemble pluseurs instrumens convenables a son office et portoit sus la crupe ung bariseau plain d'escorpions, riagal, arsenic, uuille, plong boulant, harpois, azil et morteles poisons. Quand ceste plutonique matrosne se trouva sur les rendz accompagnie de Crudelité, Famine, Fraude, Rapine, Sacriliege, Conspiration, Murtre et Felonnie, elle appella par propres noms pour conduire son oost Cacus, Nemproth, Denys, Dyoscorus, Datien, Marchien, Simphronien, Rictiovaire,

Olibrius, Agricolan, Matrocolus, Elmoradach, avec Neron qui portoit l'estandart, lesquelz impetueusement yssus de ce tres puissant gouffre, hydeux, crueux et fantasticques, crochus, bochus et noirs que Moriens, montez touttevoyes sus elephans, giraffes, tigres, griffons, serpens, dragons et cocodrilles, se rengerent en grosse bataille, esleverent ung terrible tonnoire, criminel fourdre et dure pestilence et en courant le plat pays commencherent a sanc espandre, bruler eglises, mutiler innocens, deflorer vierges, rostir petis enfans, fourdroier villes et patibuler gens. Et tant exploiterent de detestables et execrables faix que l'hystoire au loing recitee donroit piteuses lermes aux yeulx des escoutans. Sy tost que la lice rabice eut perpetré ce dolent vasselage par ses mignons qui le nommoient Tirannie, avec sieute de boute feus, gibelins, pirates, satellites, fueillars, bringars, nacquez, laronceaulx, cavestreaux, quoquineaulx, paillardeaux et ribaudeaux qui se fourerent en la queue de son armee, au tres grant prejudice et desercion desdis pays, et que ycelle se fut mug petit eslongee de nostre climat, sans rentrer toutesvoyes en son trou sathanicque, une tres reverente dame, prudente, sage et de grant auctorité se mit aux champs pour visiter ce grief dommage et, entre les furieuses inhumanitez par elle mises a execution, trouva une jeusne dame, selon la dicque d'une foriere, gisant comme pasmee, a demy morte et durement foullee, eschevellee et despoullie de ses nobles royaulx atours et auprés d'elle un petit enfant de l'eage de deux ans, criant angoisseusement, plongiet en lermes, oppressé de famine, querant les tetins de sa mere pour y trouver sa nouriture. Chose pitoyable et la plus douloureuse de jamais estoit a vëoir ceste desolee compaigne et n'y avoit tant riant œil qu'il ne fusist tourné en pleur. L'enfant moult haut crioit par destresse de faim, la mere se taisoit par traveil inhumain, l'enfant queroit sa vie ou sain de sa nourice, la mere queroit mort et derrenier supplice, l'enfant plourant succhoit une wide mamelle et la mere enduroit plaine doleur mortelle. Et tantost la bonne dame qui premiere trouva ceste piteuse assamblee, regarda la patiente en face, et jassoit ce quelle fusist fort deffiguree, recognu par certain secret signe que celle estoit Justice, sa sœur germaine, et l'enfant estoit le petit peuple, qui ambedeux par paresse, foiblesse ou male garde estoyent tresbuchiez ou parfont cavain de tirannique pestilence et lors, par pitié et compassion dont elle fut a cop navrée, esleva ung merveilleux cri farsy de pleurs, enterlardé de souspirs, baisa sa soeur en la face, le couvri de son riche mantel, puis print l'enfanchon en ses bras et de sa tres doulce alaine lui reschauffa les petites manottes, en ce faisant comme celle qui ne redoubtoit ame synon Dieu, car Vérité se fait appeller ; par ung ardant couroux qu'il luy monta au cœur, d'une vive voix tres agüe, sans riens celer, desgorgua son invective contre les recteurs de la chose publicque et dit en tel maniere :

VERITÉ

2. —Princes puissans, qui tresors affinez
Et ne finez de forgier grans discors,
Qui dominez, qui le peuple aminez,
Qui ruminez, qui gens persecutez,
Et tourmentez les ames et les corpz,
Tous vos recors sont de piteux ahors ;
Vous estes hors d'excellence boutez :
Povres gens sont a tous lez reboutez.

Que faittes vous, qui perturbés le monde
Par guerre immonde et criminelx assaulx,
Qui tempestez et terre et mer parfonde,
Par feu, par fonde et glave furibunde,
Sy qu'il n'habonde aux champz que vielles saulx ?
Vous faittes saulx et mengiez bonhomeaulx,
Villes, hamiaulx et n'y sariés forgier.
La moindre flour qui soit en leur vergier.

Estes vous dieux, estes vous demi dieux,
Argus plain d'yeux, ou anglez incarnez ?
Vous estes fais, et nobles et gentieux,
D'humains hostieux, en ces terrestres lieux,
Non pas es chieulx, mais tous de mere nez;
Batez, tonnez, combatez, bastonnez
Et hutinez, jusques aux testes fendre :
Contre la mort nul ne se peult deffendre.

Trenchiez, copez, detrenchiez, decoppez,
Frappez, haspez banieres et barons,
Lanchiez, hurtez, balanciez, behourdez,
Querez, trouvez, conquerez, controuvez,
Cornez, sonnez trompettes et clarons,
Fendez tallons, pourfendés orteillons,
Tirez canons, faittes grans espourris :
Dedens cent ans vous serez tous pourris.

Qu'ont emporté de ce mondain wason
David, Sanson, Perseüs, Herculés,
Hector, Paris, Alixandre, Jason,
Laomedon, Pompee, Scipïon,
Cesar, Charlon, Hanibal, Achillés,
Mitridatés, Cirus, Pirus, Xersés,
Et Ulixés ? ilz ont, pour toutte ville,
Sept piez de terre a boutter ung corps vile.

Se Dieu vous a, pour regir les humains,
Bailliet es mains la terre descouverte,

Se n'esse pas, dont je souspire et plains,
Pour semer plains ne sang avant les plains,
De gens mors plains, par grosse guerre ouverte ;
Soit gaing, soit perte oultrageuse ou deserte,
Vostre desserte arrez au darrenier :
Chascun merchier portera son panier.

Qui est celi qui s'oze mettre aux champz,
Pour gens meschans, riolez, piolez,
Qui robent gens sur la terre marchans
Et bons marchans et treuvent les passans,
Gens trespassans, murdris et esgeulez,
Temples brulez, moisnes tous desriglez,
Terres sans bledz et gibés sans pendee ?
Quand raison dort, justice est mal gardee.

On treuve aux campz pastoureaux sans brebis,
Clercs sans habis, prestres sans breviaire,
Chasteaulx sans tours, granges sans fouragiz,
Bours sans logis, estables sans seulis,
Chambres sans lis, hosteulx sans luminaire,
Murs sans parfaire, eglises sans refaire,
Villes sans maire et cloistre sans nonettes :
Guerre commet pluiseurs fais deshonnettes.

Chartreux, chartriers, charetons, charpentiers,
Moutons, moustiers, manouvriers, marissaux,
Villes, villians, villages, vivendiers,
Hameaux, hotiers, hospitaulx, hosteliers,
Bouveaux, bouviers, bocquillons, bonhommeaulx,
Pouchins, pourceaux, pelerins, pastoureaulx,
Fourniers, fourneaulx, feves, fains, fleurs et fruitz
Par vos gens sont indigens on destruis.

Par vos gens sont laboureurs lapidez,
Cassis cassez, confreres confondus,
Gallans gallez, gardineurs gratinez,
Rentiers robez, rechepveurs renchonnez,
Paÿs passez, paÿsans pourfendus,
Abbez abbus, appentis abbatus,
Bourgois batus, baguettes butinees,
Viellars vanez et vierges violees.

Que n'est exent de ces crueulx debas
Le peuple bas a vos guerres submis !
Il vous nourrit, vous ne le gardez pas
Des malvais pas, mais se treuve plus las
Dedens vos las que prins des ennemis ;

Il est remis de ses propres amis,
Perdu et mis a tourmens esprouvez :
Il n'est tenchon que de voisins privez.

Pensez vous point que de vos grands desroix
Au roy des roix il vous fault rendre conte ?
Vos pillars ont pilliet, par grans effrois,
Chappes, orfrois d'eglise et croche et croix,
Comme je croidz et chascun le raconte,
Dieu roy et conte et vicaire et viconte,
Comtesse et comte et roy et roÿnotte,
Au departir faulra conter a l'hoste.

De sainte Eglise estes vous gardiiens
Cotidiiens, vous y debvez regars ;
Mais vous mengiez, en boutant le doy ens,
Docteurs, doyens, chapitres, cytoyens,
Garbes, loÿens, greniers, gardins et gars ;
Gouges et gars, garnemens et esgars
Soubz leurs hangars ont tout graté sy net
Qu'on ne voit grain en gar n'en gardient.

Lisez par tout, vous verrez en cronicque,
Bible autentique, hystoires et haulx fais
Que toutes gens qui, par fait tirannicque,
Pillent relique, eglise catholique
Ou paganique, endurent pesans fais ;
D'honneur deffais, sours, bochus, contrefais
Ou desconfés sont en fin de leurs jours :
Qui qui paye, Dieu n'acroit pas tousjours.

Oez vous point la voix des povres gens,
Des indigens peris sans alligance,
Des laboureurs qui ont perdu leurs chens,
Des innocens, orphenins impotens,
Qui mal contens crient a Dieu vengance ?
Viellesse, enfance, aer, feu, fer, florissance,
Brute naissance et maint noble edifice
Sont vrays tesmoingz de vostre malefice.

Du firmament le grant cours cessera,
Le ciel sera cocu sans estre ront,
Jamais en mer fleuve n'arrivera,
Plong nagera, le feu engelera,
Glace ardera, cabilleaux volleront,
Boefz parleront, les femmes se tairont,
Et si seront mons et vaulx tous onnis,
Se vos meffais demeurent impugnis.

Oez vous point hurter a vos taudis
Les Turcqz maldis accourans les grans cours ?
Resveilliez vous, sans estre recrandis,
Princes hardis, appaisiez vos partis,
Soyez partis de grace sans decours ;
Vos jours sont cours, Turcz aprocent vos cours,
Donnez secours au saint pere de Rome :
Il n'est si belle ausmosne qu'a son prosme.

Accordez vous, roix et ducz, accordez
Et regardez vostre peuple en pité ;
Resuscitez justice et le gardez ;
Prenez, pendez, plantez, patibulez,
Boulez, brulez, nul ne soit respité ;
El la cité de Dieu serez cité,
Felicité arez en habandon :
Il n'est sy belle acqueste que de don.

L'ACTEUR

3. —Les parolles de verité estoyent tant haultaines, trenchans et vives qu'elles penetroyent les coeurs de tous ceulx qui les escoutoyent et fut a copy avironnee de gens de tous estas qui regarderent en pitié la miserable violence dont Justice estoit oppressee, ensemble le petit peuple, son enfant, tout affamé de longue jeusne, traveillié de criier et braire, qui n'estoit pas de prime face a rappaisier d'une hochette ; entre pluiseurs qui arriverent a ce tres douloureux spectacle, Verité, qui moult estoit sage, choisy ung homme tout meur, assez grave, de reverend maintien, discret et bien moriginé, habitué de robe longue et d'ung bel chapperon foudré et, comme celle qui reclaime au besoing son leal amy, Verité s'escria vers luy a haulte voix et se print a dire :

VERITÉ

Ha, Conseil, nostre bon amy, nostre bon amy, Conseil, se vous avez en espargne quelque nombre de lermes procedant de la pitoyable fontaine de vostre coeur, sy les desployez a cop, car mieulx emploiier ne les sçariez. Vecy Justice, vostre maistresse, ma desolee soeur et germaine a Prudence, vostre espeuze, nouvellement tombee en pamoison et le petit peuple son enfant tirant a fin dure et mortele, se n'est par vostre bon secours. Je cognoy par espreuve vostre science et proesse : Conseil, nostre bon amy, vous avez sept ars sur le doy et le droit canon en possesse et tant tiens je de vostre escolle que nul prince, tant soit haultain, ne doibt chose ardue ou doulteuse encommencier sans vostre advis. Quiconques vous prent en desdaing, ja n'ara bonne consequence : les nobles progeniteurs dont vous tirez naturele origine ont suscité Justice en pluiseurs regnes, eslevé sceptres royaulx jusques aux estoilles et entretenu jadis en glorieuse renommee Assiriiens, Italiians, Troyens, Cartagiiens, Belgiiens, Lacedemoniiens, Babiloniiens, Persans, Macedoniiens, Egiptïens et souverainement la triumphant monarchie des Romains, car, par la tres noble industrie d'armes ou ilz estoyent habilitez, aveuc le cler engin, sens et praticque de vos samblables qui lors ou senat flourissoyent, touttes les nations du monde, mansuetes et barbaricques, se vindrent rendre tributaires en l'ombre de leur Capitole. Depuis ce temps, je suis certaine, nostre bon amy Conseil, que la chose publique est grandement augmentée en vos mains en pluiseurs provinces, palais, villes, chasteaulx, citez et cours et meismes de nostre vivant en la tres clere et resplendissant maison de Bourgoigne. Qui esse qui soubz la chevalereuse baniere du duc Philippe, prince de glorieuse memoire, a debrisié les pointes des guerres apparantes, humilié les rebelles et nourri le petit peuple du fruit de paix, d'amour et de leesse ? Conseil. Qui esse qui soubz la tres flamboyant espee du tres illustre duc Charles, que Dieu absoile, a soustenu Justice haultement auctorisie en parlement honourable et en audience publicque, concordé le rice et le povre ? Conseil. Qui esse qui soubs la tres victorieuse main du duc Maximilien peult susciter Justice en convalescence, corrigier les delinquans, subvenir aux oppressez et conduire le petit peuple au bien heuré temple de paix ? Conseil. Conseil dont, nostre bon amy leal,b en qui flourit, croiu t et resplend noblesse, sens et preudhomie, aveuc la tres recommandee science de medecine, tesmonigz grans et horribles playes par vous sanees en pluiseurs bonnes villes, donnez soing a vostre engin, regard a vostre œil et labeur a vostre main, sy reduisiez en estat de prosperitéJustice aveuc son petit peuple qui expirent devant vos yeulx.

L'ACTEUR

Adonc Conseil, vaincu par les prieres de Verité, sans faire longue excuse pour la hastivité du cas, regarda en face Justice, tasta son poulx, vista son urine et lui pria tres instamment, s'elle avoit esperit en elle, qu'elle monstrast signe de vie et, se possible lui estoit de parler, elle s'en mesist en paine pour plus a plain congnoistre la cause de sa doleance. Et lors la desolee patiente, Dieu scet a quel traveil de corps, leva ung petit le chief en hault et de une voix bassette et casse en faisant ses dures complaintes, complaindant ses griefves doleurs, dolousant ses piteux regrés, en regretant ses bons amis proposa ces motz :

JUSTICE

4. —Justice suis, privee de solas,
Ez las
helas !
De fausse tirannie,

Car j'ai perdu, par guerres et debas,
Esbas ;
Au bas
Est ma grant baronnie ;
Je suis fort desgarnie
De gens et de maisnie ;
N'est ame qui manie
Les malfacteurs ;
Ma perverse ennemie,
Qui pour lors ne dort mie,
M'a la force endormie
Et mes facteurs.

Roÿne fus de haulte renommee,
Armee,
Amee
Ou regne des vertus ;
Maintenant suis, sans terre et sans contree,
Oultree,
Entree
Ou port des mal vestus.
Salomon, Ligurgus,
Torquatus, Trajanus,
Codrus, Fabricius,
Charle le Grant,
Cambissés, Camilus,
Et Marcus Regulus,
Furent, quand je valus,
Mon seul garant.

Ma voix avoit la force de Sampson ;
Par son
Reson
Baritonnant tonnoye.
Helas ! mon Dieu, sans tourner a bas ton,
Par ton
Baton
Les basteurs bastonnoye,
Mutineurs matinoye,
Hutineurs hustinoye,
Haussaires haussagove ;
A tout endroit,
Opresseurs opressoye,
Deffenseurs deffendoye
Et aux perdans rendoye
Raison et droit.

Et maintenant me faillent bras et mains ;
Romains,
Germains,
Dont me vient cest erreur ?
Je hue et pleure et crie soirs et mains ;
Du mains,
Je mains
En l'ombre de terreur ;
Ma valeur m'est malheur,
Ma doulceur m'est doleur,
Mon oudeur m'est ardeur,
Plouris m'est ris,
Mon long heur m'est langeur,
Ma vigeur m'est rigeur,
Mon honneur m'est horreur,
Mon pris m'est pris.

Je suis, combien que tres fort je cancelle,
Courcelle
Et celle
Ou droit se clarifie,
Fille de Dieu, tres sage jovencelle,
Ancelle,
Et celle
En qui foy se confie,
Qui les maulx purifie,
Qui torfais rectifie,
Qui guerre pacifie,
Quant j'ay vaillance,
Qui les loix saintifie,
Qui les bons perlifie,
Qui les coeurs justifie.
A la balance.

Quand j'eux en main roy, roc, regne et regent,
Argent
Et gent
Qui regenter volloyent,
Mettre je fis, je vous ay en convent,
Souvent
Au vent
Les hars qui harceloyent ;
Laboureurs labouroyent,
Recepveurs recevoyent,
Pastoureaux pastouroyent
Joyeusement,

Chevaucheurs chevauchoyent,
Navieurs navioyent,
Et marchans marchandoyent
Paisiblement.

Par les debas et les crueulx desroix
Des roix
Trop roidz
Le monde se desroye,
Tout est ravi par ravace on par roitz ;
Parois,
Terrois
Sont mis au bout de roye ;
L'ung ronge, l'autre roye,
L'ung froisse, l'autre froye,
L'ung charbon, l'autre croye ;
Char et charoy
L'ung brise, l'autre broye ;
L'ung fiert, l'autre fourdroye,
L'ung pille et l'autre proye :
C'est povre arroy.

Je suis couchié ou lit de desconfort ;
Mon fort
Confort
Me laisse perissant,
Je vis envis, car mon espoir est mort,
La mort
Me mord
Et suis amenrissant ;
J'amenris languissant,
Je languis gemissant,
Je gemis en pelourant,
Je pleure en voye ;
Je voy en empirant,
J'empire en souspirant,
Je souspire en morant,
Mort me desvoye.

Dames de court, quie le bon temps menez,
Venez,
Tournez
Pitié devant ma face ;
Et vous, mignons, qui chantez et dansez,
Pensez,
Visez
Au meschief qui m'efface;

Gemissemens j'amasse,
De bruit n'aray ja masse,
Mieulx a morir j'amasse
Que compasser
Deul, dont j'ay l'outrepasse ;
Sans respas je trespasse ;
Le pas que chascun passe
Me fault passer.

CONSEIL

5. —O Justice, ma chiere dame, donnez chez a vostre complainte, vostre doleur n'est pas mortele, prenez une onche de joye contre deux livres de tristesse : vous n'avez quelque playe ouverte, le cief est sain, si est le coeur, mais les membres vous sont faillis par leur maulvais gouvernement ; pestilence de guerre vous a ferue, tirannie vous a batue et piteusement flagellee, non pas de fer agu, mais seulement de sombres copz, par quoy vous ne poez courrir ne secourrir le petit peuple, lequel s'est tant enforcié de crier aprés vous que certainement il est tout derompus. Et pour ce, mas tres honouree maistresse, que vostre miserable inconvenient cause un tres horible dommage a la chose publicque, et de ce j'en appelle saint Augustin en tesmoingnage, distant que les royalmes sans justice ne sont que larronnieres, j'ay decreté, a mon possible, de donner souffissant remede a vostre griefve oppression ; premier touchant vostre noble personne, affin que ne demourez affolee et que les humeurs superflues ne vous empeschent le ceur, il est necessité que vous soyez sainye de la vaine du foye, car par faulte de foy estes vous en partie toutte sangmellee. Et se le malvais sang n'est tiré de vostre corps, jamais n'arez jour de santé. Au regart du petit peuple qui est tout derompu, s'il porte une petite restrainte, il n'en vauldra que de mieulx cy aprés, il en sera plus humble, plus cremeteux et mains adonné a folie. Exemple, le peuple d'Israel dansoit devant un veau, lorsqui'l fut cras et dru ; quant il fut fameilleux es desers, il prioit Dieu souvent et menu. Le peuple des Romains, lorsqu'i fut orgueilleux, perdi ses regions ; quant il fut humble et povre, il fut signeur et sire de toutes nations. David, en sa prosperité, fut homicide et adultere et, durant son adversité, fut devot plain de saint mistere. Ainsy donc, se le petit peuple est restraint par bonne mesure en sa jonesse, il n'y para en sa viellesse. Et se ce non, les entrailles luy descenderont ez boursettes, sy que jamais ne porra pain gaignier. En oultre, se vous souffrez taillier le petit peuple, il est perdu a tousjours mais, de dix il n'en eschape deux, puisqu'il sont touchiez du rasoir ; apres rere n'y a que tondre ; il est tant jus, tant povre et tant debile qu'il n'a que le pel et les os. Mais s'il vous plaist avoir vostre petit peuple nettement gueri de sa derompture, sans violence de taille, incision ou playe, selonc l'usage de medecine, il seroit besoing de faire une decoction de consaudes, lesquelles aulcunes gens appellent marguarites et,

se vous poiez finer de deux tres nobles marguarites resplendissans en ce val de misere, lorsque toutes gracieuses fleurs sont hors de saison, vous ariez santé recouvree : l'une est la grande Margerite d'Iorcque, la precieuse perle d'Angleterre, la fleur de beaulté redolente, espannie en cestui quartier, glorieusement flourissant ou plaisant vergier de Bourgoigne, celle qui nuit et jour labeure au bien de paix, celle qui s'est puis nagueres transportee outre la mer pour subvenir au bien publicque, celle de si exellente bonté que, se le petit peuple pooit sentir son oudeur et incorporer sa melliflueuse vertu, jamais n'aroit deul ne grevance. L'autre consaude est la petite Marguarite de Bourgoigne, sa fileule, apparue puis ung an au tres fructueux jardin du duc d'Austrice, belle, blance et tres debonnaire et pour ce qu'elle est tendre, pure, vermeillette et bien coulouree, s'elle estoit mixtionnee aveuc quelque fleur de lis ou d'englentier, qui mieulx m'agree, espoir que, se le petit peuple en pooit gouster la douceur, il oubliroit merancolie. Helas, Justice, pendant le temps que vous estiés en bruit, vous entreteniés noble estat et estiés honouree et assistee des grans et des petis, des dames et des damoiselles et lorsque vous avez le bont, il n'est ame qui vous compagne : Clergiet vous habandonne, Chevalerie vous delaisse, Marchandise ne peult courrir et Labeur ne vous peult nourir. Touttefois il est besoing, se vous vollés retourner en santé, que quelque dame forte et rade vous administre en vos necessitez et ne porriez, pour souhaidier, mieulx choisir que d'avoir Puissance. Puissance est fiere et deffensable pour vous garder a tous endrois et pour vous remettre en estat, s'elle y voloit mettre la main ; et ne souffit seulement avoir puissance de corps, mais il loist qu'elle soit sortie d'or et d'argent, de nobles et de hardis pour aidier son maistre au besoing et subvenir au petit peuple et, avec ce, doibt estre sage, leale et amoureuse du prince auquel elle s'assert : Alexandre concquist Judee, Surie, Caldee et les isles orientales, jusques au port des Bragmans, plus par le sens de sa puissance que par le trenchant de l'espee ; Cesar fut tant aimé de ses chevaliers qu'ilz amoyent mieulx a morir que prester foy aux ennemis : Puissance dont leale et bonne vous peult aidier plus que nulle aultre.

JUSTICE

Conseil, nostre leal amy, vous mettez avant choses assez fortes et dificiles, ne say qui les achevera ; nous cognoissons assez que Puissance nous peult plus tost remettre sus que nulle rien ; les experiences en sont cleres en mainte noble region, mais ou esse qu'on la prenra ? C'est le plus fort de l'avoir en personne.

COUNSEIL

Justice, ne vous soussyez, Puissance n'est si eslongee de vostre maysonnette que brief ne seroit pres de vous, s'elle avoit bonne volenté ; Puissance sieut la cour du prinche et se tient en Flandres, en Brebant, a Bruges, a Gand, en Hollande et Zelande et en Namur et est trop plus flamengue que walonne ; elle est de moyenne taille et scet le tour de son baston, dont elle se fait a prisier. Et, comme dit Vegece, la petite puissance hardie et fort exercitee parvient a son intention et la grande pussiance folle et estourdie se contourne en confusion ; plus bateille le ceur et la juste querelle que le robuste bras et la dure alemelle. Se vous desirez enquerrir la forche et la proesse de la puissanche de ce quartier, parlez au ramanant des francqz archiers qui demourerent en la bataille de la Viesville, vous trouverez, et Verité le vous tesmoignera, comment elle queru ses ennemis aux pointes des espees, ordonna ses batailles, soustint les escarmuces, brisa sa lance, charga raddement, servi son prince, secouru ses amis, habandonna ses joyaulx, concquist honneur et appoingna les culeuvres et horribles serpentes de ses adversaires jettans feu et flame pour le destruire ; la furent en valeur les nobles de Gant, la furent en cours les hardis du pays ; tant feri, tant lancha, bati, percha, marcha et desmarcha ceste puissance flandrine, nourrie de bonne queute, que, a petite perte des siens, synon de ses atours, gaigna le vin, le champ, les engiens et le bruit de la journee. Maintenant repose a son aise, maintenant fait son rice amas, non point de grans doubles, de placques, de malvaix doffins ne d'acroupis, mais fait tresors de bons amis du temps passé, des desirés, des fins bretons, des aidans de Liege et des lyons de Flandres et certes s'elle pooit avoir des nobles d'Angleterre avec cheulx de Gand, elle en seroit plus riche et mieulx paree ; sa force croit de jour en jour, son sçavoir multiplie au double, sa santé prospere au centisme et, pour nouvelle recreation, tient en main une Orenge naguaires de sy precieuse vertu que son oudeur a rebouté pluiseurs fois les anemis du pays de Bourgoigne. Orenge lui donne corage, Orenge lui soustient le ceur et lui donne grant appetit de conquerre les vins franchois. Vivez tousjours en bon espoir, Justice, ma tres chiere dame, et prenez consolation, car vous arez hastif secours, moyennant la grace de Dieu, en laquelle, quoy que vous faites, vous debvez du tout confyer. Requerez vos leaulx amis a vostre singulier besoing et les glorieux sains et saintes ou plus avez d'affection ; pryez premier Dieu vostre pere qui vout retirer son enfant de la main du roy Herode, son peuple du roy Pharaon, Daniel de la fosse aux Lions et Susane des malvaix juges ; qu'il veulle vostre petit peuple preserver des pervers tirans ; priiez Marie, nostre dame et princesse, plaine de grace et tres large aulmosniere, qu'elle vous preste son petit Philippus pour offrir a Nostre Signeur, affin qu'il ait misericorde de son petit peuple indigent ; priiez saint Pol, vostre mignon, vostre secret et leal amoureux, affin que par le meritte de la foy qu'il a a Dieu et a vous, aveuc l'ardant amour qu'il a a la chose publicque, vous puissiez recouvrer puissance et regner en prosperité ; priiez vos amis espiritueulx, tres reverentz peres en Dieu, monsigneur le Cardinal de saint Vital, evesque de Tournay et Monsigneur l'evesque de Cambray ; ilz ont les ames de vostre petit peuple en cure ; ilz sont nouvellement promus as dignités saintes, ilz flourissent en vertus et prosperent en santé ; soiiez confirmee de leurs benedictions, jamais n'arez espoantement ne terreur de vos ennemis ; priiez les nobles jherarchies de la haulte cour temporelle, potestés, dominations, thrones, vertus, ducqz, marquis, contes et barons, affin que par force d'armes veullent dompter vos envieux et vous redrescier en chaÿere, qui du tout estes mise au bas ; soyez en oroisons, mettez vous en vos devoirs et faittes bons pelerinages, affin que vous puissiez acquerre la grace de Dieu, des sains et des homes. Je voy penser a vostre fait, espoir que brief serez resuscitee.

L'ACTEUR

Sur cest estat se departy Conseil, qui print congiet aux dames et chemina vers Puissance, pour avancier sa venue ; Verité, Justice et le petit peuple, qui a grant peine souffroit le charier, monterent en ung chariot pour faire leurs pelerinages ; bon Vouloir, un tres amiable chareton, amena Desir de Paix, Ardeur de foy, ses deux chevaulx et Pacience, une jument chastree, qui tant avoit porté la malle fortune qu'elle en avoit la peau moult deschiree. Neantmoins elle tira jusque au jour failli et descendirent ces pelerines en ung petit logeÿs appellé Treves, charpenté depuis demy an et ralongiet depuis trois mois, de sy povre et fresle matere que les pillars d'avant les champs luy brisoyent huis et parois et entroyent dedens a force par les troux et par les fenestres, pour quoy Justice n'y reposa guaires, ains desloga hastivement et sans trompette. Tant charia ce bon Volloir qu'il trouva une petite mongoye, se parvint a Bonne Esperance, une tres grosse abbaiie plaine de convers, de rendus, de dames et de damoiselles, ensamble planté d'amoureux qui la faisoiient leurs noefvaines, pour guarir leurs griefves dolours. En Bonne Esperance fut Justice amiablement recoeullie de Charité et des soeurs de l'ostel qui le menerent en une chapelle plaine de corpz sainctz et, de prime venue, esclaira les ymages d'aulcuns saintuaires qui la furent presens, se rua a genous, fondi en lermes, leva les yeulx vers le ciel, fit joindre au petit peuple les manottes ensamble, puis a haulte voix prononça ceste oroison :

JUSTICE

> 6. —Prenez pitié du sang humain,
> Vray Dieu, souverain roy des roix ;
> Sil est formé de vostre main,
> Doibt il porter si grief desrois ?
> Vostre petit peuple est perdu ;
> J'ay le ceur triste et esperdu,
> Tant suis batue et fourmenee,

Je suis, mon cas bien entendu,
La plus dolente qui soit nee.

La plus dolente qui soit nee
Je suis, qui fus la fleur des belles ;
Mes juges m'ont habandonnee
Pour lever tailles et gabelles ;
Vray Dieu, corrigiez les rebelles,
Faittes tout tirant inhumain
Doulx et simple que colombelles :
Prenez pitié du sang humain.

Prenez pitié du sang humain,
Noble roy, Loÿs de Valois ;
Vous nous tourmentez soir et main,
Par guerres et piteux explois.
Souviegne vous que povre et nud
Bourgoigne vous a soustenu
Et soef nourri mainte anee ;
Mais vous avez mal recognu
La plus dolente qui soit nee.

La plus dolente qui soit nee
Est au debout de ses roeles ;
Par vous santé lui soit donnee.
Vous guerissiez des escroeles,
Mettez jus debas et quereles ;
Tantost n'arez point de demain.
Ains que mort happe vos mereles,
Prenez pitié du sang humain.

Prenez pitié du sang humain,
Noble Edouart, roy des Angloix,
Mon espoir, mon frere germain,
Qui gardez mes drois et mes loix,
Regardez le peuple menu
Qui meurt de fain, prins et tenu
De tirannie foursenee,
Et moy qui l'ay entretenu,
La plus dolente qui soit nee.

La plus dolente qui soit nee
Se veult logier desoubz vos eles ;
Pour Dieu, qu'elle ait, quelque journee,
De vous gracieuses nouveles.
Et vous, dames et damoiselles
D'Austrice et du pays romain,

En plourant aveuc mes sequeles,
Prenez pitié du sang humain.

Ainsy faisoit son oroison,
Au temple de Bonne Esperance,
Justice querant guerison
Et de joye la recouvrance ;
Servant les sains de brance en brance,
Je le leissay devant l'autel
Et pour en faire ramembrance,
Je retournay en mon hostel.

Ainsi que l'anee presente
Est dure et desplaisante a voir,
L'histoire que je vous presente
Ne peult guaires de mieulx avoir.
Puisque chascun pert son avoir,
Son heritage et son bien meuble,
Prions Dieu que nous puissons voir
La resource du petit peuple.

NOTES

Notes

Introduction

1. Unless otherwise noted, the translations are our own. When we do textual analysis of the medieval material, we occasionally must translate it as closely as possible to the original French. To those readers who are used to more literary translations, our style may well appear inelegant or clumsy. (In this case, our translation corresponds to Act 2, scene 4.)

2. From the 1876 "and all that is not verse is prose," translated by Henri Van Laun (*Dramatic Works of Molière* 5 [Edinburgh: William Patterson], p. 294), and the 1894 "and whatever is not verse is prose," translated by Katherine Prescott Wormeley (*Molière* 1 [Boston: Robert Bros.], p. 320), to the 1957 "and everything that's not verse is prose," translated by Herma Briffault (Molière, *The Middle-Class Gentleman* [Woodbury, New York: Barron's Educational Series], p. 47).

3. Princeton: Princeton University Press, 1957; rev. ed., 1973, p. 13.

4. To take just one illustration, there is ancient Greek: "[W]hile the last half of the fifth century begins to see the acceptance of prose as a viable means of publication, acceptance does not become complete until the fourth. This is three hundred years after the invention of the alphabet had rendered the monopoly exercised by poetry over the contrived word theoretically obsolete." Eric A. Havelock, *Prologue to Greek Literacy* (Cincinnati: University of Cincinnati, 1971), p. 59.

Havelock is, in contemporary times, virtually alone in drawing this so cogently to our attention. Why, prior to him, was this situation left so unexamined, this particularly since it was pointedly remarked upon more than 100 years ago by Frank Byron Jevons?

> For the history of literature, the importance of Xenophanes, Parmenides, and Empedocles is that they show how difficult a thing it was for a nation, which for centuries had composed in verse alone, to learn to write in prose. About the same time that Xenophanes in Elea was formulating his philosophy in hexameters, that is, about B.C. 570, Pherecydes, a native of Scyros, one of the Cyclades, and a pupil of the famous Thales, was making the earliest attempt to write in prose. Some few specimens of his work have come

231

down to us. In everything but meter they are poetry, not prose; and whereas in poetry an author could compose artistic sentences of some complexity, in prose at this time he could only ejaculate short and simple expressions, in their baldness rather resembling a child's attempt at writing than a philosopher's. A little later than this, about B.C. 547, another philosopher, Anaximander of Miletus, again made an effort to write prose, with more clearness but scarcely less awkwardness than his predecessor. Half a century later, although the philosophers Anaximenes and Heraclitus had carried on the work of establishing prose, and the logographers Cadmus, Hecaeus, and Acusilaus, the predecessors of the historians, had written geographical, genealogical, and semi-historical works in prose, we find that Parmenides preferred poetry. Prose in the hands of Heraclitus was even less well fitted for an intelligible exposition of philosophy than was poetry. Even as late as B.C. 444, the year in which Thurii was founded, a time when Herodotus had already composed and recited much of his history, the first great work in prose, Empedocles still wrote in verse. (*A History of Greek Literature from the Earliest Period to the Death of Demosthenes* [London: Charles Griffin and Company, 1886; reprinted in New York: Scribner's, 1904], pp. 93-94)

5. Omer Jodogne, "La naissance de la prose française," *Bulletin de la Classe des Lettres et des Sciences Morales et Politiques* 5 (Bruxelles: Palais des Académies, 1963), pp. 296-308.

Also, after reviewing some comparative data, H. J. Chaytor states: "The whole process is illustrated by the history of the French national epic, the history of its transformation from assonant verse to prose." *From Script to Print* (Cambridge: Cambridge University Press, 1945), chap. 5, p. 87.

There are the ninth-century *Anglo-Saxon Chronicles*, but they give no immediate rise to a vernacular prose tradition.

6. Gabrielle M. Spiegel has recently shown that the various translations of the *Pseudo-Turpin*, which initiated prose vernacular historiography in France, were all produced in a certain geographic area and patronized by the members of one particular group: the French-speaking Flemish aristocracy, for whom such writings were one way of closing ranks around a shared *knightly* culture in crisis due to the *royal* ambitions of Philippe-Auguste. ("*Pseudo-Turpin*, The Crisis of Aristocracy and the Beginning of Vernacular Historiography in France," *Journal of Medieval History* [September 1986], pp. 207-24.) The king decisively defeated most of them at the Battle of Bouvines in 1214.

7. G. Paris, *De Pseudo-Turpino* (Paris: A. Franck, 1865), pp. 44-45.

8. For example, the prose *Historia Regum Britanniae* of Geoffrey of Monmouth was translated by Wace in 1155 into the octosyllabic verse *Roman de Brut*. Even the sermons of Saint Bernard were translated into verse.

9. But insofar as the motive for the whole collective *Pseudo-Turpin* "project" on the part of the Flemish artistocracy (see introduction, note 6) is a move to construct a cultural history that justifies the knightly order against other contenders for ascendancy in the culture, the jongleur is no more corrupt than those who replace him, the clerks and *dérimeurs* whose lords assigned them particular writing tasks.

10. Prologue in verse from a prose chronicle of the reign of Phillippe-Auguste, written in 1226 or shortly thereafter, *Romania* 6: 498, as cited in Brian Woledge and H. P. Clive, *Répertoire des plus anciens textes en prose française depuis 842 jusqu'aux premières années du XIIIe siècle*, Publications Romanes et Françaises 79 (Geneva: Droz, 1964), p. 30.

11. Little has been written about prose. Our allusions, references, and notes serve to recognize those scholars whose work, in bits and pieces, has smoothed our way. But these discrete notes do not recognize, or adequately recognize, those who had already begun to think through questions of oral and written literacies, questions of performance, voice, and writing, and whose work has helped lay down the broader lines of our own: Giorgio Agamben, Jacques Derrida, Eric Havelock, Marshall MacLuhan, Walter J. Ong, S.J., and Berkeley Peabody.

Chapter 1. Signifying Practice

1. Colin Cherry, *On Human Communication* (Cambridge: MIT, 1957), p. 80.

2. Walter J. Ong, S.J., "African Talking Drums and Oral Noetics," *New Literary History* 8, no. 3 (1977): 411-30.

3. Similarly, the telegram is available to the modern world for communication at a distance. The high cost of this technology has limited its use to relatively urgent messages and also created a brief, elliptical style: it has engendered its own "language"—a language of urgency. Such urgent style can be exploited for that purpose, for example, by those who appeal for charitable donations through direct mail, although they in fact use ordinary postal letters.

4. Undeniably, an anthropologist may find that much of what keeps things together may not be recognized as such, or even as "sacred" or its equivalent, by the society itself.

5. For example, television, which began as something that contained a kind of theater stage, or the automobile, which was perceived as being merely a carriage without a horse. The printing press began by reprinting many preexisting manuscripts, seen simply as the same thing "in a different hand." "[T]he output of early presses drew on a backlog of scribal work; the first century of printing produced a bookish culture that was not very different from that produced by scribes. The more closely one observes the age of incunabula the less likely one is to be impressed by the changes wrought by print." Elizabeth L. Eisenstein, *The Printing Press as an Agent of Change* (Cambridge: Cambridge University Press, 1979), p. 26.

6. As only one example, the church in the fifteenth and sixteenth century opposed the translation of the Bible from Latin into French, which would enable the laity to read it and would raise the possibility that they might interpret it without following the lines of interpretation already laid down by the church. E.g., the condemnations of Lefebvre d'Etaples.

7. Often the language that issues forth seems incomprehensible and must be interpreted through yet another agency. (Pentecostal speaking in many tongues, *glossolalia*.)

8. See, for example, the works of Victor Turner and Richard Schechner.

9. *Major Trends in Jewish Mysticism* (New York: Schocken, 1941), pp. 349-50. Geoffrey Hartman refers to it in *The Fate of Reading* (Chicago: University of Chicago, 1975), pp. 273-74.

10. To the extent that they do not, certain modern performances take on aspects of ritual (e.g., opera), and, conversely, certain rituals take on aspects of modern performance (e.g., weddings).

11. *Alcheringa / Ethnopoetics* 1 (175): 110-11.

12. The nature of participation will also continue to change as the relation becomes one between author and reader. Chapter 6 ("Prose Literacy") concentrates on that.

Chapter 2. Written Verse

1. See Bernard Cerquiglini, *La Parole médiévale* (Paris: Editions de Minuit, 1981).

2. Using somewhat different terminology to make a similar distinction, Michel Foucault (*The Archeology of Knowledge,* trans. A. M. Sheridan Smith [London: Tavistock, 1972; original, Paris: Gallimard, 1969], 95-96), has said: "If a proposition, a sentence, a group of signs can be called 'statement', it is not therefore because, one day, someone happened to speak them or put them into some concrete form of writing; *it is because the position of the subject can be assigned.* To describe a formulation qua statement does not consist in analysing the relations between the author and what he says (or wanted to say, or said without wanting to); but in determining what position can and must be occupied by any individual if he is to be the subject of it."

3. But see H. J. Chaytor, *From Script to Print*, p. 93, for an example of a poem of the time,

a poem broken by irregularities of meter in the apparent attempt to add explanations and clarify the sense.

4. This again underlines the lack of filiation between the texts we are studying and contemporaneous Latin writing. Quotation marks in the sixteenth century were probably adaptations from such earlier Latin practices, in which either angular marks were used to separate *commentary* from *original* text, or *puncti* were used to mark the beginning and end of a *quoted author's* words within those of another writer (two dots above the word at the beginning of the citation and two vertical ones above the word at the end). (See Paul Saenger, "Silent Reading: Its Impact on Late Medieval Script and Society," *Viator* 13 [1982]: 367-414; and Richard H. Rouse and Mary A. Rouse, *"Statim invenire:* Schools, Preachers, and New Attitudes to the Page," *Renaissance and Renewal in the 12th Century,* ed. R. L. Benson and G. Constable [Cambridge: Harvard University Press, 1982], pp. 201-25.) The purpose, when there is no performer shifting from character to character but just the written words of one writer followed by those of another, was to avoid just the confusion that would face the reader of our hypothetical *rapporteur* attempting to write in the jongleur, because Herbert of Bosham justifies to his reader the use of *puncti* "lest you be led to mistake Cassiodorus for Augustine or Jerome, or the glossator for an expositor, a matter in which we have seen, not just the unlettered, but very learned readers fall into error." He is talking of his edition of Peter Lombard's *Magna glosatura* (circa 1170). (Cited in Rouse and Rouse, p. 209).

5. Although Cerquiglini *(La Parole médiévale)* is right in asserting that from the outset the written imposes its own codes on what it deals with, the reception of that writing, that is, the reading, is still within the orbit of performance. This assertion of ours can be made with some degree of certainty because it is precisely this status of the written as only virtuality that is going to be put into question in dérimage, which, far more than being a formal operation of "de-rhyming" and its attendant syntactical and prosodic changes, must be taken to be a removal of the artifact from the culture of performance.

Thus, to analyze texts only in terms of surface deictic operations, that is, in terms of attribution of *parole,* as Cerquiglini does, without delving into the signifying practice in which deixis and *parole* participate, is to grapple, no matter how impressively and usefully, with only part of the problem.

6. As Benveniste says:

> What then is the reality to which *I* or *you* refers? It is solely a "reality of discourse," and this is a very strange thing. *I* cannot be defined except in terms of "locution," not in terms of objects as a nominal sign is. *I* signifies "the person who is uttering the present instance of the discourse containing *I.*" This instance is unique by definition and has validity only in its uniqueness. If I perceive two successive instances of discourse containing *I,* uttered in the same voice, nothing guarantees to me that one of them is not a reported discourse, a quotation in which *I* could be imputed to another. It is thus necessary to stress this point: *I* can only be identified by the instance of discourse that contains it and by that alone. It has no value except in the instance in which it is produced. But in the same way it is also as an instance of form that *I* must be taken; the form of *I* has no linguistic existence except in the act of speaking in which it is uttered. There is thus a combined double instance in this process: the instance of *I* as referent and the instance of discourse containing *I* as the referee. The definition can now be stated precisely as: *I* is "the individual who utters the present instance of discourse containing the linguistic instance *I.*" (Emile Benveniste, *Problems in General Linguistics,* trans. Mary Elizabeth Meek, Miami Linguistic Series 8 [Coral Gables, FLA: University of Miami Press, 1971], p. 218)

7. *Shifters, Verbal Categories and the Russian Verb*, Russian Language Project, Department of Slavic Languages and Literatures, Harvard University, 1957. French translation available in Jakobson's *Essais de linguistique générale* (Paris: Editions de Minuit, 1963).

8. See Godzich, "The Tiger on the Paper Mat," introduction to Paul de Man, *The Resistance to Theory* (Minneapolis: University of Minnesota Press, 1986), ix-xviii. This discussion of deictics is indebted to Giorgio Agamben, *Il Linguaggio e la Morte* (Milan: Einaudi, 1983).

9. As Karl Bühler says, a signpost stands in its deictic field. Bühler provides one of the earliest modern treatments of deixis, in *Sprachtheorie: Die Darstellungsfunktion der Sprache* (Jena: Fischer, 1934).

10. For clarity of exposition, and owing to our interest in prose, we privilege the linguistic level as we recount this mechanism. In prose, the replacements are to a great extent by discourses. But the mechanism is not inherently linguistic; it takes place at a more general level: at other points in time, the nonverbal can cover for the verbal. For example, what becomes "unspeakable" at a certain moment can be transposed into mime.

11. Narrative is when that which is necessary but nonverbal in some signifying practice must be taken as said, taken as voice. Once uttered, the addressee then looks for a voice, and a possessor of that voice, an agent of that uttered. Something is considered narrative when the functions of agency become mysterious, and need their own discourse, which is thematized as voice.

12. Some signifying practices, however, formalize, make explicit their rules, their protocol. For example, there seems little in most ritual that is implicit. This may not in fact be the case, though.

13. What is necessary efficacy also changes: "The story which he [Rabbi Israel] told had the same effect as the actions of the other three." The fact that so much is shifting necessitates our remaining at a rather elevated theoretical level throughout much of our argument.

Chapter 3. *Dérimage*

1. Summarized by Georges Doutrepont, *Les Mises en prose des épopées et des romans chevaleresques du XIVe au XVIe siècle* (Bruxelles: Palais des Académies, 1939).

2. Ed. Bossuat (Paris: Société des anciens textes français, 1931-33). Our page numbers seem out of order because his edition puts the later, prose version first. There are four manuscript versions as well as an English version, the *Tale of Beryn*, which was at one point attributed to Chaucer.

3. References are to volume, page, and line. All emphasis in any of the medieval texts we cite is added by us; there was no underlining then.

4. The temporality of a fatal wound can be highly elastic, depending on the signifying practice. Opera finds a lot of opportunity in a fatal wound.

5. The difference between antecedent and referent is important. An antecedent is a grammatical and textual notion, whereas a referent here is a semantic and semiotic notion. Many of the problems of medieval philology involving pronouns have to do with the failure of the analyst to recognize that medieval linguistic practice will always put the referential ahead of the antecedent and is more concerned with the correctness of the first than with the correction of the latter. For this reason, a purely philological method of investigation is limited.

6. On endophorics, see M. A. K. Halliday and Ruqaiya Hazan, *Cohesion in English* (London: Longman, 1976).

7. *Inquit* is a defective Latin verb meaning "[he] says," and is typically used in the middle of a direct quotation. When field linguists encounter such things, they often call them "quotatives." We use the term *inquit* to refer to expressions that fulfill such a function.

8. Both versions have "Frere," but "frere" could possibly be said by either referring to the other.

9. See Erving Goffman, *Frame Analysis* (New York: Harper and Row, 1974), pp. 535-36.

10. The situation is actually more complicated, for we would have an oral jongleur quoting an oral Aigres (who is reading) quoting a written Nulie quoting an oral Aigres (this last utterance being at a third point in time: preceding the time of the writing of the letter as well as the time of its reception). (See chap. 2, note 4, on the use of *puncti* in scriptural gloss to avoid such confusion.)

11. There is a reference in Quevedo to the delivery of a letter, from one character to another, in a play. During the performance the letter was then handed to a member of the audience, who could read it and attest *viva voce* to its content for the benefit of the rest of the audience. (Margit Frenk, Mexico, 10-11 September, 1985: personal communication.)

12. Another, only partially facetious question: would the supposedly "quoted" letter be in verse? If it were not in verse, how could it be read out loud in verse? The converse is not a problem.

Similarly, if Molière had included *Le Bourgeois gentilhomme* among his verse plays, M. Jourdain could not have made his famous discovery.

Chapter 4. Versiprosa

1. With the notable exception of Paul Zumthor, *Le masque et la lumière* (Seuil: Paris, 1978).

2. The forms of lyric had been frozen for nearly two centuries.

3. The downfall of courtly love had already become thematized in Villon's poetry. Cf. David Kuhn, *Le Poétique de François Villon* (Paris: A. Colin, 1967). As an immediate example, the *Bérinus* derhymed version cuts out a long verse treatment of the nature and effects of love.

4. For example, Warner Patterson, whereas seeing the Grands Rhétoriqueurs as "A transition school of real vigor and staying power," says of Molinet: "He is a typical chief of the Rhétoriqueur school, an illustrious example of the overelaborate, oratorical, and pedantic poetry which flourished at the court of the luxurious duke of Burgundy. . . . He is one of the principal creators of the tradition of puerile search for difficult form, for recondite learned vocabulary, for an emphatic music of equivocal rimes, for a crude and bombastic art for art's sake. At his worst he achieves the most childish of jingles. At his best he is an orator, drunk with the sonorous rhythms of resounding Latin words." *Three Centuries of French Poetic Theory* 1 (New York: Russell and Russell, 1966), p. 134.

5. Noël Dupire, ed., *Les Faictz et Dictz de Jean Molinet,* 3 vols. (Paris: Picart, 1936), 1:137-61. See Paul Zumthor, *Le masque et la lumière,* for a version in a more modernized French.

6. The question of citation and the diverse strategies of the verse of performance and of prose with respect to it is taken up in chapter 6.

7. Arranging lists in columns, as Rabelais did, confirms the impossibility of applying a simple and formal verse/prose distinction to lists. Lists have a distinctive means of articulation.

8. *The Domestication of the Savage Mind* (Cambridge: Cambridge University Press, 1977), especially chap. 5, "What's in a list," pp. 74-111.

9. This makes for strange bedfellows. People have recognized the dimension of these possibilities at least since Lautréamont put an umbrella on an operating table and Duchamp put an inverted bicycle wheel on a wooden stool.

10. Were we actually in performance, there might very well have been tears.

11. Our study aims specifically at interrogating that presence, calling it rather an effect of presence, designed to produce an impression of integrity and totality in the text.

12. It will be renewed briefly in Euphuism.

On this kind of speech, Chaytor (*From Script to Print*, pp. 106-7) tells us of the *Dialogue between a Lord and a Clerke* by John de Trevisa, printed in 1482:

> [T]he lord urges the making of English translations from the Latin, for the benefit of the unlearned; the clerk objects to the translation of "bokes that stondeth moche by holy Wrytte, by holy doctours and by philosophye," to which the lord replies that much work of the kind has been done, and gives as instances Alfred, Caedmon, Bede and others. The clerk's objections to the difficulty of translation are refuted, and he then puts the question, "whether is you leuer have a translacion of these Cronykes in Ryme or in prose?" The lord replies, "in prose, for commonly prose is moore cleerer than ryme, more easy and more playne to knowe and understande." "Thene," concludes the clerk, "God grante us grace grathly to gynne, Witte and Wysedome wysely to worche, Mygthe and mynde of right menynge to make translacion trusty and trewe, plesyng to the Trynyte three persones and one God in mageste that euer was and euer shall be."

13. That is, its denomination was in compliance with its descriptive system (see Michael Riffaterre, *Essais de stylistique structurale* [Paris: Flammarion, 1971], for the definition of this term).

14. With the possible exception of the cliché "justice bafouée."

15. Identical father *and* mother, a relatively rare, and therefore particularly valorized state of affairs during the Middle Ages, when mortality affected the sexes unequally, and remarriage was the rule.

16. *Les Faictz et Dictz de Jean Molinet* (Paris: SATF, 1939).

17. Jean de Meung, *Le Roman de la Rose* (Paris: CFMA, 1966), lines 10535-650.

18. "Le Donet Baillé an Roy Loÿs Douzieme," 1: 553-76, in Dupire, ed., *Les Faictz et Dictz,* pp. 700-701, lines 553-76.

19. If they had to name what they did, they did so by reference to their role. The second half of the fifteenth century does see the development of theater groups in the schools and in certain professional groups (such as the lawyers of the *Théâtre de la Basoche*), but the individuals engaged in this movement think of themselves as schoolmen or as lawyers first. Similarly, the players in a *sotie* are more likely to describe themselves as *sotz* than as actors, especially because the *sotie* attacks the notion of representation. It is not until the introduction of professional theater groups, with which the French became familiar during the Italian campaigns of the early sixteenth century, that a term is applied on a regular basis to stage players: *comédien* copies from Italian *comediantes*. And the modern French usage *acteur* comes into being when the distinction between the genres begins to blur: someone who plays in both tragedies (a *tragédien* or *tragédienne*) and comedies is called an *acteur* or *actrice*. This latter step is the consecration of a slow process of professional formation and progressive specialization.

20. Paris, A. Vérard. 10 May 1493.

21. A different, extensive treatment of *acteur* can be found in Julia Kristeva's study of *Petit Jehan de Saintré* in her book *Le Texte du roman* (The Hague: Mouton, 1970).

22. Perhaps the discovery of perspective in painting is part of the same general transformation we are tracing here.

23. The only reason we make the distinction for this text is because we are giving a diachronic reading, seeing a new *use* of this distinction.

24. Cf. the zero, the nothing, that allows the decimal number system to work. It occupies a slot seen as necessary.

25. This is on the level of representation. In the "mean-time," on the enunciative level, *Acteur* has already slipped in.

26. The restricted familial economy of our text continues: Conseil is married to Prudence, who is a full-blooded sister of Justice, herself a full-blooded sister of Vérité, thus making Conseil the brother-in-law of both Justice and Vérité. Things get more complicated, for we read that

his *parents* also gave life to Justice: "Les nobles progeniteurs dont vous tirez naturele origine ont suscité Justice," which would make him, if not Justice's brother, at least a cousin. In this incestuous kinship system, only Common Folk's father is never named. (Conceptions are immaculate.)

27. Cf. "par ung ardant couroux qu'il luy monta au cœur, d'une vive voix tres agüe, sans riens celer, desgorgua son invective contre les recteurs de la chose publicque et dit en tel maniere:" (With a burning anger that rose to her heart and in a sharp voice, holding nothing back, she discharged her invective against the leaders of the republic and said in this way:). And "Verité . . . choisy ung homme . . . s'escria vers luy a haulte voix et se print a dire:" (Truth . . . espied a mature man . . . raised high her voice and began to say:).

28. The subject of closure will be briefly discussed again in chapter 7.

Chapter 5. Chantefable

1. We are using the edition of Mario Roques (Paris: Champion, 1965). Numbers refer to the verse or prose segment.

2. "Vers et prose dans *Aucassin et Nicolette*," *Romania* 97 (1976): 481-508.

3. Simone Monsonégo, *Etude stylo-statistique du vocabulaire des vers et de la prose dans la chantefable "Aucassin et Nicolette,"* Bibliothèque Française et Romane, série A (Paris: Klincksieck, 1966).

4. "The Cues in *Aucassin et Nicolette*," *Modern Language Notes* 47 (1932): 14-16.

5. Of heroic stature in the annuals of animal language is "Clever Hans," the horse who could count. Shown a number, he would tap it out. It turned out that he was reading the body language of his trainer, who would unconsciously communicate, probably by a release of body tension, when the desired number had been reached.

6. The versification of *Aucassin*, an assonanced laisse, is archaic even for its time.

7. As in Jean-Claude Aubailly, *Le Monologue, le dialogue et la sotie* (Paris: Champion, 1976).

8. See *La Passion d'Autun,* ed. Grace Frank, which benefits from Frank's detailed introduction (Paris: Société des Anciens Textes Français, 1932).

9. See Jean Bouchet, "Epitre familière, XCII, Aux habitans d'Issoudun":

> Du moule ay prins ce que j'ay bon trouvé,
> Et ce qui est par l'Eglise approuvé,
> Car il y a ou moule alcuns passages
> Qui n'ont passé par l'escolle des sages:
> Dont par conseil j'ay fait rescision,
> Et en ces lieux mis quelque addition.
> > (As cited in Frank's introduction to *La Passion d'Autun*)

> From the mold I have taken what I have found to be good,
> And to be approved by the Church,
> For there are in the mold some passages
> That did not make it through the school of sages,
> Which I have advisedly rescinded
> and in their places made additions.

In the following passage,

> Respont NICHODEMUS
> Helas, Joseph, tresdoulx syre,
> Ses doleurs laissés les aler,
> Quar il ne peuve maisque vous grever.

Se je pour plorer ne pour brayre
J'en puisse aultre chousz faire,
Jamais je ne fineroye de crier.
Pour quoy, las, nous fault tout laissier.
Adonc monta de sus la croix
Joseph, pour Jhesu declouer,
Et puis dit a son compaignon
Nichodemus, le vaillant hom,
Que il luy veullisse aydier
Tant qu'i fust decrucifier.
Le quel respondy piteusement
Qu'i luy aideroit diligemment
Et encore plus volentiers,
Mais comen l'ouserroit touchier?
Toutesfoy je le toucheray,
Les cloux doulcement ly trairay.
Recevés le corps doulcement
Et le convués honestement.

Lines (1658-78)

NICODEMUS answers

Alas, Joseph, most sweet sire,
Let his suffering run its course
For they can do no more than bring you grief.
If by tears and wails
I could accomplish anything
I would never stop crying.
That is why, alas, we must let it be.
And so Joseph climbed up the cross
To remove the nails from Jesus
And then he told his companion
Nicodemus, the brave man,
That he should help him
To take Jesus down from the cross.
And Nicodemus answered him pitifully
That he would help him diligently
And even more willingly,
But how would he dare touch him?
However I shall touch him,
And the nails gently I will pull out.
Receive the body gently
And carry it honestly.

Frank points out that the line we have underlined had "il disoit" ("he said") crossed out after "Mais," ("But") and that the spelling of Biard allows this line to be direct discourse, i.e., "how would I dare touch him?"

10. See Edmond Faral, *Mimes français du XIIIe siècle* (Paris: Champion, 1920). The critics of *Aucassin* are divided as to whether it was or was not a "mime," and if it was, whether it was recited and mimed by one (*jongleur? conteur?*) or more than one (*joueur?*).

11. As referred to in Emile Picot, "Sermons sur divers sujets," *Romania* 16 (1887): 494.

12. H. Lausberg, "Zum Alexiuslied," *Archiv für das Stadium der Neueren Sprachen* 191 (1955): 202-13, and 195 (1958): 141-44.

13. Brian Stock, *The Implications of Literacy* (Princeton: Princeton University Press, 1983), pp. 21-23.

14. *De Trinitate (PL* 42: 820), as cited by Erich Auerbach, *Literary Language and its Public*

in Late Latin Antiquity and in the Middle Ages, trans. R. Manheim (Princeton: Princeton University Press, 1965).

15. Eugene Vance, *"Aucassin et Nicolette* as a Medieval Comedy of Signification and Exchange," *The Nature of Medieval Narrative,* ed. Minette Grunmann-Gaudet and Robin F. Jones (Lexington, KY: French Forum, 1980), pp. 57-76.

16. *Documentum de arte versificandi* II.3 from Edmond Faral, *Les arts poétiques du XIIème et du XIIIème siècles* (Paris, 1924; reprint, Paris: Champion, 1958), 312. We owe this translation and reference to Vance, as well as the reference to John of Garland.

17. *The Parisiana Poetria of John of Garland,* ed. Traugott Lawler (New Haven: Yale University Press, 1974), bk. 1, sec. 375, p. 102.

18. Ibid., bk. 1, sec. 373, p. 132.

19. Quoted from the preface to Dufournet's edition of *Aucassin et Nicolette* (Paris: Garnier-Flammarion, 1982), p. 8.

20. Ibid.

21. Ibid. The point is also made by Vance.

22. A large amount within the reckoning of the text because the five sous are a quarter of the 20 sous that would repay the peasant (who appears in a later episode) for his lost Roget, a prized oxen.

23. Randle Cotgrave, *A Dictionarie of the French and English Tongues* (London: Islip, 1611; reprint Columbia: University of South Carolina Press, 1950).

Chapter 6. Prose Literacy

1. It is not helpful, by the way, to give a priority to the verbal and believe that the nonverbal is initially or basically verbal.

2. Foucault, *The Archeology of Knowledge,* p. 94.

3. *In primum librum sententiarum,* proem, quaest. 4. Printed in *Opera* 1, ed. Quaracchi (1882), p. 14, col. 2. See Malcolm Beckwith Parkes, "The Influence of the Concepts of *Ordinatio* and *Compilatio* on the Development of the Book," ed. J. J. G. Alexander and M. T. Gibson, *Medieval Learning and Literature* (Oxford: Oxford University Press, 1976), pp. 115-41.

4. "The compiler adds no matter of his own by way of exposition (unlike the commentator) but compared with the scribe he is free to rearrange *(mutando).* What he imposed was a new *ordinatio* on the materials he extracted from others. In the words of Vincent of Beauvais: 'Nam ex meo pauca, vel quasi nulla addidi. Ipsorum igitur est auctoritate, nostrum autem sola partium ordinatione.' The *compilatio* derives its usefulness from the *ordo* in which the *auctoritates* were arranged" (Parkes, "The Influences of the Concepts," p. 128).

5. This literacy owes a great deal to that of performance, in which the jongleur continually establishes relative positions but always under the guarantee of his presence and *his* know-how; so that despite all the changes and relativizings that he enacts, this literacy need finally be no more than a literacy of him.

6. E.g., Mallarmé, who writes "verse" that is to be read according to prose literacies; collages that contain newspaper clippings.

7. The distinction is between *literacy,* in which there is an agreement on the nature of the signs that are to be interpreted and on the kinds of ranges of meanings and effects that these signs are allowed without specifying meanings, and *interpretation,* which questions the specific meanings of given signs within a literacy. We can agree to read something allegorically but disagree on the appropriate allegorical interpretation.

Many arguments about interpretation are about literacies. The question of the appropriate competence must first be decided. Then one can proceed to hermeneutic matters.

8. *La Chanson de Roland*, ed. Gérard Moignet (Paris: Bordas, 1969). Reference is to *laisse*, page, and line.

9. Again, that kind of operation would be totally artificial with respect to performance, in that quotes are written; there is *literally* no place in performance for quotes. Recall that medieval manuscripts do not have quotation marks.

10. Gustave Flaubert, *Madame Bovary* (Paris: Garnier, 1961), p. 132. Trans. E. M. Aveling (Garden City: Doubleday, n.d.)

11. We might wonder whether performances were ever meant to be given only for single individuals. How does reception change? Did jongleurs "act" differently?

12. Both in a given text and from the emergence of prose to the sixteenth century.

13. Emulsion: an intimate mixture of two incompletely miscible liquids in which one of the liquids in the form of fine droplets is dispersed in the other. The liquid in fine droplets will come to be known as *theme*.

14. To talk about signifying practices in general as comprising discourses is to use an extended meaning of discourses to include nonverbal signifying behavior as well.

15. For economy, we simply say "the jongleur." As we said in chapter 2, it is *memoria*, it is a set of techniques, it is not the individual person as such. We mean by "jongleur" any individual who functions as such a locus.

16. Although prose is not structurally capped by an outside, *books* are physically contained, between their covers, squeezed together on the shelf. Books are in the palm of the hand. (In the Middle Ages, some were chained to their lecturn.) The book as object shows prose in this sense to be in fact subject to a kind of dimensionality and to have, along with other signifying practices, a kind of nonverbal grounding.

17. "Qu'il me soit permis d'abord (avant de vous entretenir de l'objet de cette réunion d'aujourd'hui) . . . " (May I be permitted first of all [before addressing you of the subject of our meeting today] . . .).

18. Ed. Clovis Brunel (Paris: Champion CFMA, 1926).

19. The rest of the story is as follows: asked by his father-in-law to recount the adventures of the voyage, Thibaut tells of this one but as if it happened to others and was a story he had heard along the way. He does not name the real participants. The count reacts by saying that he would have killed the lady in question. Thibaut then reveals that the lady is in fact the count's daughter. The father has the family embark on a ship, and at sea he places his daughter in a closed barrel and throws her overboard. She is picked up and saved by Flemish merchants who offer her to the sultan of Aumarie where, under duress, she consents to renounce her Christian faith and to marry the sultan. She bears the sultan children.

Her father repents, confesses, and with his son-in-law undertakes a pilgrimage to the Holy Land. During their return voyage, they are shipwrecked and cast ashore in the country of Aumarie, where they are imprisoned. As the count is about to be executed, the sultane recognizes her father and, without revealing her real identity, asks the sultan that the count, his son (a brother of hers), and Thibaut be spared on the grounds that they could provide good companionship. She forces the count to speak of his own daughter and offers a justification to him of the attempted murder of Thibaut by his wife at the time of the abduction, by stating that the wife could not tolerate the shame that she suffered before him. The count accepts this. Thus having resurrected her own self in their eyes, the sultane reveals herself to her family.

The count, Thibaut, and the brother gain the confidence of the sultan through valorous actions on the battlefield. The sultane, pregnant, gets permission to undertake a voyage with them. Once on the seas, they go to Rome, where all are absolved of sins, and the marriage between Thibaut and the daughter is reestablished. Children are born. The child she bears of the sultan is a daughter who, returned to Aumarie, is disdained in spite of her beauty and later gives birth to a daughter who will become the mother of Saladin.

20. Parataxis is not only syntactic but also a product of the unfolding of units with uniform apprehensibility.

21. A ball in soccer is kicked out of bounds. Even if it is retrieved by a player from the team appropriate to kick it immediately back onto the field, it must be given to the referee and held by him for a moment, to reestablish its integrity before it is returned to play.

22. To draw the distinction more sharply: how is the robber operating in the early version in light of the lady's state such as we are given it? It is part of *his* context as *he* understands it. How is he operating in the later version? Perhaps in the light of her state as we are given it, or perhaps with some other kind of understanding. Her state is part of *his* context as *we* understand it.

23. See Kittay, "Descriptive Limits," in *Towards a Theory of Description,* ed. Kittay, *Yale French Studies* 61 (1981): 225-43.

24. Jean Leclercq, O.S.B., *The Love of Learning and the Desire for God* (New York: Fordham, 1961), pp. 18-22.

25. See chapter 6, note 20.

26. Michael Stubbs, *Discourse Analysis* (Chicago: University of Chicago Press, 1983), p. 78.

27. We can take the disjunct as, from propositional calculus, "or." In prose, it is ultimately an inclusive disjunction, ultimately an "and/or" or an "or both."

28. Cf. studies of externalization and transactionality in research on perception and studies of that branch of linguistics known as pragmatics.

29. We are reminded of Diderot, interested in each sense insofar as it is fragmentary, as well as in the way that each impinges on the others. *Aisthesis* is freely depended on: it is all we have.

30. "Quel est la pansee d'homme qui aiant cuer trespercie de mille larmez, corps pertransy d'aspre couroux, face tainte et obscurcie de pleurs, chief anuye et bany de toute joye, chevelure detorse, voix afoibloyee, robbe deschiree, voire, et demenant la plus amere douleur qu'onquez fist dame imfortunee?" (What can a man think having a heart pierced by a thousand tears, a body surrendered to corrosive anger, a face washed and darkened with crying, a head bothered and removed from all joy, hair disheveled, a voice weakened, dress torn, and the most bitter pain ever shown by an unfortunate lady?)

31. This kind of solecism, in which the sentence starts in one kind of structure and finishes in another, is actually common to the time and is called an anacoluthon. On anacoluthon and other purely stylistic matters of the time, see Jens Rasmussen, *La Prose narrative française du XVe siècle* (Copenhague: Ejnar Munksgaard, 1958); Alexandre Lorian, *Tendances stylistiques dans la prose narrative française du XVIe siècle, Bibliothèque Française et Romane* (Paris: Klincksieck, 1973); and Samuel K. Workman, *15th Century Translation as an Influence on English Prose, Princeton Studies in English* 18 (Princeton: Princeton University Press, 1940).

Since we are referring to that book, we might mention in passing how someone like Workman takes a stab at prose. He suggests a "logic" that would be prerequisite to an "artfulness." "Asymmetrical coordination and other constructions inconsistent with logic were of common occurence in Middle English, and not only in prose. In poetry, where they are equally frequent, they cause no disruption of form; formal observations of other kinds are sufficiently conspicuous. But prose, by nature relatively amorphous, needs the presence of an abstract quality of logic in order to develop in any substantial degree an effect of artfulness" (p. 34).

32. The thirteenth-century version is performancelike. M. Soderhjelm (*La Nouvelle française au XVe siècle* [Paris: Champion, 1910], p.8) suggests that it is a *dérimage*. Brunel, the editor of both versions, rejects the suggestion: "The oldest version to have reached us is no doubt also the first to have been written in French . . . with its swift action, told in strikingly concise fashion, our tale does not appear . . . to have the features of something that would have been reworked from an older piece of writing" (p. xxiv).

33. We can ask to what extent reactions need be mirrored when reading becomes an individual and solitary experience.

34. Cf. the wringing of hands in the verse *Bérinus*.

35. When a reader's interpretation takes the form of a change or augmentation of a subsequent narrative version, we are in the practice of midrash.

36. E.g., "John said he was late" = "John said, 'I am late'." Indirect statement is neither verse- nor prose-specific, and in certain signifying practices is meant to be the precise equivalent of direct statement.

37. *"Je n'ai jamais appris à écrire," ou les incipit,* Les Sentiers te la création (Geneva: Skira, 1969), pp. 10-13. (Emphasis in the original.)

38. "The division into chapters is not the same in the two manuscripts. We did not hesitate to create a new one and to reject that of the manuscript we are basing ourselves upon, for the habits of the middle ages were quite different from ours in this respect: they sought to cut a chapter at the beginning of a speech in direct discourse, without paying much attention to the narrative" (pp. xlvi-xlvii).

39. One of the main concerns seems to be to slow down reading to the speed of speech. This of course would allow for the medieval *lectio,* mentioned earlier, to be a repronouncement and rumination. It also seems that the *cursus* was meant, at least in part, to slow down the ends of sentences: certain accentual combinations are not acceptable as *cursus,* we are told, because they go too fast.

40. M. B. Parkes, "Punctuation, or Pause and Effect," in James J. Murphy, *Medieval Eloquence* (Berkeley: University of California, 1978), pp. 127-42. He concludes with the hypothesis that

the key to the understanding of medieval punctuation lies not in grammatical theory, nor in the analysis of syntactical or intonation patterns, but in the concern of the scribe or corrector to elucidate the text transmitted to him according to the needs of his own audience. He seems to have realized that he could achieve the desired effect by means of punctuation: that the adroit use of pauses would ensure that his readers followed what the punctuator regarded as his own correct interpretation of the text. (p. 139)

41. Parkes tells us in a note:

In the Middle Ages a distinction arose between the punctuation of prose and that of verse. In prose, layout was used to indicate the beginnings and ends of chapters and paragraphs, and marks were used to indicate pauses within those divisions—to identify the *sententiae* and to elucidate the *sensus.* In verse, both layout and marks were used to indicate the metrical form. According to the grammatical theory transmitted to the West by Isidore of Seville each *versus* formed a *periodus* ("Totus autem versus periodus est": *Etymologiae* I, xx; printed *Patrologia Latina* 82.96). In most manuscripts each *versus* was placed on a line of its own. Sometimes each line was followed by a mark, but more frequently the layout alone was sufficient to indicate the metrical form, and in such cases a mark (such as the *punctus elevatus*) was placed at the end of a line only if the *sensus* was incomplete. Marks were frequently placed at the ends of lines to indicate the ends of stanzas or verse paragraphs, but in manuscripts produced from the thirteenth century onwards it became customary to place a paragraph mark in the margin at the beginning of a new stanza or paragraph. Marks were used within a line of verse to indicate a *caesura.* Where verse was written continuously marks were used to indicate the end of each *versus,* or in vernacular verse, a corresponding metrical unit. Elaborate verse forms were often indicated by elaborate layouts.

To speak of differences in layout draws us back to the question of *dérimage,* which is a process of derhyming but also describes works that often contain residues of untransposed verse (see chap. 3). A striking example of a single-minded dependence on layout as a marker of the prose-verse distinction can be found in some of the 47 manuscript versions of the prose *Histoire ancienne jusqu' à César.* Two of them from the thirteenth century have verse moralizations interposed from time to time (drawing the morals from the prose passages), verse in which the versifier will occasionally draw attention to himself, his appearance, his situation, especially in a verse prologue. See Renate Blumenfeld-Kosinski, "Moralization and History: Verse and Prose in the *Histoire ancienne jusqu' à César* (in B.N. f. fr. 20125)," *Zeitschrift für Romanische Philologie* 97 (1982), 41-46. Later manuscripts progressively suppress both the interpellations to the audience in the verse and the verse passages themselves. But in what sense is the verse suppressed? Spiegel tells us that some manuscripts (like the thirteenth-century B.N. fr. 9682)

> not only suppress the prologue but transcribe the verse moralizations in the prose format, without, however, bothering to rewrite the verses, so that they remain embedded in what appears, visually, to be a uniform prose text. The effect of this method of transcription is textually to efface authorial presence without actually silencing the author's voice, for when the passages are read aloud, that voice instantly reemerges in the octosyllabic couplets which still make up the moralizations, despite the fact that they are no longer perceivable in the written text as such. This masking of authorial presence is the first step in a steady process by which the verse portions of the *Histoire ancienne* are little by little abridged, prosed, or dropped altogether (as is the direct address to the audience) in favor of a textually coherent prose narration which has lost all traces of the author's original moral preoccupations. (Gabrielle M. Spiegel, "Social Change and Literary Language: The Textualization of the Past in Thirteenth-Century French Historiography," unpublished ms. [Department of History, University of Maryland, College Park, MD, 1985], p. 16)

42. Antoine Compagnon, *La seconde main, ou le travail de la citation* (Seuil: Paris, 1979), pp. 246-47.

43. A "pseudomorph" is a rock that has retained its shape although much or all of its original minerals have dissolved over time. They have been replaced by more recently sedimented minerals. Thus the rock is paradoxically constituted by that which postdates it. It is Spengler who applies the term to cultural phenomena over time.

44. Marcel Proust, *A la recherche du temps perdu* 1 (Paris: Pléiade, 1954), pp. 97-98.

45. *Remembrance of Things Past* 1, trans. C. K. Scott Moncrieff and Terence Kilmartin (New York: Vintage, 1982), pp. 105-6.

46. To understand, yes, but also to be puzzled anew.

47. (New York: Random House, 1951), p. 163-64.

48. Cf. the effects of a shift between other kinds of signifying practice: "The biggest difficulty in filming [*Death of a Salesman*], [Arthur] Miller found, is that it's not, strictly speaking, a realistic play."

> "In the theater, while you recognized that you were looking at a house, it was a house in quotation marks," Mr. Miller said in a recent interview. "On screen, the quotation marks tend to be blotted out by the camera. The problem was to sustain at any cost the feeling you had in the theater that you were watching a real person, yes, but an intense condensation of his experience, not simply a realistic series of episodes. It isn't easy to do in the theater, but it's twice as hard in film." (*New York Times,* 15 September 1985)

49. Whereas the movement of a heavy body was for Aristotle a movement toward the natural state of rest for that particular body, the late Middle Ages saw it as due to an internal power acquired from some outside initiator.

50. *Medieval Technology and Social Change* (Oxford, 1962; reprint 1969).

51. An unusual case of "oral residue," to use Father Ong's term.

Chapter 7. Prose History

1. *Tristes Tropiques* (Paris: Plon, 1955).

2. However, such workings may call for some interpretation so that the rules can apply.

3. See Duby, *Guerriers et paysans* (Paris: Gallimard, 1973). English translation: *The Early Growth of the European Economy*, H. B. Clarke, trans. (Ithaca: Cornell University Press, 1978).

4. The price of slaves had risen, with new demand in the southern Mediterranean and elsewhere. Duby states that turning slaves into serfs left the burden on them to establish families and raise children, thus ensuring the lords a future supply of steady labor without having to outbid others. To allow the labor force the independence minimally necessary for procreation and childraising was to set in motion a self-perpetuating process. (Ibid., p. 40)

5. Paul Aebischer, *Préhistoire et protohistoire du* Roland d'Oxford (Bern: Francke Verlag, 1972).

6. William Ryding, *Structure in Medieval Narrative* (The Hague: Mouton, 1971), pp. 117-35.

7. Cf. millenarist claims of the imminent end of the world as evidenced by current events—famines, wars, epidemics, etc., around the year 1000.

8. Ed. J. Couraye du Parc (Paris: Firmin Didot, 1884; reprint. Johnson Reprint, 1966), lines 3055-57.

9. The editor notes: "We all know what credence is to be granted to all that the authors of the epics claim about the antiquity and the origin of their works; it should be noted that the rather obscure passage we cite is to be found in only two of the manuscripts and is an obvious interpolation" (p. xxij).

10. Margaret Carruthers, "Conference on the Future of the Disciplines," University of Illinois at Chicago, October 1985: personal communication.

11. Ernest Robert Curtius, *European Literature and the Latin Middle Ages,* Bollingen Series 36 (Princeton: Princeton University Press, 1953; 1981), pp. 147-49. (See copyright page for permission statement.)

12. Marbury Bladen Ogle, "Some Aspects of Mediaeval Latin Style," *Speculum* 1 (1926): 175-76.

13. *Li livres dou Tresor*, ed. P. Chabaille (Paris: Imprimerie Impériale, 1863), p. 481.

Later, he says: "Mais comment que ta parleure soit, ou par rime ou par prose, esgarde que ti dit ne soient maigre ne sec, mais soient repleni de vis et de sens, ce est à dire de sens et de sentence. Garde que ti mot ne soient nice, ainz soient griez et de grant pesantor, mais non mie de trop grant qui les feist trebuchier" (p. 481) (Whatever your speech may be, whether in rhyme or in prose, beware that your sayings be neither lean nor dry, but that they be full of life and of meaning, that is, of meaning and of wisdom. Beware that your words not be naive; let them be heavy and weighty but not of such great weight that they fall down).

See also version edited by Francis J. Carmody, University of California Publications in Modern Philology 22 (Berkeley: University of California, 1948), bk. 3, chap. 4, p. 322.

14. "As Homer for the Greeks, so for the later Romans Vergil was the pattern of all rhetoric. The speakers in Macrobius' *Saturnalia* (V, 1, 1) agree that Vergil must be accounted an orator no less than a poet" (Curtius, *European Literature*).

15. James J. Murphy, *Rhetoric in the Middle Ages* (Berkeley: University of California, 1974).

16. Prose was often seen at this time not in binary opposition with verse but in ternary opposition with discourse marked rhythmically and discourse marked metrically.

17. For a fuller development on *ars dictaminis*, see Murphy, *Rhetoric in the Middle Ages*, chap. 5.

18. Ibid., p. 225.

19. Ibid., p. 248.

20. Writing does not necessarily obviate the need for formulas; formulas are not always and only mnemonic—they also function, purposefully, as a means of restriction. Even when concerns of oral transmission no longer exist, this function of formulas can remain vital.

21. "Little attention . . . has hitherto been paid to the fact that, in addition to the artistic prose [*Kunstprosa,* 'rhetoricus sermo', 'eloquentiae prosa'], which required a great expenditure of time, talent, and erudition, there was also a plain prose of factual communication. Seneca already insisted (Epistle 40,4) that the language of the philosopher should be 'incomposita et simplex'. Pliny complains that the press of business forces him to send letters lacking in literary style ('inlitteratissimas litteras') (*Ep.,* I, 10). Plain prose was indispensable when one was in a hurry; hence Jerome calls it 'subita dictandi audacia' in contradistinction to 'elucubrata scribendi diligentia' (*PL,* XXVI, 200). Ennodius correspondingly distinguishes between 'sermo simplex' and 'sermo artifex', or, as alternative terms, 'plana' and 'artifex locutio'. Aldheim makes the same distinction ('cursim pedetemptim, non garrulo verbositatis strepitu')" (Curtis, *European Literature,* p. 149).

22. Bernard Guenée, *Histoire et Culture historique* (Paris: Aubier, 1980), p. 215.

23. Ogle, "Mediaeval Latin Style," p. 178.

24. Benoît Lacroix, O.P., *L'Historien au moyen age* (Montréal: Institut d'Etudes Médiévales, 1971), p. 130.

25. Guibert de Nogent, *Gesta Dei per francos, Patrologia Latina* 156.682 (cited by Lacroix, *L'Historien au moyen age,* p. 114).

26. After having discussed how Latin prose is finally translated into French prose, and giving the argument of "rhyme constraint" its due, the historian Omer Jodogne adds a parting personal remark that we consider admirable:

> On devrait en conclure qu'après s'être excusés d'adopter une autre façon d'écrire, la plus méprisable puisque c'est le vers que voulait la littérature, des auteurs ont délibérément opté pour l'expression affranchie des servitudes du rhythme et des finales homotéleutes qui les obligeaient à triturer le texte de leur modèle alors qu'il eût été si aisé de le suivre à la lettre. *J'ajouterais qu'ils me paraissent avoir exagéré les entraves de l'octosyllabe, ce vers si commode.* ("La naissance de la prose française,"p. 306; emphasis ours)

> One ought to conclude that after having excused themselves for adopting another kind of writing [prose], the more contemptible one since what literature wanted was verse, authors deliberately opted for a means of expression free from having to impose rhythm and similarity of endings that forced them to rework their model text, when it would have been so easy to follow it literally. *I would add that they seem to have exaggerated the shackles of the octosyllable, that so commodious verse.*

27. History in verse continued longer in Germany. And when the English language succeeded the Norman culture (1338), its first histories were in verse.

28. *Chronique de Jean le Bel,* ed. Jules Viard et Eugène Déprez (Paris: Libraire Renouard, 1904).

29. If we take a common modern definition of fact—an occurrence, quality, or relation the reality of which either is manifest in experience or can be inferred with certainty—"truth" in Jean Le Bel is seen here to move toward the former, the brute event, and the truth of performance leans more toward the latterO.

30. Myths and tales require the application of hermeneutical rules to determine how they apply to the world as it presently is. They must be mediated by interpretation. The new historical writing is going to present itself as unmediately dealing with the world. Truth in Le Bel should be immediate, and the mediation required to get it to us should be minimal.

31. Questions surrounding the early work of Froissart are discussed by Normand R. Cartier, "The Lost Chronicle," *Speculum* 36 (1961): 424-35. Cartier says at one point: "Liberated from the crippling framework of versification, he found new satisfaction in painting his vast canvas of the endless wars, and in re-weaving the intricate web of human activities of his time. The immense success of the prose version brought widespread fame to Froissart, and helped him shelve his first love forever."

32. Froissart, *Chroniques de J. Froissart,* ed. Siméon Luce, Variantes du Premier Livre 2 (Paris: Renouard, 1891), (Emphasis ours.) Note that the method is spoken of as "attainment" or "reach," the goal as "matter." Also: *"Pour atteindre et venir à la matière* que j'ai emprise de commencer . . . je me veux fonder et ordonner sur les VRAYES CHRONIQUES . . . [de] JEHAN LE BEL" (from the prologue to Froissart's first book, as cited in the preface to the edition of Le Bel) (To reach and arrive at the matter that I have undertaken . . . I want to base myself and align my work on the TRUE CHRONICLES . . . [of] JEHAN LE BEL).

33. *Chroniques de Jehan d'Auton* (Paris: Silvestre, 1834).

34. It is a common, one might even say necessary, technique for news as broadcast: "I am standing on the sight where . . ."

35. The first stanza of his epitaph (p. ix of his *Chroniques*) is of more than passing interest:

> Ci-dessous gît en ce bien étroit angle,
> Un bon seigneur autrefois abbé d'Angle
> Religieux: c'est frère Jean d'Auton,
> Noble de sang, qui vécut, ce dit-on,
> Par soixante ans et plus en bonne estime:
> Grand orateur, tant en prose qu'en rime,
> Il ordonnoit comme en prose ses vers,
> Sans rien contraindre à l'endroit ou envers;
> Il étoit grave en son mètre et facile:
> Bref, on ne vit jamais de plus grand style.

> Here below, in this narrow corner, lies
> A good lord, formerly abbot of Angles;
> A man of the cloth: it is brother Jean d'Auton
> Of noble blood, who lived, it is said,
> For sixty years and more in high esteem.
> A great orator, in prose as well as rhyme,
> He ordered his verse like prose
> Without constraining anything forward or backward;
> He was serious in his meter and easy;
> In short one never saw any greater style.

36. It will have been noted that the author makes reference to his own presence but that what he "saw" were such abstract entities as the workings of God's grace. His ability to see the invisible, made acute in the prose in which he constantly sees the past as present in the trace, comes in handy here.

37. Presence is not a problem for an orator, who purposefully stands as a focus of attention. In discussing varieties of mediation, it would be useful to contrast *acteur* with the orator, who does not want to do away entirely with his own mediation, for although he proposes his own discourse as one to which hearers will adhere as if transparent, he still clings to his discourse as powerful and mystifying, to his own presence, his own word as a screen. He will not abandon the communicational situation of his own utterance, for in that he has a personal stake. The *acteur*, on the other hand, does not want to concentrate on the communicational situation between him and his receiver, for he has no somatic qualities and is not engaged in a personal exercise. He is not engaged in a struggle with a real or possible audience; his grip on his commu-

nicational situation is minimal—he is really only a textual function, leaving a place for statements that would otherwise be displaced.

38. He was the king's ambassador to Italy.

39. Influence: "an ethereal fluid thought to flow from the stars and to affect the actions of men"; "the act, process or power of producing an effect without apparent exertion of tangible force or direct exercise of command and often without deliberate effort or intent"; "the exertion of force at a distance"; "the power or capacity of causing an effect in indirect or intangible ways: dominance, sway, ascendancy."

40. Les Faictz et Dictz de Jean Molinet 1, ed. Noël Dupire (Paris: SATF, 1939), pp. 232-50.

41. But our terms still have the potential of betraying us. We are elaborating a theory of discourse containment that no longer sees the container as a "body." Yet we must use terms like "incorporation." See Brian Stock, The Implications of Literacy, on how literacy reconstrues the role of the body and of nature in the practice of the eucharist.

42. To a great extent, our "in-fluence" can channel the "flow." Prose emerges in an era of great advances in water wheels, windmills, and gears of all types.

43. Phillippe de Commynes, Mémoires, 2 vols., ed. J. Calmette and G. Durville (Paris: Champion, 1924-25), vol. 2, bk. 5, chap. 18. The translation is from The Memoirs of Philippe de Commynes, trans. I. Caseaux, ed. S. Kinser (Columbia, SC: University of South Carolina Press, 1969-73.)

44. Jean Dufournet, Etudes sur Philippe de Commynes (Paris: Champion, 1975), p. 134. We also take it as meaning: "Commynes is not pronounced, one does not pronounce Commynes."

45. Commynes tells us of the siege of Liège by the baron d'Humbercourt, in which the baron realizes that he is undermanned and cannot sustain an attack that might issue forth from the city. Reinforcements are expected in the morning. Humbercourt sends a proposal of ceasefire into the town, where he knows it will be debated among the officials. He then sends another. These messages keep the townsmen distracted throughout the evening, and the next morning Humbercourt's strength is reestablished and the siege continues unrelentingly.

Although no doubt couched in the trappings of officialdom, and thus fairly calling out to be quoted, these messages were used as empty communications. Commynes does not bother to quote them or tell us anything about their substance.

46. Mémoires, vol. 2, p. 293.

47. "Et monta bien en ung an ses veuz et ses offrandes et reliquaires qu'il donna et chasses, comprins la grisle d'argent de Saint-Martin de Tours, qui pesoit près de dix huict marcs d'argent, et la chasse monseigneur sainct Eutroppe de Xaintes et autres reliquaires qu'il donna à Coulongne, aux Trois Rois, à Nostre Dame d'Ez, en Almaigne, à Sainct-Servés d'Utrecht, la chasse sainct Bernardin à l'Aquille, au royaume de Naples, et les calices d'or envoyéz à Saint-Jehan de Latran, à Rome, et plusieurs aultres presens d'eglise, tant d'or que d'argent, en son royaume, le tout se monta bien sept cens mille francs." (Ibid.) (In one year he raised his vows, gifts, and reliquaires, including the silver screen of Saint Martin of Tours which weighed nearly eighteen marks of silver, and the reliquary of our lord Saint Euthropius of Saintes and other reliquaries which he donated to Cologne, Trier, Our Lady of Aachen, all in Germany, to Saint Servus in Utrecht, the reliquary of Saint Bernard in Aquilla, in the kingdom of Naples, and the chalices of gold he sent to Saint John Lateran in Rome, as well as several other gifts to churches, of both gold and silver, that he distributed in his own kingdom, the whole coming to seven hundred thousand francs).

48. Mémoires, vol. 1, bk. 1, p. 93. The translation is from Philippe de Commynes, Memoirs, trans. Michael Jones (Middlesex: Penguin, 1972), p. 58.

49. This is not necessarily to deny a tragic view of history that Commynes may have. One could make the case for his participation in certain lines of thought put forward by the tradition

of Christian historiography, where human agency is constantly blinded and undone by divine direction.

"Plans emerge and get themselves carried into effect, which no human being has planned; and even men who think they are working against the emergence of these plans are in fact contributing to them. They may assassinate Caesar but they cannot arrest the downfall of the Republic; the very assassination adds a new feature to that downfall. Hence the total course of historical events is a criterion which serves to judge the individuals taking part in it." R. G. Collingwood, *The Idea of History* (London: Oxford University Press, 1946), p. 53.

50. Walter Benjamin, "The Storyteller," in *Illuminations,* ed. H. Arendt (New York: Schocken, 1969).

51. Prose is more like the game of "Go," in which there is an instability and substitutability as to where territory is, than like chess, in which territoriality is more situable, staked out, and confrontatory. In "Go," you construct lines. At one moment, they delineate your territory—on the left, say—from hostile territory on the right. At another moment, just when your territory on the left becomes threatened, the same line can function to lay claim to your opponent's territory on the right.

52. *Mémoires,* vol. 2, bk. 4, chap. 11, p. 74.

53. The Carolingian Reform for a "correct Latin" put an end to this move for a more vernacular Latin, and Grégoire had no successors. There was another attempt to bring Latin closer to a simple, speakable style in the fourteenth and fifteenth centuries, but that ran into a humanistic reform of the Renaissance seeking to purify Latin, i.e., bring it back to Ciceronian norms.

54. *In gloria confessorum (Monumentae Germaniae Historiae Scr. rer. Mer.,* vol. 1, Bk. 2, pp. 747ff), as cited and translated by Erich Auerbach, *Literary Language and its Public in Late Latin Antiquity and in the Middle Ages* (Princeton: Princeton University Press, 1965), pp. 104-5.

55. Trans. Ernest Brehaut (New York: Octagon, 1965), p. 248.

56. Rasmussen, *La Prose narrative française, p. 25.*

Chapter 8. Prose Fiction

1. Note the parallels with the remarks in our introduction on the situation of the jongleur in the thirteenth century.

2. See the prologue to his *Chanson de Saisnes,* cited in Robert Bossuat, *Le Moyen age* (Paris: Del Duca, 1967), p. 46.

3. See Mikhail Bakhtin, *The Dialogic Imagination,* ed. Michael Holquist, (Austin: University of Texas Press, 1981), pp. 84-258.

4. And we see how totally reversed the situation is for Commynes: whereas the performer must follow and recount several strands to prepare for one event, an event seen as made up of prior events, for Commynes one single significant event is already complex enough. Why? "When such events occur," says Commynes, "there is seldom only one account."

5. However, the strategy is not an exclusively prose one. In the late Chrétien (the *Conte du Graal*), we find similar, linking articulations.

> De mon seignor Gauvain se test
> Li contes ici a estal.
> Si parlerons de Perceval.
> Perceval, ce conte l'estoire,
> Asi perdue la memoire
> Que de Deu ne li sovient mais.
>> (Ed. G. Baist [Freiburg, 1909], vv. 6176-81. See William W.
>> Ryding, *Structure in Medieval Narrative* [The Hague: Mouton,
>> 1971], pp. 141-42)

Of my Lord Gawain
The story keeps quiet for some time.
And so we will speak of Perceval.
Perceval, the story goes,
Has become so forgetful
That he does not even remember God.

6. Ferdinand Lot, *Etude sur le Lancelot en prose* (Paris: Champion, 1918).

7. Whereas one school of thought sees this kind of textual organization as a failure to syn-thesize, another school sees it as revealing "un véritable sens de la composition." (Joël Blan-chard, *Le Roman de Tristan en Prose* [Paris: Klincksieck, 1976], intro.) This is all part of the established debate about the genesis of epic: a string of preexisting folktales or a single and dominating artistic stroke of genius? For our part, and with Commynes retrospectively in mind, we see here a reluctance to posit a consciousness with a grip on the whole, even if the grip is clearly not dominating. A reluctance to exercise the possibilities of an inside position.

8. *The Death of King Arthur,* trans. James Cable (Hammondsworth, Eng.: Penguin, 1971), p. 210.

9. Ibid., p. 220.

10. Other mechanisms involving myths and national identity are touched upon in J. W. Fernandez, "Folklore as an Agent of Nationalism," *African Studies Bulletin* 5 (1962): 3-8.

11. See Thomas Pavel, *Fictional Worlds* (Cambridge, Mass.: Harvard University Press, 1986).

12. Malory, *Works,* 2d ed. (Oxford: Oxford University Press, 1971), pp. vii-ix.

13. We do not have Malory's original manuscript, but we do have the 1485 printed edition made by the first English printer William Caxton. Malory's text was apparently relatively continu-ous, with only seven points at which he noted (in words) divisions or conclusions in his French sources, but Caxton tells us in his preface that it is he, the printer, who divided it into books and chapters: "And for to understonde bryefly the contents of thys volume, I have devyded it into XXI bookes and every book chapytred as here after shal by Goddes grace folowe." Here are compositional devices being developed at the beginning of printing to accelerate the charac-ter of narrative as writing.

Of more interest to our discussion of fictionalization is Caxton's explanation about why he published the work. He says he was asked by "many noble and dyvers gentylmen of thys royame of Englond" why he had not yet printed the story of the Grail and of King Arthur, "whyche ought moost to be remembered emonge us Englysshemen tofore al other Crysten kynges." Caxton had already published a book on Godefrey of Boulogne but says he was told he should rather have published on Arthur, "consyderyng that he ws a man borne wythin this royame and kyng and emperour of the same. . . . To whome I answered that dyvers men holde oppynyon that there was no suche Arthur and that alle suche bookes as been maad of hym have ben but fayned and fables, bycause that somme cronycles make of hym no mencyon ne remembre hym noothynge, ne of his knyghtes." He was told there was much evidence to the contrary, including sculptures and shrines, and many books about him. "Wherfor it is a mervayl why he is no more renoned in his owne contreye, sauf onelye it accordeth to the word of God, whyche sayth that no man is accept for a prophete in his owne contreye." Unable to deny that there was such a noble king, Caxton finally "enprysed to enprynte a book of the noble hystoryes of the sayd Kynge Arthur and of certeyn of his knyghtes, after a copye unto me delivered, whyche copye Syr Thomas Malorye dyd take oute of certeyne bookes of Frensshe, and reduced it in to Englysshe" (*The Works of Sir Thomas Malory,* ed. Eugene Vinaver [London: Oxford University Press, 1954], pp. xv-xvii).

The implication is clearly that Caxton was about to choose a hero on his usual basis, which was without any regard to his national origin, when he was told that his market should now be differentiated along the lines of nationhood as well. Although he had apparently rejected

Arthur on the grounds of fictionality, he did not ultimately allow such lack of historical standing to get in his way. He accepted the evidence of those who wanted a foundational national myth, part of a newly constituted national literary history.

14. From the proem to "Filostrato," *The Story of Troilus*, trans. R. K. Gordon (London: Dent, 1934), pp. 28-29 (emphasis ours) . . . :

> And knowing very clearly that, if I kept the grief I felt wholly hidden in my breast, as I had purposed, it was impossible but that at some time, out of the thousand times when it came upon me in its fullness, exceeding all measure, it should so triumph over my strength, already very much weakened, that death would certainly follow, and therefore I should see you no more. Governed by more sober counsel, I changed my purpose, and determined to give it outlet from my sad breast in some fitting lamentation, so that I might live and be able, moreover, to see you again, and by living to remain longer in your service. And such a thought no sooner came to my mind than, along with it, I straightway perceived the means to my end. And in that circumstance, as if I were inspired by a mysterious divine power, I found the surest augury of future happiness. And the way was this: that, in the person of someone stricken with love as I was and am, I should tell my sufferings in song. And so with zealous care I fell to turning old stories in my mind to find one which I could fitly use as a cloak for the secret grief of my love. Nor did another come to my mind more suited to meet my need than the valiant young Troilus, son of Priam, most noble King of Troy. For inasmuch as his life, *if any faith be put in old stories*, was saddened by love and by his lady being far from him after Criseida, so dearly loved, was restored to her father Calchas, my life after your going hence has been much like unto it. And therefore in his person and his fortunes I found most happily a frame for my idea; and afterwards, in light rhyme and in my Florentine idiom, in a very moving style, I set down his sorrows and my own as well.

15. With Troy, it is a question of going from the one culture to the many, the opposite of what Europe was undergoing in drawing many local cultures into one national one.

Those interested in the relationship of Trojan history to prose, as well as in the conflict between literal and critical translation and derhyming, should consult Brian Woledge, "La Légende de Troie et les débuts de la prose française," *Mélanges de linguistique et littérature romanes offerts à Mario Rogues* (Genève: Slatkine, 1976), pp. 313-24.

The Prosaic World

1. "Antidosis," secs. 46-47 in *Isocrates* 2, trans. George Norlin (Cambridge, MA: Harvard University Press, 1962), p. 213. Cited in James J. Donohue, *Ancient Classifications of Literature* 1 (Dubuque: Loras, 1943, p. 31.

2. From *Isocrates Orations* 2, ed. Benseler-Blass (Leipzig, 1895), p. 275. Cited by J. W. H. Aitkens, *Literary Criticism in Antiquity* (Gloucester, MA: Peter Smith, 1961).

3. See introduction, p. xi.

4. *Orator*, chap. 20, secs. 66-67, in *Cicero* 5, trans. Hubbell (Cambridge, MA: Harvard University Press, 1971), p. 355.

5. Prose can borrow rhythm from poetry and poetry can borrow variety from prose, as Dionysius of Halicarnassus says. See Donohue, *Ancient Classifications of Literature*, pp. 41-42.

6. *Institutiones Oratoriae of Quintilian*, trans. H. E. Butler (Cambridge, MA: Harvard University Press, 1976-80), bk. 10, sec. 1, p. 31.

7. Eric A. Havelock, "The Preliteracy of the Greeks, *New Literary History* 8 (1977): 371.

8. From *Aristotelis De Interpretatione*, cited in G. L. Hendrikson, "The Origin and Meaning of the Ancient Characters of Style," *American Journal of Philology* 26 (1905): 255, who has followed closely for us many of these fine philological distinctions. See also his "The Peripatetic

Mean of Style and the Three Stylistic Characters," *American Journal of Philology* 25 (1904): 125-46.

9. *The "Art" of Rhetoric*, trans. J. Freese (Cambridge, MA: Harvard University Press, 1926; reprint, 1967), bk. 3, sec. 1, pp. 347-48.

10. But he himself does not escape grandiosity.

11. *De Pythiae oraculis*, secs. 46-47, in *Plutarch's Moralia* 5, trans. Frank Cole Babbitt (Cambridge, MA: Harvard University Press, 1962), pp. 327-29.

12. "As Greek *prose began with history*, οι λόγοι came to have the general sense of *prose-writing, prose*, like Lat. *oratio*. . . . [F]urther, since at Athens the most valued and influential prose-writings were *speeches*, hence again like Lat. *oratio*, λογος came to be *a speech*." Liddell and Scott, *A Greek-English Lexicon* (Oxford: Oxford University Press, 1968).

Jevons (*History of Greek Literature*, p. 384) was quite clear on this long ago: "The early Sophists, as Hippias and Gorgias, when they wished to display their skill in the new accomplishment of prose composition, did not attempt to do so by publishing their compositions, but attended the great festivals of Greece and there recited their work."

13. Isidori, Hispalensis Episcopi, *Etymologiarum Sive Originum* 1, Libri 20, ed. W. M. Lindmsay (Oxford: Oxford University Press, 1911), bk. 1, xxxviii. His specific etymology for *prose* remains unsubstantiated. The passage continues:

> Prosum enim antiqui productum dicebant et rectum. Unde ait Varro apud Plautum "prosis lectis" significari rectis; unde etiam quae non est perflexa numero, sed recta, prosa oratio dicitur, in rectum producendo. Alii prosam aiunt dictam ab eo quod sit profusa, vel ab eo, quod spatiosius proruat et excurrat, nullo sibi termino praefinito. Praeterea tam apud Graecos quam apud Latinos longe antiquiorem curam fuisse carminum quam prosae. Omnia enim prius versibus condebantur; prosae autem studium sero viguit. Primus apud Graecos Pherecydes Syrus soluta oratione scriptsit; apud Romanos autem Appius Caecus adversus Pyrrhum solutam orationem primus exercuit. Iam exhinc et ceteri prosae eloquentia contenderunt.

> That is why the ancients said that prose was extended and straightforward. Hence Varro says that in Plautus "prose readings" are meant to be straightforward; hence also a discourse is said to be prose if it is not pervaded by meter but is straightforward, extended straight ahead. Others say that prose is so called because it is overflowing, because it runs hither and thither all over the place, without any predetermined boundary to itself. Moreover, among the Greeks as well as among the Latins, song was an object of concern far longer and earlier than prose. Everything was first established in verse; the taste for prose developed later. Among the Greeks, Pherecydes Syrus was the first to write in prose; among the Romans it was Appius Caecus who first applied prose against Pyrrhys. Since that time several have contended for the eloquence of prose.

14. Martin Heidegger sees *logos* as coming from *legein*, to bind, as in collecting shafts of wheat. (*Vorträge und Aufsätz* [Pfullingen: Neske, 1955], pp. 86-88.)

15. "Literacy" in some specialized Western sense is also regularly misapplied to other cultures that have writing.

16. Franz Boas, "Stylistic Aspects of Primitive Literature," *Journal of American Folklore* 38 (1925): 329-39. As cited in Dennis Tedlock, "On the Translation of Style in Oral Narrative," *Journal of American Folklore* 84 (1971): 114-33, who asserts that such a *caveat* notwithstanding, Boas himself did not escape from presenting such narratives as equivalents of modern short stories.

17. See introduction, note 10.

18. Nithard, *Histoire des fils de Louis le Pieux*, ed. P. Lauer (Paris: Champion, 1926).

19. Can the vernacular do what Latin does? Can it do so only by imitating Latin? Must it do so only by keeping Latin at a distance and drawing on its indigenous sources? Etc., etc. In

France the most recognized treatise is Joachim du Bellay's *La Deffence et Illustration de la Langue Françoyse* (Edition critique par Henri Chamard [Paris: Didier, 1966]).

20. The shift becomes itself a stylistic move within a given work, like that of Rabelais. See Kittay, *From Telling to Talking: A Study of Style and Sequence in Rabelais, Etudes Rabelaisiennes* 14 (Geneva: Droz, 1978), pp. 111-218.

21. Cf. Harold A. Innis, *Empire and Communications* (Toronto: University of Toronto Press, 1950, rev. ed. 1972).

22. For the church, the vernacular functions only as an extension of its Latin. Thus it is permissible for preaching.

23. This is the ideal toward which Flaubert will strive.

24. Aristotle understood this. His critique of ornament was basically the search for a style that would not draw attention to itself.

25. Reinhard Bendix, "Bureaucracy," *International Encyclopedia of the Social Sciences* 2 (New York: Macmillan, 1968), pp. 206-19.

26. This is what is at stake in the fatal wound.

27. A culture that would confront, within a few years of each other, the early prose of the Senlis translation of the *Pseudo-Turpin* (1202) with the early imposition of centralized control, which was the Battle of Bouvines (1214). (See introduction, note 6.)

28. See Barbara Johnson, *Défigurations du language poétique* (Paris: Flammarion, 1979).

INDEX

Index

Wlad Godzich is professor of comparative literature and French studies at the Université de Montréal as well as professor of comparative literature and director of the Center for Humanistic Studies at the University of Minnesota. He serves, with Jochen Schulte-Sasse, as editor of the series Theory and History of Literature.

Jeffrey Kittay is a visiting scholar in the department of French and Italian at New York University. His publications include studies on language in Rabelais, on theories of description, and on anaphora and antecedence. Kittay formerly taught French literature at Yale University.